You're On!

*Consulting for
Peak Performance*

You're On!

Consulting for
Peak Performance

Kate F. Hays
Charles H. Brown, Jr.

American Psychological Association

Washington, DC

Published by
American Psychological Association
750 First Street, NE
Washington, DC 20002
www.apa.org

To order
APA Order Department
P.O. Box 92984
Washington, DC 20090-2984
Tel: (800) 374-2721; Direct: (202) 336-5510
Fax: (202) 336-5502; TDD/TTY: (202) 336-6123
On-line: www.apa.org/books/
E-mail: order@apa.org

In the U.K., Europe, Africa, and the Middle East, copies may be ordered from
American Psychological Association
3 Henrietta Street
Covent Garden, London
WC2E 8LU England

Typeset in Meridien by Stephen McDougal, Mechanicsville, MD

Printer: United Book Press, Inc., Baltimore, MD
Cover Designer: Minker Design, Bethesda, MD
Technical/Production Editor: Casey Ann Reever

The opinions and statements published are the responsibility of the authors, and such opinions and statements do not necessarily represent the policies of the American Psychological Association.

Library of Congress Cataloging-in-Publication Data

Hays, Kate F.
    You're on! : consulting for peak performance / Kate F. Hays and Charles H. Brown, Jr. — 1st ed.
        p. cm.
    Includes bibliographical references and index.
    ISBN 1-59147-078-1 (hardcover : alk. paper)
    1. Counseling. 2. Performance—Psychological aspects. 3. Success—Psychological aspects.
I. Brown, Charles H. II. Title.

    BF637.C6H366 2003
    158'.3—dc21   2003012670

British Library Cataloguing-in-Publication Data
A CIP record is available from the British Library.

Printed in the United States of America
First Edition

"When the bird and the book disagree, always believe the bird," said James Audubon. I am inspired by the skills and knowledge, the doing and being, the essence of performance and performers. To Jeff, and our dance of life.

Kate F. Hays

To Janet—my soulmate, partner, and dreamweaver in this adventure we call life, who keeps me anchored, laughing, and in childlike wonder of life's gifts and endless possibilities.

Charles H. Brown, Jr.

Contents

Preface

We firmly believe that events are best understood when viewed in context; therefore we wish to share with you the context or "back story" in which this book came to be. The evolution of this work has been influenced by certain pivotal life events and a number of wonderful people who have been both "front-" and "backstage" through this process.

For me (Kate Hays), it began in 1986, in Concord, New Hampshire. A few years previously, I had discovered the joys of running. Curious about the mental changes that accompanied this activity, I began exploring the vast knowledge base that is sport psychology. Offering workshops on the psychological skills involved in optimal sports performance gave me the opportunity to begin thinking about the parallels between sport and another of my great passions, music. I shared some of these ideas with the conductor of an auditioned chorus I had recently joined. The chorus' conductor was intrigued by mental skills techniques and began incorporating some into the chorus' rehearsals. Then, on January 28, 1986, the shuttle Challenger exploded, and Christa McAuliffe, a Concord teacher, died. It seemed fitting that our already-planned concert repertoire, Fauré's sublime *Requiem*, be dedicated to her memory.

Concord may be the state capital, but it is also a city small enough for two degrees of separation. All of us either knew Christa or knew someone who did. How would a community chorus contain their grief enough to perform so an audience could experience their own? With our conductor's approval, I led a guided imagery session during part of a rehearsal. I learned a lot about issues of entry (some still recall that evening as important; others felt their own privacy compromised) and a lot about transfer and generalizability.

By the time that the idea for this book was a gleam in APA Books Assistant Director Mary Lynn Skutley's eye, in 1999, I was three work settings, two community choruses, and one country beyond Concord. In my new big city life (Toronto), it really was proving possible to have a practice that encompassed not only sport psychology but also work with performing artists and people in business. Mary Lynn's "piece o' cake" idea: interview some people in the field, find out what they do, and write it up. You'll know you have enough, said trusted Margaret Schlegel, Acquisitions Editor, when you reach saturation—when you're hearing the same thing from various people. (In fact, we never actually experienced a saturation point. We never tired of interviewing great performers, as they shared their emotions and insights and for a brief moment, invited us into their lives.)

Enter Charlie Brown, my good friend and colleague. With a similar background in psychology practice and developing expertise in sport psychology, Charlie could bring to this work his own expanding practice in working with businesspeople as well as the perspective of a different locale.

My own (Charlie Brown) sojourn to this point was the result of a carefully considered, conscious decision. My wife and I periodically take stock of the path we are following to ensure that our efforts and directions are consistent with our personal dream. We refine our vision, weigh our resources, and look for paths that will make that vision real. Performance psychology and this book are part of my dream.

In the mid-1990s I was well established as a marriage and family therapist with expertise in broad systems consultations, when my wife and I engaged in one of our "life planning retreats." While my practice was financially successful, it still entailed constant on-site nurturing, for hourly wages. I dreamed of taking longer breaks and spending two to three weeks at a time traveling abroad. As I reviewed my practice, I was most energized when providing performance consultation with clients seeking excellence. This work formed a nexus of all my knowledge, talents, skills, and beliefs. A performance consulting practice could be done from virtually any locale and would be amenable to seasonal work, an active lifestyle, and travel.

Pursuing this dream required a bold move: going back to being a student and cutting back my practice and income in order to reach the eventual goal. It has been a grand and glorious journey. Along the way, I have met wonderful colleagues, made new friends, and discovered the powerful impact of integrating the richness of sport psychology within my clinical practice. When Kate asked me to join her in this project, the synchronicity of resources, goals, and interests was staggering.

In a long discussion prior to beginning the process, we set out our priorities. We share these here because they have remained our guiding principles and have helped us maintain our reason through this process. The first priority was maintaining our own physical and spiritual health; second, our primary relationships; third, our friendship; and fourth, the book. This set of priorities has perhaps made the process a bit longer. It has, however, made the book possible.

The other thing that has made the book possible has been the wonderful and extraordinary cooperation and participation of the people whom we interviewed. At times when the project seemed most overwhelming, what kept us going was the sense that what they had told us was so valuable and so important to share. In particular, we would like to thank Mary Alice Adams, Dr. Tim Adamson, Dr. John Baker, Dr. Sarah Benolken, Chrys Bentley, John Cane, Michael Colgrass, Mike Collins, Dr. Stephen Covey, Lindsay Fischer, Dr. Sandra Foster, Dr. Ron Fox, Nathalie Gilfoyle, Rick Githins, Dr. Dan Gould, Kim Griffith, Dr. Linda Hamilton, Kitty Carlisle Hart, Dr. John Hipple, Celeste Holm, Dr. Peter Jensen, Dr. Stan Jones, Karen Kain, Leslie Knowles, Dr. Roberta Kraus, Jeffrey Kuhn, Jeanne Lamon, Rosa Lamoreaux, Dr. Frank Landy, Sheri Lynch, Susan Macpherson, Joseph McCambley, Dr. Sean McCann, Dr. Ellen McGrath, Richard McMillan, Dr. Andrew Meyers, Dr. Shane Murphy, Dr. Robert Nideffer, Allan Oxman, Dr. Dennis Selder, Peggy Senter, Fred Sherry, Dr. Richard Suinn, Dr. Jim Taylor, Dr. Adrienne Leslie-Toogood, Chet Walker, and Dr. Dan Wiener, as well as several other contributors who wished to remain anonymous.

The skillful advice and shaping provided by our APA Books development editor, Ed Meidenbauer, sustained us through the exciting yet arduous process of bringing our interviewees' knowledge and thoughts to life. We have benefited immeasurably from the thoughtful assistance of a number of friends and colleagues. Among them are Janet Blanchard, John Carter, Dr. Kristen Dieffenbach, Dr. Christy Greenleaf, Helen Jones, Paul Mack, Jim McHugh, Dr. Michael Miller, Dr. Artur Poczwardowski, Heidi Powell, Dr. Emily Roper, Chiz Schultz, Steve Unger, Cheryl Weiss, Alexa Wing, and Carolyn Youren. The assistance of our transcriptionists, Judith Abramham, Delores Berendt, Jennifer Fodden, and Kristen Johnston, was invaluable.

Setting the Stage

Introduction: The Roots of Performance Consultation | 1

I am finding it really fascinating to see the parallels between athletic performance and what musicians do. We both have to practice skills until things become automatic; then we have to get out of our own way to show them to others.

—Diane (musician)

n recent years, practitioners, performers, and the general public have been actively involved in the systematic application of psychological principles to the improvement of performance. This explosion of interest has been most evident in relation to elite athletes. Largely through the study of these extraordinary performers, sport psychology in particular has taken the lead in the research of principles and practices of peak performance. More recently, this interest in enhancing performance has broadened from the confines of athletics to the entire spectrum of human performance. This new and burgeoning field is generally described as *performance psychology,* and the services provided are referred to as *performance consultation or coaching.*

As we considered this broad specialty, we were aware that performance psychology has often been approached from different perspectives, each with varying focus and emphasis. For us, this raised numerous questions. Is there a specific array of knowledge that can be described as performance psychology? What does it include and how does one gain that knowledge? Is sport psychology the best route for gaining that knowledge, or are there better paths for learning the skills and techniques for enhancing performance in different domains?

Our intention in writing this book is to provide a descriptive account of the still-evolving field of performance psychology as we try to answer these questions. We hope to assist psychologists and other mental health professionals in making use of the currently available information, in finding the commonalities across areas or domains of performance, and in differentiating among domains where warranted.

Intention of the Research

In approaching the topic of performance psychology, we were guided by those same principles that served as the foundation of the practice of applied sport psychology. This practice focus was not created in a laboratory or classroom; rather, it began through studying the experiences of top athletes and coaches. Psychologists have sought to understand these "best practices," albeit in conjunction with knowledge from more formal research and laboratory settings (Gould & Pick, 1995).

In a similar fashion, we began our research by interviewing elite performers about the mental, emotional, and psychological aspects of performance. We were aware of the large extant literature within sport psychology that speaks to these questions. Instead of duplicating that information, we decided to draw from it to frame our questions and to understand our interviewees' responses. Therefore, we deliberately chose to interview performers in "nonsport" areas. We considered three other general domains of performance: business, high-risk professions, and performing arts.

We also interviewed consultants in these performance domains, people who can be considered "elite" in their own right, given their extensive work with performers. We found that the consultants often brought their own particular theoretical framework or template to their practices and that these perspectives varied. Like the Indian fable of the three blind men attempting to describe an elephant, no one perspective seemed to quite represent the "beast"—performance consulting—in its entirety.

Even though consultants have established practices in these performance domains, the vast majority of performers we interviewed were unaware of the practice and concepts of performance psychology. This lack of familiarity could be considered a liability: When discussing performance consultation, were the performers merely projecting vague notions and impossible expectations that have little practical application? However, we saw their newness to this area as an opportunity to learn performers' actual experiences and needs firsthand. Their descriptions of the mental, emotional, and psychological aspects of peak performance reflected their direct experiences, untainted by jargon or constructs of organized psychology.

From this experience, we came to understand better what *performers* experience, understand, and need. To best inform consultants and potential consultants, our ultimate intention became (to paraphrase Freud) a further clarification of the question, "What is it that performers really want?"

Among our central questions were ones that asked performers to reflect on their own experiences:

1. Are there critical or unique features of your performance domain?
2. What are the key mental factors involved in excellent performance?
3. What kind of mental preparation is necessary in order to accomplish this?
4. What are the major stresses of performing in your field, and how do you cope?

We also asked questions more directly related to consulting and consultants. Performers who had prior experience with consultants typically were clear about what they wanted and did not want. The responses of the majority of performers (who were unaware of the resources of performance consulting) ranged from an unfettered "wish list" to an attempt to incorporate the concept within their existing performance paradigm. We also specifically asked the following questions:

1. What assistance or skills might be helpful?
2. What would you consider to be the characteristics of an ideal consultant?
3. Are there ways in which a consultant could hinder performance?

We wanted our understanding of performance to be guided primarily by the experiences of the performers, but we did not want to neglect the knowledge of consultants. Curious about consultants' understanding of these same questions, we asked them to elaborate specifically on matters of training, competence, and ethics. With these many and varied voices and perspectives, our intention in this book is to create a synthesis, or even better, a collage: information with distinctive features that yet provides an overall pattern and whole.

Organization of You're On!

In the remainder of this chapter, we explore the roots of performance psychology, that is, the underlying information, perspectives, research, applications, interests, and motivation. The next chapter describes the research that forms the basis of this book.

One of our questions throughout this research has been the extent to which the mental aspects of performance are generic and can be generalized and the extent to which they are domain-specific. Although much of the book looks at general aspects of performance, we thought it important to ground that work by highlighting the different and unique aspects of each domain. Part II details critical and unique information concerning the business domain, the high-risk domain, and the performing arts domain.

In Part III, we focus on the major psychological, emotional, and mental elements of optimal performance. We begin with the basic information, preparation, and mental skills required for such performance, recognizing that stress and stress management are necessary elements as well. Chapter 11, "You're On," describes the outcome of appropriate preparation.

Our final two sections shift from performance per se to performance consulting. In Part IV, we describe various aspects of performance consulting, maintaining an emphasis on performers' thoughts and preferences. We review the assistance for which performers express interest, a sense of ideal consultant characteristics, and efforts that consultants might make that would interfere with or hinder excellent performance. Part V is directed to consultants and derives largely from our interviews with consultants. We look at the interrelated areas of training, competence, and ethics. In our final chapter, we consider the metaphor of consultant as performer.

The Roots of Performance Consultation

To understand the model and outcomes of this research, it is useful to appreciate the sources of performance consultation. An overview of the history and approach used by each of the "blind men" of the Indian fable (also known as performance consultants) provides a background and framework to synthesize the research and develop new patterns of practice. In addition, understanding these roots can assist readers in assessing their own particular background, with a view to furthering their knowledge and training.

The roots of performance consultation lie in three general areas: applied sport psychology, consultation and coaching, and psychotherapy. Each comes from a somewhat different framework, with distinct bases of history, knowledge, practice, and assumptions.

APPLIED SPORT PSYCHOLOGY

The field of sport psychology is a goldmine of insight about issues of performance. As psychologist practitioners with combined experience of more than half a century, let us state our bias at the outset: The applied research and practice of sport psychology provide psychologists and other mental health practitioners interested in performance consultation a wealth of directly applicable knowledge and skills, yet is unknown to many psychologists. Although sport psychology contains the word "psychology" in its title, this field, with its long history, has seemed of little interest to psychologists (Brewer & Van Raalte, 2002; Murphy, 1995; Petrie & Diehl, 1995). The primary investigators of this domain have been educators and academicians from departments of exercise and sport science (physical education and kinesiology).

The 20th-century roots of sport and exercise psychology lie in a couple of late 19th-century studies: One probed the effect of hypnosis on muscular endurance, and the second, by Norman Triplett in 1898, included the first experimental research on the performance effects of competition (Gill, 1986).

The history of sport psychology in the United States is often described as beginning in the 1920s and 1930s when Coleman Griffith, a psychologist at the University of Illinois, conducted laboratory and field research on the subject. Psychology historian E. G. Boring (1950) described Griffith as one of a select number of researchers with the potential to influence the entire field of psychology. Griffith was the consummate (pre-Boulder) scientist–practitioner, setting the standards for the systematic integration of laboratory findings with practical application to "real world" situations. In fact, he was probably the first psychologist to leave academia for a career in performance consultation. Griffith studied the best practices of his day; he interviewed athletic greats such as Notre Dame football coach Knute Rockne and running back Red Grange, and he consulted with the Chicago White Sox baseball team. He also wrote books on applications of psychology to coaching and athletes (Carron, 1993; Gould & Pick, 1995; Singer, 1989).

Griffith was something of an anomaly, however, and attention to his research remained sporadic until the1950s, when interest developed in motor learning and other areas of academic sport psychology. Generally such research was conducted within physical education departments (also known as departments of kinesiology, movement sciences, human performance, or more generically, sport sciences). Applied sport psychology—the application of principles of psychology to athletic performance—came into its own in the 1960s with an initial clinical focus on personality variables and the psychological management of the elite athlete.

Interest in exercise and sport psychology surged during the 1970s and 1980s. The public became more aware of sport psychology during the 1984 Olympic games, when televised coverage included several presentations on the mental aspects of sport. Applied sport psychology organizations began to emerge during this period, with the founding of the

North American Society for the Psychology of Sport and Physical Activity (NASPSPA) in 1984, the Association for the Advancement of Applied Sport Psychology (AAASP) in 1985, and Division 47 (Exercise and Sport Psychology) of the American Psychological Association in 1987. During this same time the first professional journals dedicated to sport psychology began to emerge. The first issue of *The Sport Psychologist* appeared in 1986, followed in 1989 by the *Journal of Applied Sport Psychology*. Research, courses, and graduate programs proliferated, primarily within sport sciences departments. It was during the mid-1980s that Orlick and Partington (1987) conducted their landmark Olympic Excellence Study of Olympic athletes. This was one of the first of several efforts to identify the psychological and mental aspects of athletic excellence (Smith & Christensen, 1995; Williams & Krane, 1997).

As key aspects of athletic performance were identified, efforts in the field immediately focused on how best to cultivate these abilities. It is difficult to distinguish between the *zeitgeist* of cognitive–behavioral techniques that were developed and popularized at this time and the good "fit" between these techniques and performance issues. Whatever the reason, fairly rapidly a "canon" of cognitive–behavioral intervention techniques (Andersen, 2000b) was developed and applied in the training of competitive athletes (see the meta-analyses by Greenspan & Feltz, 1989; Meyers, Whelan, & Murphy, 1995).

These techniques, often described as peak performance or psychological skills training, are based on the assumption that aspects of thoughts and feelings can inhibit effectiveness and that the use of mental skills can enhance optimal performance. Psychological skills training programs typically include training in relaxation, imagery, goal setting, concentration, and cognitive self-management. Research suggests that educational psychological skills intervention improves competitive performance (e.g., Gould, Guinan, Greenleaf, Medbery, & Peterson, 1999; Meyers et al., 1995; Williams & Krane, 1998).

This practical aspect of enhancing performance has become the most popular and popularized aspect of sport psychology. Information for interested practitioners is becoming progressively more available (see, e.g., Andersen, 2000a; Brown, 2001; Cogan, 1998; Hays & Smith, 2002; Lesyk, 1998; Petrie, 1998; Simons & Andersen, 1995; Van Raalte & Brewer, 2002; Wildenhaus, 1997).

An increasing number of sport psychologists have expanded their perspective on consulting to include work with other performers. (A recent special issue of the *Journal of Applied Sport Psychology* was devoted entirely to the theme "Moving beyond the psychology of athletic excellence"; Gould, 2002.) In part, this decision is financially driven. Consultants who restrict their practice to athletes may limit their business or sources of funding, especially considering that these services are typically

I was speaking to a group one time and they said, "These are marvelous skills, so useable, how come we're just hearing about them now?" I said to them, "If I'd come in 15 years ago and said: I've got this great group of skills that Buddhist monks are using, you wouldn't have listened to me. But coming in and saying athletes use them, you suddenly perk up."

Athletes are seen as very practical people, very goal oriented, very achievement oriented, certainly not interested in anything frilly or at the fringes. It better be solid, meat and potatoes stuff, or the athletes aren't going to take it on. They're seen as being very conservative. And so the business world has no trouble embracing anything from there.

Dr. Colin Cross (consultant, business)

not reimbursable by third-party payers (Meyers, Coleman, Whelan, & Mehlenbeck, 2001).

This broader perspective has other causes as well. For at least the past 20 years, the business community has focused on the psychology of excellence (Weinberg & McDermott, 2002). Peters and Waterman (1982), for example, focused on performance excellence in business in their popular book, *In Search of Excellence*. Many businesspeople experience a logical connection between athletic peak performance and business excellence (Jones, 2002; Strauss, 2001). Furthermore, with the corporate downsizing of recent years, a number of executives have experienced isolation and loneliness; hence the need for key "soft skills" with which consultants can be helpful (Jones, 2002).

In a journal typically more noted for its sport psychology research than its descriptive practitioner articles, Jones (2002) recently detailed his own transition from sport psychologist to business consultant. Known for his research on competitive anxiety and his work with elite athletes, Jones was approached by a senior executive of an international business organization interested in increasing the performance of its senior management. Jones described the parallels between sports and business: organizational constraints, stress resulting from the high visibility and public nature of performance outcomes, transformational leadership, and the importance of team functioning.

One business consultant with whom we spoke described how he was recruited by a well-known business training organization. They invited him to train with and work for them because of his consulting experience with high-achieving athletes. As Dr. Dean (as we call him) explained:

They have worked with some other folks who had some sport background and they've found that executives really connect with it. Some of the other folks who have started in this area without the sports background have felt really intimidated. It is hard for those consultants to challenge some of these people.

> For me, the background of working with elite athletes has been very useful. Business folks need to be challenged and enjoy being challenged.

The transfer of information, skills, and techniques from sport psychology to other domains has been investigated in the past few years. Presentations, articles, and chapters addressing the links between sports and the performing arts indicate the increasing interest within the practitioner community (Hays, 2000, 2002; Martin & Cutler, 2002; Poczwardowski & Conroy, 2002; Schoen & Estanol-Johnson, 2001). Sport psychology techniques are being applied in ever-widening areas of performance, such as public safety and other high-risk professions (Le Scanff & Taugis, 2002; Newburg, Kimiecik, Durand-Bush, & Doell, 2002).

Dr. Andy Meyers, a recent president of AAASP, spoke with us about the future of the field and its expansion to performance domains beyond sport.

> I would hope that sports might always be the core of what we do, because in fact, in our Western culture, it is the best example of performance enhancement opportunity. No matter how much someone loves ballet, the average person in the audience may have a very hard time saying "This ballerina is better [now] than she was a year ago and better than the ballerina I just saw." What we know in sport is because it fits our culture in a very special way. When the Yankees score more runs than the Texas Rangers, we all know it and we don't have to guess at it.

CONSULTATION AND COACHING

During the same years that applied sport psychology was emerging, the processes and practices of consultation and coaching were likewise evolving and being refined. The initial sources of some of these methods developed within social psychology during and following World War II. Community psychology, developments in systems theory, and applied methods in industrial–organizational psychology provided initial models of interaction that have subsequently evolved into particular applied perspectives. These perspectives, now manifest in community psychology, family and systems psychology, organizational development, business consultation, and, recently, coaching, have shared certain essential tenets. Depending in part on *who* one is working with and in part on *what* is emphasized, consultation and coaching share a recognition that individuals do not operate in isolation and that there is a powerful interaction between the person and his or her environment. This emphasis on the system offers important information concerning such issues as gaining access or "entry" into a sys-

I think in terms of people as members of an integrated unit rather than as a bunch of individuals. A system reacts as a whole. It doesn't just react as individuals. They've got a history, they've got ways they handle stuff, and you have to be ready to pay attention to that because that may be more dominant than an individual's inclination. A given individual may be willing to be confrontational, but he may be in a family where that is just not done. So it never comes up and never occurs to him. As a result, even though it is a skill he might have himself and might be willing to use, things don't get confronted within the family and thus within the family business.

Dr. Brian Bell (consultant, family businesses)

tem, formal and informal power, strategic interventions, role function, situational determinants, a focus on solutions to current issues, and a collaborative perspective (Sarason, 1967; Wynne, McDaniel, & Weber, 1986).

The area of family/systems consultation has provided a framework for describing the rules and structure of the context in which the performer works and through which the consultant endeavors to navigate. A systematic approach contributes to performance psychology in two distinct ways: theoretical and interactive. The theoretical perspective offers models and frameworks that can guide a consultant in gaining entry to a performance setting, as well as in developing support from administrators and others with whom the consultant has indirect contact. Family and systems consultation has also contributed to a more complete understanding of the ways in which external and interactive issues can affect optimal performance, whether positively or negatively.

Described as "goal-oriented and collaborative" (Foster, 1996, p. 9), "executive coaching" has been in vogue in the business world for about a decade (Tobias, 1996). Executive coaching involves the use of an outside consultant who meets on a regular basis with a company executive to "improve the executive's managerial skills, correct serious performance problems, or facilitate long-term development" (Witherspoon & White, 1996, p. 125).

Coaching has certain features in common with psychotherapy, such as reframing, active listening, empathy, and a focus on solutions; however, coaching explicitly excludes the treatment of psychopathology (Dean, 2001). Recently, Harris (2002b) has conceptualized the similarities and differences between coaching and therapy as existing along two different continua: the vulnerability of the client (e.g., as a function of level of mental health or psychopathology) and the similarity of types of topics that are discussed to those traditionally dealt with in psychotherapy. Coaching is designed to build on a person's strengths, resources, and passions to actualize growth and potential. Even in situations where problems are addressed, the focus is on strengths and solutions.

Transference or intrapsychic interpretation is not part of the coaching paradigm. The interaction between coach and client is geared more toward facilitating growth rather than treating illness (H. Levinson, 1996). In terms of consultative models, executive coaching can be considered "client-centered consultation." Meetings with executives may extend over a number of months but often occur at infrequent albeit predictable intervals. The goal of executive coaching is to assist executives in improving overall performance, with a view to improving the performance of the larger organization (Kilburg, 1996).

Within psychology, practitioners in both industrial–organizational and consulting psychology have been increasingly attending to the lucrative market of executive coaching (Caironi, 2002; Kampa-Kokesch & Kilburg, 2001). Vicki Vandaveer, founder and chief executive officer of The Vandaveer Group, suggested that industrial–organizational psychology, with its emphases on organizational theory, human motivation, learning theory, and problem identification and analysis can provide a strong initial base for coaching (Caironi, 2002).

The terminology for this coaching process varies, depending on the domain. Perhaps because in athletics the title of "coach" is already established as the term for a physical skills leader or consultant such as a conditioning coach, a one-on-one session between an athlete and a performance psychologist is likely to be described, deferentially, as "consultation." (On the other hand, for just this reason, some athletes prefer terms that modify *coach*, e.g., *mental coach* or *concentration coach*.) The same process in a business setting would more likely be considered "coaching" (Jones, 2002).

Although *executive coaching* may be the term most familiar to people, the concept of coaching has expanded to include a wide array of performance settings. Today one can find coaches for virtually any aspect of modern life, including adjusting to midlife, dealing with procrastination and burnout, or, increasingly popular, "life coaching" (Cole, 2000; Dean, 2001).

In the past few years, with increasing emphasis on the value of diversification from a dependence on the managed health care market (Haber, Rodino, & Lipner, 2001), the area of "business psychology" has experienced particular interest and rapid growth (Walfish, 2001). Business psychology, noted Perrott (1999), is

> the application of Clinical Psychology's [sic] traditional knowledge and skill base, modified and augmented by related knowledge and skill areas bases (such as organizational development theory) to people working in business settings, for the ultimate purpose of enhancing the business' performance. (p. 31)

Ben Dean (2001), whose MentorCoach program specializes in training therapists as coaches, proposed that therapists' skills in relationship-building, communication, and change techniques make them uniquely suited for the world of coaching. He cautioned, however, that the transition requires new learning. In addition, mental health practitioners need to make attitudinal shifts, moving from their original pathology-focused training and orientation.

In advising clinicians who are transferring their knowledge and skills, some focus on the importance of shifting from an illness-based model to a strengths model. Others emphasize the importance of increased understanding of systems and organizations. Richard Kilburg (2000), one of the founders of the Society of Psychologists in Management, has expressed skepticism about therapists' ability to make the transition from one to the other perspective:

> I do not think that the majority of therapists could work
> successfully as consultants or coaches in organizational
> contexts. There are many attitudes, values, behavioral patterns,
> and personality traits that would make it difficult for them to
> adapt their ideas and methods to the typical corporate
> setting. (p. 17)

Many see coaching as the wave of the future; but the mushrooming number of coaches also raises some concerns. At present, anyone can call himself or herself a coach. The absence of clear professional standards and core knowledge results in exceptionally diverse and sometimes questionable qualifications. As one of the consultants that we interviewed exclaimed:

> You've got everything! Hell, one I ran into was a barber. He got
> started advising people about hairstyles and their clothing.
> They liked his taste and that led to décor. And then he got into
> office arrangements and personnel and how to relate to people.
> And the son of a bitch is a barber!

No standard definition of coaching or regulated certification for executive coaching currently exists. Rather, executive coaching is an "umbrella term" that can have various meanings and implications, both for practitioners and businesspeople (Foxhall, 2002). Postgraduate education and training is available through both continuing education and free-standing programs. At the time of this writing, the International Coach Federation (ICF) has attempted to address some of these concerns and has rapidly become the largest professional group that accredits coaches (Cole, 2000). The ICF has identified four core competencies for

> You can go too far in either direction. You can become a very narrow coach who says "I just want you to land that part or to be able to sing that aria. How you get there is something that concerns me only insofar as the result." There is a place for people who are coaches only, but that may not be very helpful to performers, if that's all that's being done for them. And then there's the psychotherapist who brushes aside the specific questions of what's going on in the client's career and performance in order to say, "It all has to do with who you are as a person" and reduces it to being generic psychotherapy. That doesn't serve the client either.
>
> Dr. Owen Osborne (consultant, theatre)

coaching: ethics and professional standards, relationship skills, communication skills, and skills that facilitate learning and results (ICF, 2002). Various levels of certification are available, based on hours of formal training in coaching and hours of supervised coaching experience. By the end of 2002, ICF had accredited 13 free-standing programs that provide training in coaching; it also certified numerous individuals and workshops that provide "Approved Coach Specific Training Hours."

The ICF provides a direction and focus to the legitimization of coaching. Nonetheless, there are ongoing concerns that despite the development of ethical standards, the organization has no way of monitoring or enforcing ethical compliance or assuring the quality of training. One of us (CHB) recently encountered a bright, enthusiastic young woman who was delighted to have attained certification as a "Life Coach." After several years as a personal fitness trainer, she was excited about opening a practice designed to help people deal with life's challenges. She explained that the difference between coaching and therapy was that "therapists focus on a person's past, and coaches focus on the present and the future." This oversimplistic differentiation between therapy and coaching, one that is not infrequently touted by non-therapist-trained practitioners, is naïve. It ignores the contributions of positive psychology, solution-focused therapies, cognitive–behavioral therapies, and other well-established practices used by therapists that are action- and future-oriented.

It is ironic that what is often promoted as coaching's greatest strength—that it does not focus on psychopathology—may be a serious liability: ignorance or lack of understanding of pathology. Many of the consultants we interviewed expressed apprehension that coaches who do not have adequate clinical training may simply be unaware of all that they do not know. In such cases, there is risk of practicing beyond one's competency, maintaining coaching efforts when instead a client would be best served by referral for psychological treatment. This topic of qualifications and certification for coaches will undoubtedly continue to be closely watched and debated for some time to come.

PSYCHOTHERAPY

This is a time in the history of psychotherapy practice when the influ-ences of certain areas are in confluence with a focus on performance and performance issues. Contemporary psychotherapy often attends to indi-viduals' desire and ability to grow and change, to solve problems, and to become more effective. Certain perspectives and methods, such as cogni-tive–behavioral therapy, solution-focused methods, and positive psychol-ogy, seem to provide a particularly good "fit" with performance consulta-tion. Although clinical psychology programs at times provide this perspective, counseling and counseling psychology, in which the em-phasis is more on growth than on fixing illness, have been specifically noted as intellectually and methodologically aligned with performance enhancement (Petitpas, Giges, & Danish, 1999; Poczwardowski, Sherman, & Henschen, 1998).

When we asked AAASP President Meyers about his general perspec-tives on training issues in psychology, he commented:

> I think what we do is pretty consistent with this new or reasonably new emphasis in applied psychology and to some extent in some research areas, and that is that we don't necessarily have to focus on the pathological client who walks through the door. We may in fact spend some very productive time helping reasonably healthy people to perform well, to perform better, to cope in a more productive and helpful way.

Meyers's comments are consistent with the emphasis of positive psychology most recently spearheaded during Martin Seligman's presi-dency of the American Psychological Association (APA) in 2000. Al-though Maslow (1968) and other humanists in mid-20th-century American psychology attended to human possibility, Seligman (Seligman & Csikszentmihalyi, 2000) was deeply concerned that for the most part, the field of psychology had focused since its inception almost exclu-sively on mental illness and a disease model of human functioning. The price of this preoccupation with the worst things in life was "knowing very little about how normal people flourish under more benign condi-tions" (Seligman & Csikszentmihalyi, 2000, p. 5). His mission as APA president was to change the focus of psychology to include the positive aspects of life and human potential. The energy of positive psychology is that of a nonpathology-based system, one that attends to people's capacities. Positive psychology has been described as focusing on "what works, what is right, and what is improving" (Sheldon & King, 2001, p. 216). Seligman and Csikszentmihalyi (2000) have argued that "the field of positive psychology . . . is about valued subjective experiences: well-being, contentment, and satisfaction (in the past); hope and optimism (for the future); and flow and happiness (in the present)" (p. 5). Performance psychology is an example of applied positive psychology, addressing many of these same issues and embracing the potential of the individual.

The psychotherapy skills and approaches that have been most closely aligned with the tenets of positive psychology work well in the arena of performance enhancement. Solution-focused techniques (DeShazer, 1982, 1985; O'Hanlon, 1987) share with performance consultation an emphasis on present behavior and practical solutions to problems. As mentioned earlier, cognitive–behavioral methods have been adapted with considerable effectiveness to the domain of sport psychology and to work with athletes.

Within sport psychology, there has been a similar shift from a deficit model of human nature to one with a growth perspective in addressing performance enhancement. During the 1960s, psychologists with a traditional clinical focus made initial forays into working with professional sports teams. Ogilvie and Tutko (1966) focused on problem athletes and how to handle them; Beisser wrote *The Madness in Sport* (1977), a collection of bizarre behaviors and activities observed in sport settings. This emphasis on the problematic and pathological created a negative impression about the value of psychological services among many athletes and coaches (Hardy, Jones, & Gould, 1996; Ravizza, 1988). In contrast, Le Scanff and Taugis (2002) described the ways in which consultation to Special Forces police in France occurred specifically because of the acceptance of the sport model of performance improvement rather than a pathology perspective.

The terms *psychology* and *psychotherapy* evoke varying interpretations. In many performance settings, psychologists must confront and counter the "shrink" stereotype to be accepted (Gould & Damarjian, 1998; Linder, Pillow, & Reno, 1989). In our interviews, we found this to be particularly true among performers in settings where the role of emotion is minimized during performance, areas such as business, medicine, and law. Dr. Cross, who consults with businesspeople, commented:

> I had a heck of a time labeling these mental skills when I first
> started presenting them to businesspeople. As soon as you start
> using the word *psychology* or *psychological*, it carries a lot of
> baggage with it. It had a bit of a stigma in the sense that, "well,
> who needs that? That means you're weak."

In contrast, other settings with different histories, such as the performing arts, may conflate psychology and psychotherapy, in this case from a positive perspective. That this apparent increased receptivity can also be problematic is explored more fully in chapter 5.

INTEGRATION OF THE ROOTS

At present, it would be difficult to argue that there is one true route to performance psychology practice. The field of performance psychology is being shaped by practitioners who come from various fields, some of which are in the process of self-definition. We would suggest that the three roots that we have described each bear close examination. A practitioner's skills and energy can be strengthened through "cross-training," in which one develops expertise in several of these strands (Brown, 2001). Sport psychology is a well-defined field with rich quantitative and qualitative research concerning one specific dimension of performance: performance excellence in athletes. Consultation and coaching emphasize the contextual and systemic knowledge that is a vital complement (or antidote) to the individualistic focus of therapy. Cognitive–behavioral methods also offer relevant tools; solution-focused and positive psychologies have direct relevance to performance psychology in their directed attention to the constructive elements within individuals and situations.

Terenzini (1993) proposed that effective consultation requires three different types of knowledge: basic skills, knowledge of issues, and knowledge of the specific group with which one is consulting. We would suggest that performance consultants bring varying skills to their work, often depending on which of the three roots described above has had greatest salience for them. Ultimately, we suggest that the fully competent performance consultant should have basic proficiency in five areas: relationship skills, change skills, knowledge of performance excellence, knowledge of the physiological aspects of performance, and knowledge of systems consultation.

With an understanding of some of the background, or roots, of the field of performance consultation, we now turn to the research that informed this book. In the next chapter, we describe the research participants, the process of interviewing, and our method of analysis.

The Back Story: Research in Performance Consultation | 2

A s we sought to broaden the notion of performance beyond athletics, we realized that every working person performs a job or task and, hence, might be considered a performer. An accountant completing income tax forms is performing his or her job but is typically not thought of as a performer. On the other hand, people in the performing arts are readily accepted as performers. What makes a dancer's performance different from that of an accountant?

For the purpose of this study, we recognized that performers must meet certain performance standards: They are judged as to proficiency or excellence, there are consequences to poor performance, good coping skills are intrinsic to excellent performance (McGrath, 1970; Poczwardowski & Conroy, 2002). In addition, a performer is expected to bring talents and skills into action at a given point in time (thus, the title of this book, *You're On!*). The temporal aspect of performance was central to our selection. People who have the option of starting and stopping a task (e.g., the accountant) were excluded.

A wealth of information is available about athletes as performers, and we deliberately chose to avoid duplication. We attempted to consider all other possible areas of performance that fit this criterion. Performing artists were clearly included in this group. In expanding our search, we also recognized that some "players" have already been included in the field of performance psychology: Certain work domains have acknowledged concern about improving performance and have been receptive to performance consultation. Business, the sales industry, and the military have long histories of using consultants to maximize performance. We added certain groups from the domain of medicine, those in which the temporal demands of performance were clear: surgery and the emergency room. In the end, our selection of performers could be classified into three broad groups: those in the performing arts (music, dance, and theatre, the latter including live and film, on stage or behind a microphone), those in business (including the law, marketing, and sales), and those whose professions or outcomes are characterized by a high level of risk to human life, whether one's own or that of others (including surgery, emergency room medicine, public safety officers [firefighters, police personnel], race car drivers, astronauts, nuclear engineers, and military personnel).

These groups are extremely diverse, but they all require that a specialized set of skills be brought into action at a given point in time. In the text that follows, we refer to each of the three groups as "domains," and the specific professions within them as "areas."

In developing our analysis of performance psychology, we opted to be guided by performers and consultants who have demonstrated expertise. Our definition of *expert* included both those whose authority derives from their work and identity as performers and those whose authority has developed through their work in consulting with performers. Thus, we subsequently refer to our experts, separately, as performers and consultants.

Participants

Purposive sampling (Patton, 1990), in which participants are chosen on the basis of perceived suitability for the research, was used to recruit expert performers. Selection of performers was based on the following criteria: that the person be considered successful and expert in his or her field, as indicated by a national or international reputation and more than 10 years' experience in the field (Ericsson, 1996a). We interviewed people we knew and people we did not know beforehand. None of the participants was a client of the interviewers or the consultant-participants. Our own geographical distribution, professional networks, and varied practice emphases expanded the available pool of interviewees.

To the extent possible, we attempted to select a heterogeneous sample of interviewees. We actively sought participants who could bring fresh knowledge or a divergent perspective. For example, one of the interviewees was a male ballet dancer; another was a female attorney. Fifteen of the performers were male, and nine were female. Eighteen of the consultants were male, five female. We were aware that ethnic minority status was underrepresented in our sample. Only one person (a consultant) was so identified.

We had access to a number of classical musicians, and so we did not tap into other types of musicians (e.g., jazz, rock, country, or pop musicians). Even with some potential leads, we were able to directly interview only one public safety officer and no astronauts or nuclear engineers.

The one area of performance that we found utterly impenetrable was that of successful television and film actors. Despite various leads, possibilities, and connections, the phalanx of people who surround and protect movie actors prevented us from interviewing people whose primary livelihood comes from that field. (Some of those who are in broadcasting or are stage actors have also been in film and on TV, and their comments on those media are included in the information that follows.)

Of the people we actually contacted, there were only two direct refusals: one was a performer who expressed regret for lack of time, and the other was a retired consultant who was uninterested in the project.

In all, then, we ended up interviewing 24 performers: five businesspeople (two lawyers, one insurance broker, one banker, and one advertising executive); four people in high-risk professions (three physicians and one person who is a Special Forces medic and has additional training as a police sniper); and 15 performing artists (three actors, two broadcasters, three dancers, and seven musicians). The disproportionate number of performing artists, compared with those in the other domains, reflected ease of access. Their voices are therefore at times more actively represented in the text.

Among the businesspeople we interviewed, four were male and one female. Each lawyer has practiced law for 25 years in major national law firms and has partnership experience. One now is deputy general counsel in the nonprofit sector; the other has recently stepped down as managing partner of his firm. The insurance broker, also in the field for 25 years, has been recognized as one of the top insurance salespeople in the United States; the banker, having worked in traditional banking for 20 years, currently heads a global investment arm of a major national bank system. The advertising executive, in his early 40s, is president of a firm working with Fortune 1000 companies.

The performers in the high-risk field were all male. One of the physicians has chaired the department of neurosurgery for a major metropolitan hospital and is neurosurgeon for two professional sports teams; another, a practitioner and chair of the emergency medicine department of a major metropolitan hospital, also has research and administrative responsibilities for a physician corporation; the third, similarly, is active as a surgeon, administrator, researcher, and teacher. The other high-risk performer has two distinctive roles and careers: He has been a noncommissioned officer in the U.S. Special Forces, and he has had ten years of experience in a police tactical unit as a sniper.

The performing artists we interviewed included three actors, one at the beginning of his career, one in midcareer, and one who has been acting for 60 years. One is known for film and TV work, whereas the other two have spent most of their work life on stage. Both broadcasters have also had experience in TV, theatre, and film. Three dancers were interviewed: Two are retired ballet dancers, one teaches at a ballet school and is primarily-engaged as an arts administrator. The third dancer still performs (as a modern dancer) but currently is primarily engaged in teaching and administration. Seven classical musicians were interviewed. One is a member of a large symphonic orchestra; two freelance, one as a singer, the other an instrumentalist; one serves a dual role as musician and conductor of a chamber music ensemble; one is a musician and music organization administrator; and two are conductors, one primarily of orchestras, the other, of choral groups. Along with their own particular individual personalities, temperaments, and skills, there are differences between the different art forms, and even within the same art form, differences of role (e.g., conductor vs. player).

Because performance consulting has been of such interest within the community of sport psychology practitioners, we initially turned to that population to select interviewees. We targeted those consultants who have extended their practices from working with athletes to working with a broader population, especially businesspeople. We supplemented this selection with consultants from the broader community of consultants who work with performers in various fields. Again, we looked to expertise and longevity in selecting those to interview. Ultimately, we interviewed 23 consultants (nine identified primarily as consultants in business; six in high-risk performance; six in performing arts; and two in broader issues of performance consultation). Most were people we knew as professional colleagues. A few were consultants whose work we had read or who we knew of or who were suggested to us by other consultants. The consultants had doctoral level training, and most were psychologists.

During the review process, three participants were dropped from the analysis. Two were consultants and one a performer, all three were involved in the same program. Each of these individuals expressed concern that the interview questions did not capture the essence of their methods. Through mutual agreement, their information was not included in this book. A fourth participant was deemed too new to the field to qualify as an expert.

Each potential interviewee was initially contacted by telephone, letter, or electronic mail. A letter was sent confirming the interviewees' willingness to participate, and, when requested, a copy of the interview questions was sent as well. We also assured anonymity in the final written product. Because we wished to preserve the reality of our interviewees and their thoughtful responses to our questions, we decided to retain the integrity of their spoken words but gave them pseudonyms. In Appendix A, we have given brief descriptions of each interviewee, along with his or her respective pseudonym. In order for the reader to be able to distinguish between performers and consultants, we have used the convention of indicating the performers by a pseudonym first name only; the consultants were given fictitious first and last names along with their honorific title.

Interview Process

We developed a semistructured interview protocol, based on the questions of concern. We asked the same questions of performers and consultants about the key elements of preparation and performance, as well as critical information in their particular field and consultant characteristics. Questions about performance stress were directed to performers only. Questions about aspects of training and competence were restricted to the consultants. In addition to the open-ended questions, we prepared a checklist of services and skills that are commonly offered by performance consultants working with athletes. At the conclusion of the open-ended interview, both performers and consultants were given the checklist and asked to indicate which skills or services might be helpful for a performance consultant to provide.

After the questions had been developed, each of the authors conducted two pilot interviews, one with a performer and one with a consultant. The questions were further refined for clarity. The final interview questions are available as Appendix B (Performers) and Appendix C (Consultants).

The actual interviews were conducted primarily by telephone; some interviews were conducted at either the participant's home or office or the interviewer's office if that was considered more convenient for and preferred by the participant. Prior studies using similar techniques indicate no difference between interviews conducted by telephone and those made face-to-face (Weinberg, Butt, & Knight, 2001). All interviews were tape-recorded and subsequently professionally transcribed. Transcriptions were reviewed and corrected for accuracy by the original interviewer prior to analysis. The interviews were conducted as conversation, using the questions as guide rather than specific sequential protocol. In some instances, this resulted in extensive follow-up questioning on certain items or aspects of the conversation. In certain interviews, not all questions were asked, either because they seemed irrelevant to the conversation or already had been covered in some other way.

Each interview lasted approximately 1 to 1 1/2 hours. A few were a bit shorter, and a few somewhat longer. Most were conducted in one sitting or phone conversation, although because of personal time constraints, a few had to be conducted in two sessions.

Interview Analysis

We considered a number of methods of interview analysis. We kept in mind our ultimate goal—sharing information derived from these interviews—and our ultimate audience—practitioners with an interest in performance consulting. We wished to develop a qualitative analysis that would retain the meaning and intention of the interviews themselves. Various numeric methods of information analysis were not used because they required a nominal or ordinal process that was not present in the data and therefore would not capture the meaning of participants' comments.

The eventual method of analysis was the simplest and most direct: Following an initial joint review procedure for two transcripts to ensure similar methods of analysis, each transcript was separately read and coded for "meaning units," the smallest unit of analysis (Lincoln & Guba, 1985). For example, Faith, a professional singer, described her process of learning and memorizing music: "I view things from the inside of my head. If I'm singing from memory, the page is more or less there, the song is laid out." This performer's process was categorized as *imagery*.

We subsequently jointly grouped meaning units into lower and higher order themes (Conroy, Poczwardowski, & Henschen, 2001; Gould, Eklund, & Jackson, 1993). This classification of themes and categories was developed initially with the performers' transcripts. Analyses of consultants' transcripts were then fit to the performers' clusters, with additional categories added as needed.

The initial transcript analysis was done by the investigator who had not conducted the interview. This procedure allowed optimal freshness of analysis. The second researcher, the one who had actually interviewed the individual, then reviewed the initial analysis, conducting a "study audit" (Patton, 1990). If there was a discrepancy in the analysis, items were discussed at length in order to arrive at a consensus. If a consensus could not be reached, the perceptions of the actual interviewer were given preference in determining meaning units.

A further means of ensuring accuracy of analysis involved "member checking" (Patton, 1990). Each interviewee was sent a copy of the analysis of their interview, with a request that he or she indicate either acceptance of the analysis as representing their perspective, modifications of the analysis that they would suggest, or preference for reviewing the entire manuscript. With the exception of the interviewees who chose to withdraw from the process at this point, as mentioned above, all interviewees accepted the analyses or made minor modifications.

The checklist of potential services was analyzed by calculating the percentage of respondents who endorsed each item as desirable for a consultant to offer. These percentages were also broken down according to major performance domain: business, high-risk, and performing arts.

II

Domain-Specific Information

Unique Aspects of the Business Domain | 3

Always remember that you are completely unique . . . exactly like everyone else.

—Anonymous

The consultant interested in performance psychology faces a dilemma: To what extent should one be a generalist; to what extent, a specialist? Is it important to have skills applicable to a wide range of performers, or should one understand deeply a certain subset of performers? Our answer is: both. For the most part, we discuss elements common to both areas of emphasis. In our interviews, however, especially those with performers, we became aware of differences particular to each domain. Accordingly, before we look at the common features, we focus on some of the essential aspects that set these domains apart.

We recognize that our descriptions of differences are painted with broad strokes and risk falling into stereotypes. There are exceptions to all cases. In fact, even within the same domain, no two consulting situations are exactly alike. Each business, troupe, orchestra, or unit has a unique history, a distinctive set of values, and an idiosyncratic interaction of personalities.

In part II, we address the characteristics that are essential within each domain but differ between domains. In subsequent parts of the book, we focus more on issues common to all aspects of performance.

We asked our experts (both performers and consultants) what they considered unique about their particular domain and what information about that performance setting would be critical for a consultant to know. We have organized their responses into five categories. *Milieu* characteristics describe the general context of the domain, including such aspects

> Every performance, however broadly we define that, is an attempt to communicate and to publish a private or individual viewpoint. If that's a lawyer presenting a case or if that's a dancer dancing a ballet, that to me is the element of performance. I don't think dance is unique in that way.
>
> —Jerry (dancer)

as the role of competition, systemic issues, the role of subjectivity, time and tradition, gender issues, stresses unique to this domain, and contemporary changes in the domain. *Role function* pertains to the various expectations beyond the immediate performance, including attention to business aspects such as marketing and running a profitable enterprise, maintaining relationships with the public or "political structure," and dealing with relationships within a group or team. *Characteristics of performers* within the domain relates to personality types and attitudes that are typically found in the domain. We acknowledge the danger of succumbing to stereotypes; there are always exceptions to any description of this kind. Nonetheless, research in career development and occupational success suggests that certain personality types tend to gravitate toward and to be more successful in certain occupations (Hamilton & Hamilton, 1991; Hamilton, Hamilton, & Meltzer, 1989; Marchant-Haycox & Wilson, 1992). A well-prepared consultant is aware of these typical characteristics while being open to the exceptions. The *nature of performance* looks at dimensions such as the role of memorization, the role of emotions, physical demands, and interactions with the audience. Included in this category is a discussion of what is "at risk" during a performance. For example, some may be risking their reputation, pride, or public embarrassment; for others, the consequence of failure may mean death itself. Understanding the emphases of these various dimensions helps a consultant appreciate the differences between the performance domains. Finally, we discuss the *familiarity with consultants* within the specific performance domain. Consultants entering a field that readily accepts performance consultation confront different issues from those forging into "virgin territory."

Although most of the performers we interviewed perceived their particular domain as unique, a few did not. Arthur said that there was little that was singular about the practice of law. Harold (conductor) also questioned whether the music domain was unique, pointing out that whether a person is a musician or athlete, anyone who has to compete or perform needs certain key skills: to be able to focus, relax, and prepare thoroughly. We hope to demonstrate that the situation is a "both/and." The key skills Harold described are indeed generic, but each performance domain contains specific critical elements. We begin with a discussion of the business domain.

The Business Domain

What does it mean to "perform" in the business domain? In general, business involves commercial or mercantile activities, the production of commodities, and financial transactions. Interviews with performers and consultants working in or with the fields of law, insurance, banking, and advertising were considered representative of this domain. Although one can make distinctions between these professions, several common characteristics can be clearly identified by both performers and consultants engaged in business. These are addressed in detail below.

> What is happening now is when a lot of folks go to apply for a job, there is a psychological contract. There is something in the air in the room that you are interviewing in, but it is not the actual business contract. The person that is conducting the interview is thinking to themselves as they are interviewing you: "We will use you here as long as we need your skill, but as soon as we don't need your skill we are going to show you the door." The person being interviewed is thinking: "What skills am I going to learn by coming to work for your company that will make me employable elsewhere? Because I know there is no security in companies any more."
>
> —Dr. Barbara Benton, (consultant, business)

MILIEU

A primary feature identified within the business domain was the extraordinarily rapid pace of change. Technological advancements in communication have vastly expanded or removed physical boundaries for many businesses. Company personnel no longer need to be located within the same physical space, and organizations now exist within an expanding global marketplace. More than 20 years ago, John Naisbitt (1982) predicted a number of "megatrends," such as the increased value of a postindustrial information society, a global marketplace, decentralization, and networking. One of the people we interviewed, world-renowned consultant Dr. Andrew Adams, described the actualization of this process:

> They're all going into a new economy with a vortex of seismic sea changes. The globalization of markets and technology is changing everything. It's creating a free agency market in which top talent goes to the highest bidder. Intellectual capital is replacing financial capital as the main source of wealth. How do you manage knowledge workers? It's a totally different approach and it's causing tremendous insecurity, fear, and uncertainty everywhere.

In this world of acquisitions, buyouts, and downsizing, our interviewees suggest that company loyalty is no longer a relevant value. Consultant Dr. Alice Austin explained:

It's a very crowded marketplace, and more than ever it's moving very fast. People are always thinking about what they will leave with when they go. With the majority of the people that I coach, developing an exit strategy is most important. They don't expect to stay in a position. And this is different from job hopping as people have done in the past. It's a brand new era, and for me, it's a pretty frightening one in terms of its potential damage to the psyche.

> Over the past two months, things have been so hectic that I go to meeting after meeting after meeting and there is no buffer zone, no time to think and plan and really even to find what success looks like. As a consequence, there have been times over the past two weeks when people have come to my office and honest to God, I thought, "I can't remember why we are meeting. I have no idea why they are here." You just kind of have to let them talk and try to remember. It is embarrassing.
>
> —Barry (advertising executive)

Competition is common to all performers, but a unique factor in the business world is the rapidity with which the entire scope of competition can change. Within the insurance industry, for example, Carl commented about the competitiveness of the organizational, rather than interpersonal, climate. When Carl started in the business, it was simple: Insurance polices were sold by insurance companies. With recent changes in federal regulations, insurance policies can be purchased through any number of institutions and organizations, resulting in a dramatic shift in the insurance arena. "I'm in a relatively competitive business that's service oriented, and nowadays everybody in the world wants to be in it. Banks are in it now in the United States, [as well as] the CPA firms, and stock brokerage firms."

In contrast to the rapid pace of most facets of the business world, long-term investment offers its own brand of stress. As David, a global investment banker, explained:

We're not worried about what the stock market does this week or this month or frankly, this year. We're looking at businesses that we think should do well over a three- to seven-year time period. Earlier today I was selling some shares in a public company that we own and we've been selling just a little bit. We were able to sell a fairly large number of shares today at what we think are pretty good prices. But yet, I don't know. Tomorrow somebody may announce they are acquiring the company at 30% higher. So now I feel good today but you always don't know if that was a good decision. The very long-term nature of our work is very, very different from most of the rest of this institution. Almost every other part is short term. It may be hour to hour, day to day, on up to quarter to quarter, but nothing beyond quarter to quarter as far as measuring performance and results. The long-term nature—it kind of eats at you as to whether you're doing well.

The enticement of rapid monetary riches creates a special stress in the business world. Instead of a gradual, predictable accumulation of savings, fortunes can be gained and lost in a matter of moments. David (banker) described the world of commerce as "a very competitive but difficult environment with high stakes." In this environment, several consultants discussed the challenge of working with businesspeople to maintain a sense of perspective that incorporates a work–life balance. As Dr. Austin explained, "It's very easy to lose sight of other things of value, of importance. And that's why I can feel quite at a loss against the lure of: 'If I can just hang on, if we can just do this one more thing, then I'll cash out. Then I can turn my attention to my family, my health, my exercise program,' and so on."

The importance of balancing work and family is recognized by highly skilled performers. Elite athletes recognize that having a sense of identity outside their area of performance is a critical factor in preventing burnout and has been found to actually enhance performance (Danish, Petitpas, & Hale, 1993; Gould, Udry, Tuffey, & Loehr, 1996; Miller & Kerr, 2002). Most of the businesspeople we interviewed considered this work–family balance important to their own success. As David (banker) explained, however, this is not necessarily the norm: "There are plenty of people who don't have that attitude. They're just so driven. They think they've got to do it, and they've got to do it now, and that they'll eventually take time out for their family. What they haven't figured out is the family is going to grow up and be gone."

REPORTED CHARACTERISTICS OF PERFORMERS

Successful performers in banking were described as having drive, determination, a bit of greed, competitiveness, and a fear of failure. In the field of insurance, Carl said, "Most guys in my business are controlling type of guys, and they don't want to let go of anything." Creativity is required for success in advertising. Our advertising executive, Barry, noted that creative people are often motivated by idealism and may be arrogant. A reasonable degree of intelligence is considered a prerequisite in all areas of business.

More generalizable information appears to exist about lawyers than any of the other subgroups. Our personal experience working with lawyers is consistent with Arthur's description. He commented that attorneys "don't have a lot of patience" and described them as having a short attention span, being skeptical, and thinking they're unique. Anna, also an attorney, added that people in her profession often feel uncertain and insecure but are typically able to hide these emotions behind a "good front."

Anna mentioned characteristics of lawyers and the legal profession that we have frequently observed in our practices: The grueling hours, constant competition, and adversarial nature of the profession take a toll. Anna described the emotional fallout that may ensue:

> A lot of lawyers are desperately unhappy. While my decision to leave private practice wasn't a career change, it was a big change in terms of type of practice. One of the most depressing things about my decision was the number of people who just came into my office, closed the door and said, "Oh my god, how do I get out of here? How did you do this?" Even worse was the number of men who said "I wish I could afford to do this," but who just felt that making money was their raison d'être.

These observations echo concerns expressed throughout the legal profession (Benjamin, Sales, & Darling, 1992). An estimated 40% of young attorneys are dissatisfied with their jobs, resulting in more dropouts from law than from any other profession (Drogin, 1991). A study by the American Bar Association noted that most lawyers perceive their work environment as the major source of dissatisfaction (Benjamin, Darling, & Sales, 1990). Ninety-seven percent of the senior lawyers surveyed had changed jobs three or more times in the course of their careers. Increasing numbers of disillusioned lawyers are realizing that "they were never suited to legal practice in the first place" (Drogin, 1991, p. 119) and are seeking careers elsewhere. Lawyers suffer clinical depression at four times the rate of the general population (Benjamin et al., 1990). A random sample of attorneys in the state of Washington in 1987 ($N = 802$) indicated that approximately one third of the lawyers responding suffered from clinical depression, problem drinking, or cocaine abuse (Benjamin et al., 1990). Discontent is rampant within the profession. Lawyers struggle with a sense of declining professionalism as there is increasing emphasis on number of billable hours and decreasing attention to personal relationships with clients.

One of the business consultants, Dr. Benton, made two observations comparing athletes and people in the business world. Although these points are anecdotal, they have also been observed in our own practices and are worth noting. First, businesspeople tend to be receptive to techniques used by athletes, especially the use of imagery. However, imagery is used differently in the two domains:

> Athletes will do imagery before the performance; businesspeople use more imagery *after* the performance. The businessperson will do very little prepping, but when he gets in the train on his way home, he goes back through and replays the team meeting or his presentation in his mind. Depending on his thinking, he either beats himself up or compliments himself.

The second observation is that

> athletes who are trying to be consistent top performers really do know the power of using these mental training techniques both in their sport and away from the Olympic arena. They realize the only way these techniques work is when they can be on automatic pilot. And the way to get on automatic pilot is lots and lots of practice in *different* arenas. Businesspeople do not get that yet. They seem to think that their business stresses are separate from their life stresses. They do not understand that there is such a correlation in terms of how one impacts the other.

ROLE FUNCTIONS

The primary or ultimate purpose of businesspeople is financial profitability. David's comment highlighted this perspective and provided contrast to the performers in the other domains: "Greed, within bounds, is very good. It is a necessity in business." Our advertising executive, however, noted occasional difficulties with young, idealistic talent who sometimes struggle with the pragmatics of the business. "Creative people tend to be motivated by idealism. When it becomes a primary motivator, it's a very difficult management challenge. [They think] we should handle this business pro bono because it's the right thing to do. Well, we just laid off 24% of the work force and we don't have the money. Who cares if it's the right thing to do?"

Virtually all of the business performers emphasized the centrality of work relationships to optimal functioning. Barry, in advertising, said: "Everything comes down to relationships in our business. It's often not what you know, it's who you know. It's political." In the field of insurance sales, Carl described the process as essentially "selling a relationship." David (banker) emphasized the importance of trust and respect in all business undertakings.

Our consultants were even more emphatic about the value of rela-tionships and a work environment that nurtures excellence. Whereas executive coaching often focuses on the needs of an individual, numer-ous consultant programs emphasize changing the entire culture and en-vironment of an organization (Covey, 1989; Covey, Merrill, & Merrill, 1994; Jones, 2002). In the past several years, many businesspeople have paid increased attention to the importance of relationships and the emo-tional aspects of business, using the concept of emotional intelligence (Goleman, 1995).

Among our interviewees, the attorneys reported little difficulty be-ing prepared for the technical aspects of practicing law. However, they reported being not as well prepared for the requirements of managing relationships, both within the firm and with clients. Anna commented that lawyers need to possess a nearly impossible array of technical knowl-edge, salesmanship, and people skills.

> You have to have an incredible combination of technical skills; you have to know your profession; you have to know what you're doing; and you have to sell that to your client. You have to have the personality to bring in business and to maintain those relationships, and at the same time, deal with your partners and get your share of the pie. There are people in law school who are Number One in the class, have fabulous legal skills, and then get out in the real world and can't do anything with it. Conversely, there are lawyers who have all the people skills but don't have the technical skills.

Arthur, a former managing partner of a major national law firm, said that team building is difficult with lawyers, describing the process as be-ing akin to "herding snakes."

Our interviews suggested that clients may place unique demands on their attorneys. The French term for lawyer, *avocat*, is taken literally by some legal clients. They expect their attorney not only to represent them but also to be their *advocate* at all cost, sometimes in a way no mere mor-tal can accomplish. The sobering truth is that, in the adversarial context in which the majority of law is practiced, inevitably one side has to lose.

THE NATURE OF PERFORMANCE

While business performers must have a large amount of technical knowl-edge, memorization is not typically required for performance in this do-main. Emotions are typically minimized during performance, an ability that our banking executive, David, talked about with pride: "The style I prefer is one that has very moderate emotion involved in it. It's business.

It's not about personality; it's not about emotions at all. That is one of my strengths."

Although decisions in business are best made on the basis of logic rather than emotion, emotions are an important element in managing the group process to successfully accomplish a task. For a trial attorney, this may involve a dramatic show of emotion to elicit a certain response from jurors. Or the performances that are played out in boardrooms may require a leadership style that draws on the emotions of the participants. For example, Arthur (lawyer) described one of his most memorable experiences: He was faced with a deadline on a critical case in which all the parties had struggled until the wee hours of the morning. They were at a stalemate, but he refused to let them leave.

> I just basically said, "It's two o'clock and if you leave we will never get this done. So we are going to stay here until five o'clock, and we will either make this happen or we won't, but we are not going to walk away just because we are tired." Somehow, I was able to cajole everybody into staying. Everybody had to be there. If anybody had left, the whole thing would have fallen through. And we did it. We finished about seven o'clock and then we all went out to breakfast.

Performance in business is typically more demanding at a mental than physical level. Yet there are subtle physical demands. Arthur's anecdote reflects the aspect of performance that is most likely to take a toll on one's body: working long hours under high stress conditions.

In most situations, the stakes of performance in business are pride, ego, and money—at times vast amounts of money. On most occasions, failure is not experienced publicly. The increasing media attention focused on public trials, however, affects trial lawyers' visibility. The attorney's actions, mannerisms, and even attire may become subject to public scrutiny. In a limited number of situations, the risk of poor performance is literally a matter of life or death. A poor performance by a trial lawyer can result in an innocent person being put to death; a poor performance by a prosecutor can mean that a criminal is released, perhaps to molest, abuse, or kill again.

FAMILIARITY WITH CONSULTANTS

With the possible exception of the military, it is hard to imagine a domain that has more experience with consultants than business. When social psychology first began to emerge during the 1930s, business and industry became applied laboratories in the effort to better understand human behavior and motivation (Mayo, 1933). In the mid-1940s, Kurt Lewin conducted field research. The movie *Pajama Game* was reportedly based on a collaborative effort between Lewin and Alfred Morrow to increase productivity in a pajama factory (Leonard & Freedman, 2000). In the 1950s, companies such as Esso, Proctor & Gamble, and General Mills worked with consultants to improve organizational climates and group functioning (Leonard & Freedman, 2000; McGregor, 1960). The applied focus broadened in the 1960s to include both industrial and organizational factors, spawning the increased visibility and utility of industrial–organizational psychology. Team development began taking center stage within industry during the 1980s. The total quality management model (Deming, 1982) gained recognition and acceptance in several industries, as Americans competed with Japanese businesses. The 1990s witnessed a growing interest in the use of individual consultants or coaches to assist executives and middle managers in honing skills and coping with a rapidly changing world of business. A demand has developed for organizational consultants who can focus on creating and developing environments for fostering excellence.

The widespread use of consultants can be both an asset and a liability. Gaining entry into organizations familiar with consultants is likely to be much easier than in domains not as accustomed to them. However, with the proliferation of consultants in any field, there may be much more competition among consultants or executive coaches. Skills and knowledge may vary widely. Arthur, a former managing partner of a large law firm, articulated the down side: "One bad consultant will ruin it for the next three good ones."

Recommendations to Consultants

- Consultants working in business must be mindful of the rapid pace of change within the entire domain. Advances in technology and communication, and the globalization of markets, have created conditions in which drastic changes can occur in an extremely short span of time.
- With these rapid changes has come a corresponding shift in the ties and expectations concerning employment: Now, both management and employees see their relationship as temporary. It is increasingly important for individuals to have "exit strategies" in mind, even as they assume a new position.
- Greed is often an asset for performers in this environment.
- The enticement of financial gain poses a challenge for performers in establishing a balance between work and personal life.

- Although the primary goal of performers in this domain is financial profitability, the management of emotions and relationships is crucial to long-term success. Relationship skills are likely to be a major focus of any consultation in these domains.
- Effective performance in these areas typically requires a certain amount of deliberation, even if instantaneous: attention to various factors, evaluation of situations, and then selection from an array of alternatives. In general, performers report making the best decisions when they rely on logic, often with a correspondingly calm emotional state. Emotions may later be used, behaviorally, as one aspect of a performance strategy.
- Mental skills are typically more critical than physical abilities for successful performance in these areas.
- In most circumstances, money, pride, and ego may be at risk when performing. In some legal cases, the stakes may be greater.
- There is a substantial amount of data indicating that the prevailing stress on lawyers results in higher rates of depression, alcoholism, and substance abuse. Consultants working in this domain must have knowledge concerning the diagnosis and treatment of these conditions. They should be aware of appropriate community resources. In assessing these areas, they may want to consider a change in career as a viable option for unhappy attorneys. These risk factors also suggest that performance consultation may be particularly beneficial for individuals in this domain.
- Businesspeople, especially businessmen, are especially receptive to consultants' analogies and comparisons between sports and the world of business.
- Of the three domains we discuss, people in the business domain are most familiar with the concept of performance coaching and are most comfortable with using consultants or executive coaches. They are also likely to have the means to pay well for such services.

Unique Aspects of
High-Risk Professions 4

The stress of some operations is not the technical exercise. We could do a technically perfect operation time and time again with some types of problems and still end up with a 2–3% stroke rate. It's not because of any factor that you have control over; it's just the nature of the disease you are treating.

—Eric (neurosurgeon)

e have included a broad and diverse range of performers in the category *high-risk professions*, defining the domain by what is at risk during the performance: human life. Whereas athletes or performing artists may comfort themselves about an approaching event by saying, "It's not like this is a matter or life or death," for these performers there is no such reassurance. A human life may indeed hinge on one's performance. In this grouping we have included those whose performance involves saving life and performers who place their own lives at risk. We have also included those whose performance not only involves risk to themselves but may also involve the risk of taking another person's life.

One could argue that all physicians fall within the first category, "performing to save a life." However, as noted earlier, throughout this book we focus on performance in situations with a component of temporal urgency, in which abilities are brought into action at a given point in time. This definition directed us toward surgeons, emergency room physicians, and military medics. Our selections of those who risk their lives in performance were guided in part by domains that have shown growing interest in performance consultation. These areas included public safety workers (e.g., firefighters and police), race car drivers and their teams, and nuclear reactor personnel. We recognize that people in this latter group perform in isolation and operate in much more controlled environments than other performers in this domain; however the consequence of poor performance similarly involves direct risk of loss of their own as well as other people's lives. The cluster of professions that trains recruits to actually take a person's life includes the military and certain police specialty units, such as SWAT teams and snipers.

The High-Risk Domain

MILIEU

Each individual area in this domain is unique and deserves special attention, yet the areas are similar in relation to the intensity of stress: Death waits in the wings for these performers. It hovers. It is omnipresent. For some—those trained in the military—the death of another may even climax a successful performance. As unsettling as some may find the profession, police snipers must have extraordinary mental skills. As George commented, "You're not pulling the trigger in a reactive way. It's a proactive thing. It's a planned shot. You are the last resort for the police department and law enforcement. So there's time to think about it."

To those unfamiliar with North American Stock Car Auto Racing (NASCAR), it may seem unusual to include this domain as part of our study. Our decision to include it was guided by three factors: First, although we personally view auto racing as a sport, it has not been included in traditional studies of athletes and athletic performance. Second, this is a performance area where a mistake may cost a person's life. Third, in recent years, performers in this domain have shown a growing interest in consultation on the mental aspects of performance.

> I was in Haiti when a French police officer was shot by a sniper. I went along with my team to go after the sniper and take care of the injured parties. This was at night and an interpreter tried to be helpful by giving me more light. He actually put me in serious danger by back-lighting me, giving a shot—a sight picture—to a possible sniper out there. As soon as he lit me up I had an adrenaline dump. My fine motor skills went; I had auditory exclusion, tunnel vision; I couldn't find things in my aid bag—it has been arranged the same way ever since I became a medic. I just couldn't find anything. I lost it for about a minute. I finally took some deep breaths and got it together. The guy was med-evacuated into Port-au-Prince and, fortunately, lived.
>
> —George (medic–sniper)

Dr. Gordon Gates, who has experience with both Olympic teams and NASCAR teams, had no doubt that these are elite performers:

They are passionate. They are athletic. When they jump over the wall as one of the pit crew or climb into the cockpit, they need to be confident. They approach it like an athletic event. They are not a bunch of mechanics just changing tires. They are a high-performance team. They are athletes, and you need to treat them like that.

The mental demands of this sport are extremely high and extremely dangerous. To have some appreciation of the difficulty, one need only to think of the concentration required to navigate busy freeway traffic bustling along at 60 miles an hour. Now imagine going three times that fast while maintaining a high level of intensity, concentration, and competitiveness, throughout a four-hour period. During the few stops, the pit crew must work with flawless precision to service the car in under 18 seconds. A half second slower may mean dropping six places in the standings.

These high-risk areas are predominately composed of male performers, high in tradition, with rigid hierarchies and, typically, a militaristic mentality. The military metaphor was used by the physicians we interviewed. Eric, a neurosurgeon who received his training in both the United States and abroad, said that "the tradition of surgery is kind of militaristic; the training traditionally is very militaristic. The philosophy was if you were tough enough to do it, then you did not need anything, the stand-alone and take care of things yourself philosophy." Emergency room physician Frederick commented that

> the camaraderie that develops amongst house officers is very much akin to the camaraderie of people in the military together, in combat together. This plays into a macho-ism associated with physical stress: "I just put in a 110-hour week."

In addition to the macho attitude, one is likely to encounter a sexist stance within these areas. This is particularly true in the world of stock car racing, as described by consultant Dr. Gates:

> The old motor oil calendar with the gal who is quite well-endowed and wearing something low cut embodies the prevailing attitude toward women. Women are sexual objects in the sport. It's even endorsed and perpetuated by the women involved in the sport. The secretaries all wear mini-skirts and flirt with the guys. I may be over-generalizing a little, but they think it's normal for guys to whistle at you, and kind of like it.

The stresses of dealing with death are constant, but rarely discussed in these groups (Katz, 1999; Le Scanff & Taugis, 2002). Given the opportunity to talk one-on-one, our performers in each of these areas admitted wrestling with the specter of death. Emergency room physician Frederick confided,

Many, many years ago, I interviewed a cop in Kansas City. Although he had only been on the job 15 years, he told me he was retiring in a week. Usually, you'd go for 20 or 25 years to get a full pension. He explained, "Well, a couple of months ago I was sitting in my squad car and a black guy came up and asked me for directions to a particular area. I leaned over the glove compartment to pull out the map, and when I turned around he had a gun in my face. He pulled the trigger and it misfired. He ran off. We got him, and it turned out that he had an old grievance because of something that had happened to his brother. You know, he was just drunk or high on drugs or something, and this is the way he was acting out. The issue is that from now on every black man who approaches me, I'm going to have my hand on my gun because I'm scared. I'm not afraid they're going to kill me, I'm afraid I'm going to kill them."

—Dr. Irving Ingram (consultant, public service)

Nobody ever talks about making a mistake and a patient dies. If you talk to people in medicine, you talk about mistakes. If there is a bad outcome, they say, "I'm going to get sued." You don't want to think about having caused a death, which we've all done; but if you can transfer it and say "Well, the damn lawyers are going to get all over me," you can push it aside.

Neurosurgeon Eric remarked on the ripple effect of patient death:

Dealing with an unexpected complication like death can be really devastating to the physician. Unfortunately, it's the nature of what we do. There are going to be a number of people that we will maim or injure in some way. That is the horror of what we do. That's what we try to get away from. It may not be apparent to the patient, but to us, we know it was not an expected outcome. That can be incredibly frustrating, and takes its toll on family and other relationships.

Fear of litigation is a growing pressure experienced by performers in all of the areas of this domain. Malpractice insurance premiums are skyrocketing to the point that many physicians question the financial feasibility of practice (Johnson, 2003). Frederick routinely faced this issue with residents rotating through the emergency room:

There is this constant fear of making mistakes in the medical world. A lot of incredibly inefficient medicine is practiced because of that fear. We overorder lab tests; we overdiagnose people. I'm forever telling our residents, "Don't use malpractice as a crutch and an excuse for ordering a lab test. You are a doctor. You are professionally trained. You've got to learn how to take chances and play the odds. And medicine is a game of odds, absolutely a game of odds. You are going to miss things because ultimately, you have to get down to playing the odds."

Physicians are also frustrated by having to make decisions driven by the "business of medicine." They often entered the field because of a sense of calling and a desire to help people. Now, they struggle with the increased emphasis on running a profitable business. Time management, cost management, the labyrinth of insurance demands—all are factors that can create a dehumanizing experience for both patient and performer (physician) in today's medical culture.

Knowing that one can debrief after critical instances is important for maintaining the ability to isolate emotions during performance. For surgeons, discussion may occur with a trusted colleague who has been through a similar situation. For others, special personnel are brought in for this process. As described by George:

> The real concern for me is what happens after I take the shot. Many times a sniper is the only one who sees what he could see. So he has to make that life or death decision [alone]. And later, he thinks about the person he shot. Even though that person could be the biggest dirt bag in the world, there's probably somebody who loves him. And you're taking that human being away from the other person who loves him.

Frederick provided telling insights concerning the emergency room physician. In this setting, both speed and efficiency are essential. "One of the things you can measure in emergency physicians is how fast they are; you don't necessarily measure how good they are," he explained. However, success in this area of performance requires more than technical expertise, speed, or efficiency. The most important skill, Frederick suggested, is the ability to develop rapport rapidly with a patient and the patient's family. He thinks of the patient as part of a larger system, attending not only to the physical symptoms that are present, but taking into consideration the relationships in the patient's life as well.

> I do two quick reads when I walk into any room. Number one is, how sick is the patient. The other thing that is important is to absolutely figure out the dynamics of the human beings in the room. It is absolutely critical. What you have to do is find out what it is that you think is wrong with them [the patient] and treat that. But that is secondary to finding out what they think is wrong with them and treating that. You have to treat both.

He gives the following example of "diagnosing" the relationships and dynamics of those accompanying the patient.

> Say you walk into a room and there is a young woman and an older man. You say, "Hi. How are you?" You shake hands with the old man and the first person to open their mouth is the young girl and she's carrying on the conversation. And you say, "Do you live together?" and she says, "No, this is my grandfather and I'm visiting from somewhere else." And then you have this instant read where, okay, here we have guilty granddaughter with grandfather who comes in and has something wrong and there is this dynamic. How are you going to address the dynamic.

Medical practitioners have increasingly emphasized the influence of psychological and social factors in the healthcare setting on healthcare outcomes (Cassell, 1985; Quill, 1983; Williams, Frankel, Campbell, & Deci, 2000). This perspective is frequently referred to as a *biopsychosocial model of medicine* (Engel, 1977), a focus that is not limited to biological explanations and treatment of disease (Glass, 1996). Those who subscribe to this broader perspective are often said to practice "patient-centered" or "relationship-centered" medicine, in contrast to "physician-centered" medicine. "The relationship-centered approach involves physicians understanding the patients' perspectives, being responsive to the needs of patients (and in some cases their families), and sharing treatment-relevant power with patients and their families" (Williams et al., 2000, p. 80).

Elaborating and underscoring this point, Frederick rank ordered the skills necessary for his work:

> In emergency medicine, like anything else, the most important tool that you use in your job is your interpersonal skills. The second most important thing is time management and in our world, in my world, truly, the third most important thing is medical knowledge—third place.

Several studies have established a clear relationship between this collaborative approach and patients' satisfaction with their health care (Williams et al., 2000). Primary care physicians who are collaborative and relationship-centered are far less likely to be sued by their patients (Levinson, Roter, Mullooly, Dull, & Frankel, 1997). Collaboration may, however, be a function in part of the medical specialty. This same research indicates no correlation between a surgeon's attitude and the probability of legal action. This discrepancy may be explained by patients' expectations for the specific task at hand. Patients typically want to believe that their surgeon has extraordinary skills and judgment if they are facing an operation, and thus, more readily accept a physician-centered relationship. For dealing with day-to-day healthcare matters and general illness, they prefer and expect a more collaborative relationship.

Even though emergency room physicians were not specifically studied in the research described above, Frederick understands the power of the relationship-centered approach: "I am no more competent than any of the other physicians in the emergency room, but all of my patients like me—even the ones I hate. And I'm not going to get sued."

The most prevalent stresses experienced by police workers often involve organizational and political factors (Alexander, Walker, Innes, & Irving, 1993; Biggam, Pwer, MacDonald, Carcary, & Moodie, 1997; J. M. Brown & Campbell, 1990, 1994; Le Scanff & Taugis, 2002). Organizational stresses include lack of adequate funding and resources, time pressures, and work overloads. In their study of stress encountered by the French Special Forces police, Le Scanff and Taugis (2002) reported that officers felt pressured to overlook certain criminal acts during election periods. They were expected to maintain a desired "public image," even though some officers felt this image directly interfered with their actual job function.

The current litigious atmosphere affects performers in all of these high-risk areas. As noted earlier, physicians often order tests and alter their practice solely to protect themselves or to offer good defense in the case of a lawsuit; as a Special Forces medic and police sniper, George fears losing his house and finances if he makes a bad decision; and public safety officers are constantly aware of risks to their lives as well as potential legal repercussions to all of their efforts.

CHARACTERISTICS OF PERFORMERS

The people who are drawn to these professions typically must be reasonably bright and physically fit. They frequently have a sense of "calling." Consultant Dr. King described the sense of purpose for those pursuing military careers: "They are motivated to preserve a way of life, to protect freedom, their country—those kinds of things. They are not motivated to put money in their bank account." They often have a preference for adventure. The macho "he-man," however, is not necessarily the person who will excel in the military. Typically, out of a class of 120 who start the Navy SEALs program, only 15 will make it through. One of our consultants, Dr. Lindsay, has been involved in identifying the factors that predict successful completion of the program. Surprisingly,

> the person who had this Rambo image of the Navy SEALs just didn't make it. We found the key factor to be when the motivation an individual had was tied to something of high

personal importance. Several of these recruits, for example, had not excelled in school, but came from high achieving families. This was a chance to prove themselves to somebody, a significant other like their mother or father. Those were the ones who made it through.

ROLE FUNCTION

One interviewee, George, was unique in that he performed in two domains: He was both a Special Forces medic and a sniper for a special police unit. These roles may seem at odds with one another; yet for him, both are about saving lives: "The way I look at it, in both cases I'm saving somebody. I may be shooting to kill somebody, but I'm doing it to save an innocent person. That's what keeps me motivated in my training for sniping: saving an innocent person."

These performers must achieve a high level of technical proficiency that often includes preparation for every conceivable variation of performance. Eric, a neurosurgeon, explained how the excitement and challenge of variety is part of the appeal about his specialty:

> There is an attraction for people who go into this profession [neurosurgery], because it is incredibly varied. There are very few surgical specialties where you can operate from the head to the feet—a whole range of different structures all in the same week. The breadth is pretty huge. One of the things that steered me away from cardiac surgery was it was the same operation every day. There was no variety. You did the same thing. It is very intense when you do it, but there is no variety. In remembering some conversations with my partners, one of the common traits seems to be that people are attracted by the intensity and the variety.

Virtually all members of a NASCAR pit crew have dual roles: Each person is expected to have the technical expertise to work on the car in a specialized capacity; but each also has a specialized role within the elite team that goes "over the wall." When a car pulls in for a pit stop during a race, only seven people are allowed to cross the restraining barrier or "wall" to service the car. Within 18 seconds, a good team is able to change all four tires, refuel the car with 22 gallons of gas (without spilling any), and make adjustments to the suspension of the vehicle. Dr. Gates, consultant to a NASCAR team, explained: "It is complicated because if they are a pit crew, most of them have another job. They are under another car, getting it ready, and all of a sudden, they've got to run out and service the car that is racing."

Working a shift in the emergency room involves perpetual changes of role in relation to patients: being a consoling comforter with a family that has just lost a loved one, an optimistic purveyor of hope to a person waiting for test results, and a jovial and entertaining examiner as one distracts a 5-year-old child who is being sutured. "Having to change pace and to change your personality—not your personality but the way you are relating to patients—over and over again, over and over again, over and over again—it just makes me really tired," reflected Frederick, our emergency room physician.

> Everybody knows me and I am in a position of power. Nobody argues with me. They don't say "Why are you calling me?!" They say "Thank you very much" and they take care of things. If I am talking to somebody in the Emergency Department I have this air of being in control and people become much more efficient when they work with me. It is all team. There is no question what everybody's role is and it never deviates.
>
> —Frederick (emergency room physician)

In each of the high-risk domains, teamwork is essential. As Frederick described, "The absolute key to my efficiency is everybody else's efficiency. The key is to mobilize your team. The key is to make the people around you operate as efficiently as possible, and then you will operate as efficiently as possible."

Teams in high-risk professions develop a clear hierarchical order for making decisions. William Nolen (1970), a surgeon, described this in his autobiography: "I wasn't God by a long shot, but as far as power was concerned, I was closer to Him than anyone else at hand" (p. 272). Within the field of medicine, there is even a hierarchy among the various subspecialties. Eric, the neurosurgeon, commented: "We [neurosurgeons] are kind of known as the bullies in surgery. Normally when we have to do something, we have to do it then and everyone else has to get out of the way." On any given day, one's role and input may vary according to the team composition. For example, two surgeons may work together on a case, but "no matter what, the relief guy will never have the same stress responsibilities as the guy who starts. You are always going to feel like it is your case because you started the case and you are the one responsible for it—which you are, technically. There is a different level of preparedness if you are the assistant compared with the guy who starts it."

THE NATURE OF PERFORMANCE

In addition to technical knowledge, typically the physical demands in this domain are extreme. One consultant, Dr. Leo Lindsay, who has worked with both the Navy SEALs and elite athletes, marveled at the physical requirements of the military program.

What they were engaging in was more physically demanding and stressful than what most people experience in a lifetime. I am not denigrating the tremendous training that athletes go through, but they don't have to go through a week with three hours of sleep while at the same time putting up with mental abuse and huge physical stress.

In athletics, virtually all the variables that we're talking about are under your control. In gymnastics, the "horse" is always going to be exactly the same height from the floor. The marathon is always 26.2 miles. It ain't changing. The unpredictability in public service comes from the fact that there are so many variables out of your control. The environment that the firefighter or the police officer is in is incredibly malleable, volatile, changing.

—Dr. Irving Ingram (consultant, public service)

The physical demands are not limited to the military, police, or firefighters. Some surgeries can last eight to ten hours. Emergency room personnel and nuclear reactor monitors typically have rotating shifts that play havoc with their sleep cycle. According to emergency room physician Frederick, "Emergency medicine is unlike any other part of medicine. It is sort of assembly line shift work. You work two days, two evenings, two nights, and then you are off. You recycle."

The margin of error in these performances is virtually nil. These performers prepare by overlearning and rehearsing in a multitude of adverse situations, all geared toward maintaining the ability to focus, concentrate, and perform under any circumstance. Neurosurgeon Eric explained that he "focuses more on preparing for the worst-case scenario, knowing what could possibly go wrong and then hoping that if you prepare for the worst, it won't happen." George, a Special Forces medic, prepared by creating practice conditions to tax both his mental and his physical abilities. By controlling his stress response during practice, he has found it easier to manage his reactions in actual combat situations.

For performers whose work entails risk to life—their own or others—camaraderie, teamwork, and loyalty are essential. Fear of letting down the team is experienced as being even more critical than fear of losing one's own life. As George (medic–sniper) described it:

My greatest fear as a medic is letting my teammates down. It could be one of my friends on my team that I can't save. I've got to be able to face my teammates and say I did everything I could, I did things right. I've got to be able to live with myself if I couldn't save that person.

This camaraderie also breeds a unique, often irreverent, sense of humor as a means of coping with stress. This type of gallows humor formed the basis of the movie and subsequent TV show, *M.A.S.H.* Interviewee Frederick advised: "Consultants working with emergency room physicians would need to know what the environment was like. They would need to know the place of humor in our environment and why we are constantly telling bizarre jokes to each other."

Teamwork is essential in these domains, yet at the same time, each performer must be able to function independently. Describing practitioners in his field, Eric said, "Most neurosurgeons are fiercely independent people who tend to be rather nonconformist in their thinking. They may be fairly formal in their behavior, but how they get from A to Z is probably widely different." In a high-stakes profession, the person at the top is often lonely. The rigid hierarchy within these areas and the taboo concerning admission of doubt often create a sense of isolation for these performers, one that they must learn to accept and integrate into their lives.

In marked contrast to the performing arts, in which conveying emotion is central to peak performance, the suppression of emotions is essential for performance in the high-risk domain. In the midst of performance, there is no place for self-doubt. Taking an anthropological perspective on the world of medicine, Katz (1999) viewed this emotional distancing as essential to surgeons' effective development. Anesthesia has only been available for slightly more than 100 years; prior to that all surgeries typically involved excruciating pain. The emotional "coldness and insensitivity to patients were likely to have been necessary to enable them to distance themselves sufficiently to take necessary risks with frightened patients" (Katz, 1999, p. viii). The culture of surgery in the present day still contributes to this emotional distancing. The medical culture—including patient expectations—perpetuates surgeons as modern-day action heroes. A patient facing an operation does not want a surgeon with doubts, nervousness, or hesitancy. Patients want their doctor to have "the right stuff," explains Eric, the emergency room physician. This term—referring to the valiant and daring mentality of the first U.S. astronauts depicted in Tom Wolfe's novel (1979)—encapsulates the macho, determined, and certain style presumed necessary by physicians who regularly encounter high-risk situations. Similarly, a common motto among surgeons is "Sometimes wrong; never in doubt" (Gawande, 2002, p. 54). Le Scanff and Taugis's (2002) work with the French Police Special Forces corroborates the expectation that police officers act "without expressing doubt or feeling, blocking any emotional reactions" (p. 331). The ability to carry out an action and inflict pain or suffering on another person for the purpose of reestablishing order or domination is referred to as *virility*. Le Scanff also noted how virility and the suppression of anxiety or doubt are critical for effective performance in this domain. George's (police sniper) elaboration on the burden of "taking the shot" demonstrates the importance of not having doubts.

It's a decision. You can't make a mistake, you know, not even talking about the liability—the legal aspects. Hell, I could lose my house. I could lose my family. I could end up in jail the rest of my life if I made a bad decision.

Those performers who successfully isolate emotions in order to complete their required tasks may struggle with cutting off all emotional experiences in their lives. The total suppression of emotion can take a tremendous toll on interpersonal and professional functioning. "Even if emotions are repressed they still exist and can arise and threaten professional efficacy if a problem occurs, especially as most police officers are not ready to cope with stress" (Le Scanff & Taugis, 2002, p. 332). George (sniper and medic) demonstrated one method for dealing with this dilemma: By acknowledging his emotions, he was able to put them aside long enough to complete the task.

The first thing that I had to do in using any of this [mental skills training] was to acknowledge that I am an emotional being and that I could not deny that, no matter what. In our professional culture, we tend to be very stoic and quiet. And that's fine, in terms of professional bearing; but in terms of being able to deal with the emotions and how they translate into physiology, I had to acknowledge what I am. This is what I am. Okay; now I have to deal with it. I see a lot of guys just refuse to acknowledge it because maybe it's not how they think a man should be.

The suppression of emotions is echoed by Frederick's description of the ideal emergency room physician: "You may lose control of the environment, but you should not lose self-control. When the Hells Angels drive their motorcycles into the lobby of your emergency room, chaos ensues; but you must absolutely never lose your temper."

In his consultative work with a professional race car driver, one of Dr. Gates's goals involved assisting his client in suppressing emotions.

Basically, this was a guy whose wife had left him. He was really messed up. He went to a couple of clinicians—as he probably should have done. When they [the team] asked me to consult, I said, "I am not a clinician," and they told me they didn't want one. He owned the team and he had to drive. They wanted somebody who could help him focus. He had good people around him. They thought he was going to get killed because he was thinking about his wife at 180 miles an hour. I didn't have any illusions. We weren't solving the problem; we were doing triage—Band-Aids. But in the bigger scheme of things, first we needed him not to kill himself or anybody else. And it

It's acting for me. It really is. There is a certain way you are expected to behave and will behave to carry on that professional demeanor. You do it. Part of it comes from the fact that you deal with such a large number of highly unlikable people, people that there is no objective reason on this planet that you would want to be with. Not just patients, but staff and colleagues too—you get some real asshole general surgeons. You just have to have your professional mask. You undoubtedly have some patients that you despise. When you think about a person as they ought to be, they just are not there. You've got to deal with them. So you put on your professional mask. And when I put on my professional mask, I just don't get mad.

—Frederick (emergency room physician)

was putting Band-Aids on an artery that is bleeding. But sometimes Band-Aids are pretty damn important.

FAMILIARITY WITH CONSULTANTS

The relationship between performance consulting and this domain of high-risk performers provides an interesting paradox. It is visible particularly in relation to military personnel. On the one hand, these individuals and the organizations in which they work have a long history of studying the practices of "top performers." *The Art of War*, written by Chinese strategist Sun Tzu in 100 BC (Clavell, 1983), is standard reading for young military officers. It is both a resource on tactical strategies and guidance in leading troops and gaining their loyalty. As mentioned, the origins of modern day performance enhancement can be traced back to World War II, when social and behavioral scientists were recruited to study and improve leadership and team functioning.

On the other hand, these same performers view consultants with marked skepticism. With lives at stake, they are particularly reluctant to accept input from an individual who has not "walked the walk" and directly experienced similar life-threatening situations. For example, consultant Dr. Irving Ingram has gained credibility with the rank and file of firefighters and police with whom he works through spending countless hours "hanging out" with them. He has traveled in police patrol cars, ridden to fires, and spent time with officers in the aftermath of disasters. Dr. Kenneth King described a combination of life experiences as crucial to his being accepted as a credible resource to the military: having grown up in a rural area in which he was comfortable with the use of firearms, during an era supportive of the military, and then having been involved in the military himself.

Our consultants in high-risk areas suggest that having firsthand experience in the area in which they are consulting is ideal. Even without direct experience, consultants can still be accepted if they show respect, can demonstrate that they offer something of value, and acknowledge that they know their limitations.

> I think you do need to know your own weaknesses and limitations. You have to be sensitive to that. You don't have to apologize for them, but you have to be aware of them. You have to own them if you are to establish some kind of credibility with people. (Dr. Kenneth King, military consultant)

No other areas of performance evoke such intense emotions in both consultants and the general public as those that involve the taking of another person's life. It is critical that a consultant be prepared for his or her own emotional reaction and that of others. In the words of military consultant Dr. King:

> If you can't identify with their missions, if you can't in your own mind find yourself believing and feeling that there are things that you would fight for—that at times, what they do is necessary—then you are going to have a hard time working with them, both from a credibility standpoint and just from staying focused on trying to help them with what they do. I do believe that there are a lot of psychologists who are so anti-war, anti-guns, anti-violence, anti-whatever else that the hypocrisy they would feel in that situation would either affect them or be picked up by the client.

Perhaps with the exception of the physicians, these performers "don't want theories; they want to know it works" (Dr. Kenneth King, consultant). Our own consulting experience in working with physicians is consistent with the feedback from the doctors that we interviewed. These performers are best approached by offering suggestions in a cafeteria-like fashion, where the consultant would "give options and make them feel like they are directing it themselves" (Eric, neurosurgeon). Although this is a good guideline for effective consultation in general, it is specially true in working with surgeons. Simply put, most people don't like to be told what to do. Extremely bright, talented, surgeons who are accustomed to being in charge of making life-and-death decisions on a daily basis *really* don't like to be told what to do. When consultants bring their knowledge to the table in a collaborative fashion, surgeons can choose for themselves what has the best chance of success.

As NASCAR has evolved into a multimillion dollar industry, it has experienced a dramatic shift from its origins in which "good ol' boys" honed their driving skills by illegally hauling moonshine (homemade whiskey) across the rural roads of the southern United States. Racing teams are an interesting culture of highly skilled craftsmen, high-tech equipment and resources, and business entrepreneurs. A growing number of teams have incorporated programs to address both the physical and the mental requirements of performance. It is common for a team to have state-of-the-art exercise facilities. The use of performance consultants is growing, but these activities tend to be a closely guarded secret and kept highly confidential, for a number of reasons. For one, with so much at stake, every team is looking for "an edge" and does not want a competitor to know what they are doing. Second, NASCAR is the fastest growing spectator sport in the United States (General Motors, 1998). Drivers become overnight celebrities and function in high-profile situations. "Whether we like it or not, in auto racing there is still a stigma to working with [performance consultants]," commented Dr. Gates. A consultant entering this arena must be particularly sensitive to the intense competition between teams, the importance of confidentiality in this culture, and the social pressures that go with rapid ascension to celebrity status.

From all the emphasis on "right stuff," virility, and macho mentality, one would expect that it would be difficult for a woman to be accepted as a consultant in these domains. Interestingly, anecdotal evidence suggests the opposite. Our consultant with the Navy SEALs supervised several individuals who provided psychological services for the soldiers. He reported that the most successful supervisee was a woman. Le Scanff demonstrated her effectiveness in working with police Special Forces (Le Scanff & Taugis, 2002) and candidates for space missions (Le Scanff, Bachelard, Cazes, Rosnet, & Rivolier, 1997). In each of these situations, participants were specifically addressing issues of stress. It may be that when the consultant is a woman, it is actually *easier* for a male performer from these domains to drop his emotional barriers and discuss vulnerabilities and fears. This is a topic that deserves further investigation.

Recommendations to Consultants

- The work of high-risk performers consists of performances in which human life is at stake. With little margin for error, performers prepare by overlearning and through extensive preparation for performance under adverse situations. Consultants working in these domains must be well-grounded in theories and techniques of concentration, attention, and focus.
- Successful performance typically requires the suppression of emotions and the maintenance of a calm, detached mental state in which decisions can be made and actions implemented. After com-

partmentalizing and detaching from emotions during performance, performers often struggle to integrate emotions in nonperformance situations (either after the performance or in interpersonal relationships).

- Successful performance in many areas of this domain requires extremely high levels of physical fitness, in addition to a reasonable degree of intelligence. Prospective consultants should be knowledgeable about a wide range of physiological factors that affect performance (e.g., nutrition, sleep, exercise, and recovery) and may require additional training to gain this knowledge.

- Teamwork is essential for success in these areas; performing under high-risk circumstances breeds a strong sense of camaraderie and loyalty. These teams are hierarchical in nature. Consultants are advised not only to have expertise in group dynamics but to be knowledgeable and comfortable working with hierarchical groups.

- There is persuasive evidence that within the medical domain, a physician's interpersonal relationship skills are critical to performance success. This is an area in which a performance consultant may be particularly useful.

- Individuals often have strong opinions and intense emotions about performance in which human life may be taken. Consultants whose personal values are at odds with the performer's required role are not likely to be of assistance. These professionals should refrain from attempting to consult in such situations.

- Performers in these domains are skeptical of consultants who have not had direct performance experience in similar high-risk circumstances. It is crucial that a consultant know and acknowledge his or her limitations.

- Theory is often of little value to high-risk performers; they are more interested in practicality and effectiveness: Does it work?

- A collaborative approach is often most helpful for high-risk performers who routinely make life-and-death decisions. A consultant is advised to offer suggestions in a cafeteria-like "menu" rather than attempting to tell the person what to do.

- The culture of these domains is typically male-dominated, hierarchical, militaristic, high in tradition, and sexist, one in which "macho" male behavior is accepted and often encouraged.

- Although the culture is generally sexist and male-dominated, there is evidence suggesting that female consultants may be effective, especially when the goal of consultation involves dealing with emotions and stress.

Unique Aspects of the Performing Arts | 5

If you are going to be out there on television, the radio, or the stage, you expose yourself. Whether it is spoken or unspoken, you open yourself up to a certain amount of criticism. People are looking at you and they are judging you for what they see. If you knew what they really thought, many times you would not be able to function, so you have to think of yourself as being something other than what you really are in order to get through.

—Ian (actor and broadcaster)

n describing the experience of being an actor, whether on the stage or behind a radio microphone, Ian captured the sense of vulnerability of the performing artist. The artist has nothing to rely on or hide behind. The performance may be physical or cerebral; it may involve the dancer's body or the percussionist's drums; it may be an audition or the routine iteration of a long-learned part. Yet it always involves judgment by an audience, an engagement that determines whether the performer is good enough.

In the sections that follow, we look at both the similarities and differences within the domain of performing arts, as well as some contrasts with the other major domains. We also consider the milieu, reported characteristics of performers, role functions, nature and risks of performance, and the familiarity of performing artists with consultants and their role.

The Performing Arts Domain

MILIEU

As with the business and high-risk domains, there are particular characteristics to the milieu of the performing arts. We highlight those characteristics that pertain to the role of competition and tradition in shaping and maintaining performing artists, as well as issues of gender and the stresses that are especially notable in this domain. We also describe some of the contemporary changes in the milieu.

The competitive milieu of the performing arts is sometimes unrecognized, overlooked, or minimized. We tend to think of sports as competitive but performing arts as lyrical. Yet competition is endemic to the performing arts. Each area of performing arts has a labeled hierarchy: There is the first chair of an orchestral section, the principal dancer, the "talent" of broadcasting, and the lead role in acting. Where there is a star, there are also lesser lights.

The competitive experience begins at the earliest levels and continues throughout the performing artist's career. Some performing artists, such as actors and many musicians, earn their livelihood by freelancing, competing for roles as they occur. Ballet dancers are part of a company, but they compete for particular roles or status.

The level of competitiveness is often related to the particular art form and the roles available within it. For example, violinists and cellists typically train with the expectation that they will have a solo career. Viola and double bass players, on the other hand, usually anticipate performing in ensemble settings. As an orchestral violinist, Diane described the developmental experience of competition among violinists:

> Everyone was a child prodigy. It's a very dog eat dog kind of thing. You have to be really talented to even get a halfway paying job; you have to be the "big deal" kid. All those big deal kids' parents had told them they were the next Heifetz [famous violinist], and now they're lucky if they get an orchestra job. They come into an orchestra and find themselves just not getting the kind of attention they anticipated.

Within any one area of performing arts, comparison and competition can occur along a number of dimensions. Dr. Martin (consultant, music) pointed out that musicians may be ranked not only by the quality of the music they produce, but also by the ability to sight-read music. These types of evaluations occur especially in the process of auditioning—a unique, regularly experienced aspect of competition for performing artists. The Juilliard School in New York stands as the epitome of and symbol for the highest level of musical training. Diane commented, without exaggeration, that "kids at Juilliard commit suicide from the pressure." A jury panelist at Juilliard remarked: "I hate audition time at Juilliard. The whole building shakes" (Kogan, 1989, p. 14).

The need to prove oneself over and over again, individually and against others, is a frequent and challenging aspect of acting in particular. Auditioning is a fact of life for actors. The emotional toll that it takes was described by Keith: "Auditioning is huge. That's 90% of our lives, and it's always so different and it's always so bad. I think it's important to understand performers in that context."

The audition process is also stressful because performers typically receive little feedback from those conducting the audition (Kogan, 2002). Furthermore, judgment may be entirely subjective, and to that extent, arbitrary and unpredictable. Among the many unstable elements of the performing arts milieu, one's success in competition does not in and of itself ensure the linear progression of one's career. "Unlike the business world, the amount of effort and time put in to master your craft in the arts does not pay off with predictable success" (Dunkel, 1989, p. 51). Keith commented on the general uncertainty that actors experience. Instead of a stable path involving clear steps, specific goals, constructive feedback, and accomplishments that build on one another, culminating in a definite, successful outcome, actors experience their careers as a lottery, dependent ultimately on luck. As a consultant, Dr. Osborne notes that this sense of randomness has been codified among actors. They recognize that they are likely to do well if they experience two out of three: luck, talent, or perseverance.

The milieu of performing artists also involves the heavy weight of tradition, whether they are adapting to it or rebelling against it. In contrast to visual artists, playwrights, composers, or choreographers, performing artists are noted for their interpretive rather than creative skill (Kogan, 2002). Classical musicians work from a standard repertoire, with traditions encompassing the composer, styles of performance practice, and a ready catalog of recordings of other musicians' interpretations. This sense of tradition can have various effects on performers. Diane, for example, considered the universality of music performance to have a transformative, spiritual quality. At the same time, the weight of tradition can hang heavy on the performer. As a pianist, Ilene noted the complexity of technical challenges and expectation; music, she said, involves an

> interplay of visual reading skills (reading music) that have to combine with the physical skills (of playing the instrument) that then have to combine with the whole body of interpretative tradition. As a pianist, when you're playing the standard literature, there's just so much background to it and so many years of performances and ways it "must be done."

Ballet, like classical music, is rooted in a long, specific tradition. Dance critic Deborah Jowitt spoke about the hierarchical, at times "dictatorial," culture of ballet training (2001). There is paradoxical complexity in that a ballet student looks for the teacher to criticize, or make "corrections," as a sign that the student is worthy of attention. Karen Kain (1994), prima ballerina in Canada for many years, described the role of "corrections" in her autobiography:

> In the perfectionist world of dance, teaching traditionally emphasizes "corrections." [Kain's teacher] singled me out, giving me a dozen corrections every class, while everybody else got two or three. Nobody thought for a minute that these frequent corrections meant I was making more mistakes than anyone else; in the elite world of dance, only those who have promise are given these attentions. (pp. 11, 15)

For many serious young dance students, the stress of early training encompasses not only the rigors and intensity of ballet, but the challenge of leaving home in their early teens and boarding in a distant city. In this, young dancers are not unlike young and talented hockey players or gymnasts, who also may need to relocate to obtain optimal training.

Tradition within ballet also sustains rigid expectations with regard to thinness, body proportion, and flexibility. The research literature and our interviewees, both performers and consultants, were uniform in asserting this fact of dance life.

> The quest for physical perfection . . . imposes a punishing ethic on dancers who fail to conform to cultural expectations for thinness. Ballet is anaerobic; thus, dancers must be naturally thin, because a low weight cannot be achieved through dancing alone. (Hamilton, Hamilton, Warren, Keller, & Molnar, 1997, p. 131)

Regardless of a ballet dancer's level of talent or amount of work, if her body does not meet traditional aesthetic and technical standards, she will not succeed in this profession. (We have deliberately used the female pronoun here because of the conjunction of ballet aesthetic and sociocultural norms in regard to women and weight.) "Anatomy is destiny," commented dance consultant Dr. Desmond. "You're attracted to the field from a very early age, sometimes as early as age 2. But if you don't have the turn-out or the feet or the extension, it's not going to happen."

The role of tradition can also affect the ways in which a potential consultant may be perceived by performing artists. If you are not part of the domain, you may be viewed as "other," foreign, an outsider. Consultants who work with musicians, actors, and ballet dancers all spoke of the ways in which many arts organizations maintain a narrow and self-protective stance. For example, Dr. Norris described the music business as a closed system, in which few outside consultants get hired. Dr. Osborne commented that consultants working with actors "have to know the work

One soloist, a wonderful dancer, is just below principal, but she wants to be a principal. Although she has done some principal roles and she's done them really well, she's suited to a certain kind of role. Usually it's a dramatic role where she's a bit of an oddball, a character. She has a beautiful face, she's intelligent, she's musical, she's a worker. But as beautiful a dancer as this girl is, she just wasn't born with the legs and the feet and the physique to do the real ballerina type roles.

"It's so hard for someone like her, a dancer who has everything inside but doesn't have everything from God. No matter how hard she works, she's never going to be able to dance like the ones that just were born right. Now she's 27, and each time the casting has gone up all year she's cried because it wasn't what she'd hoped she was going to get."

—Charlotte (dancer)

context. They have to know the real world and what it's like to be in that world." Dr. Desmond referred to the world of ballet as hierarchical and militaristic. She described it as

> very cloistered in some ways. If you don't speak their language, they will often write you off. If a sport psychologist tries to go into a ballet classroom and apply the same techniques, not understanding how a classroom works, they wouldn't be interested. You'd have to know how the system works. They have been training dancers the same way for a hundred years. You couldn't start saying, "Well try this or try that," they're not open to trying this or that. They do it *their* way, and you have to work their way.

Although issues of gender and other demographic characteristics are relevant in all domains, our interviewees in the performing arts commented specifically on gender more than did interviewees in other areas. Because of our limited sample size and composition, we cannot make comparative conclusions. However, gender inequalities are experienced or noticed throughout the performing arts. We heard comments in regard to ballet, theatre, and classical music. We share them as anecdotes rather than fully documented truths.

Ballet attracts a significantly larger number of female than male students. Only recently have ballet schools begun to address the differential expectations of male and female dancers within ballet culture and specific school environments (Wootten, 2001). In part because of the disproportionate number of women in ballet and the limited number of roles, greater competition is likely to exist between the women than the men. One of the effects, Charlotte suggested, is that the women who are selected tend to have more discipline and to concentrate for longer periods of time than the men.

Similarly, Larry noted the effect of disproportionate involvement of men and women in theatre: "There are more women in the business and fewer parts for women. I generally find that if you take 20 actresses and 20 actors, there will be more better actors among the women than among the men." In his consulting work, Dr. Osborne has seen the challenges that occur for women as they age: Unless female actors are well-established and exceptionally talented, the roles available to them are limited. Despite various attempts at reform and change, the social attitudes of the general culture, especially with regard to women and minorities, continue to be reflected within the film industry (Abramowitz, 2000; hooks, 1996; Null, 1993).

Among musicians, the orchestral violinist's observations on gender reflect certain socialized norms of interaction. Diane commented that men in an orchestra are generally less cooperative than women: "They're not as good ensemble players as women." Other female musicians noted, however, that at times women personalize interactions to such an extent that their reactivity can interfere with the smooth functioning of the group.

Three particular stressors may affect performing artists more than other types of performers: the longevity of their professional life, financial issues, and the use of illegal or prescribed substances. Career longevity in the performing arts can be determined by a number of factors, such as the amount of physical wear and tear exacted by the profession, work availability, and financial stability. Of the performing arts, ballet, like professional sports, by its very nature has temporal limits. Ballet has been described by Anna Marie Holmes, the former artistic director of the Boston Ballet, as "the butterfly profession. Dancers have a short-lived time of real beauty, and then you go" (Kaye, 1998, p. AR1). After an intensive period of professional performance, most ballet dancers retire when they are in their 30s to 40s (Kogan, 2002). Intensely involved with and isolated by their art, ballet dancers rarely plan for their postcareer future, even though they acknowledge its importance. The challenges of career transition from ballet are augmented by a culture in which it is atypical for dancers to be college graduates; in fact, up to a quarter may have dropped out of high school. Retirement from dance may "usher in a series of losses that encompass income, workplace, community, and most important, loss of identity" (Hamilton & Hamilton, 1991, p. 43). At the same time, it is important to recognize the potential advantage of early retirement from one's first career: Dancers may be young enough when they retire from dance to successfully change vocations (Greben, 1999). When they do engage academically, in part because of the discipline honed by years of rigorous professional engagement, their level of academic achievement is often remarkably high (Sidimus, 1998).

Performers in modern dance may experience more career flexibility than ballet dancers, in that a number of them move into their career following academic training in dance and potentially can maintain a somewhat longer dancing career. Other performing artists, whose professional lives are less dependent on total body strength and endurance, may still experience career limits in relation to the effects of their art on their physical being. Common, and sometimes career-ending, injuries among musicians include repetitive strain injuries and loss of hearing.

In contrast to dancers, whose lives during their performing years may be professionally filled to overload, actors spend a considerable amount of their time *not* performing. Actors are notoriously unemployed or underemployed. Kogan (2002) noted that at any one point in time, 95% of New York stage actors are not engaged in their craft.

Although superstars in the performing arts, like those in sports, may have immense amounts of disposable income, the vast majority of performing artists tend to be markedly more financially circumscribed. The romanticism of the "starving artist in a garret" remains a cultural attitude at some levels. Artists are often underpaid, in part because of an unarticulated assumption that their art should be enough to sustain them (Sidimus, 1998). The stresses of insufficient finances, underemployment, or unemployment may be chronic, not merely acute.

As in professional sports (Carr & Murphy, 1995), but perhaps unanticipated for those not in this field, alcohol and other substances are intertwined in the field of music. Reviewing nearly 200 years of drug use in the arts, Lanchester recently reflected on the central role of drugs especially in relation to popular music, most particularly jazz. "The history of dope-fiend jazz musicians is the history of jazz" (Lanchester, 2003, p. 84). Both legal and illegal substances are used by some musicians to alter perception and at times to cope with stress. The use of mind-altering substances especially for stress management in other performance populations has also been noted (Abramowitz, 2000; Hamilton & Hamilton, 1991).

Some percentage of performers undoubtedly use medication as a method to cope with stress, yet very few spoke with us about medication. Within the musician community, the nonselective beta-blocker Inderal (propranolol) is used with such frequency to manage per-

> I only know one guy who will admit that he takes Inderal, but you hear rumors about it. Virtually every French horn player in the world takes it, yet they don't want people to know. They *really* don't want people to know. There are some classical music email lists, and there are discussion boards for various instruments. I was scrolling through the French horn board, and there were several threads about Inderal and how much to take, like: "I took 20 mg. for the audition in Houston and it was too much because . . . ." Right down to discussing fine-tuning the dosage. If you take too much your performance will be really flat, and if you take too little it won't do anything for you.
>
> —Diane (musician)

formance anxiety that it has been described as the musician's underground drug (Dunkel, 1989). In our interview, Faith (singer) commented:

> I have a student who used to suffer just horribly from stage fright. She would just get up and be amazed at how shaky she was. She wasn't expecting to be shaky and she'd be so mad that she was shaking. She did try a beta blocker with great success. She got church solo work, and just felt like: "I'm going to get these beta-blockers so I don't fall apart. I'm not worried about it. I know my music; I know what I'm supposed to be doing."

The milieu of performing arts also changes over time. Currently, young ballet dancers have fewer dance opportunities than used to be available. Charlotte observed that this factor has major consequences for comfort with performance: Fewer performance opportunities mean fewer opportunities for practice, repetition, and general ease with being on stage. Charlotte elaborated:

> We used to go on tours for months and months and months, and I'd do a role over and over and over. In some ways you get more obsessive about every detail, but you get to a point where you can go on stage in a calm manner, normal and fully conscious, and not just "Oh my God there's a light in that wing that's right in my eyes, and I'm trying to do this step. I had no idea there would be that," that sort of horrible discovery that you get when you aren't in the first cast, and you're on stage for the first time for your first show.
>
> Young dancers today don't get nearly the same number of performances. Usually they have two shots at something: The first one is like a dress rehearsal. At the end of it, they don't know what they did, because they're coping for the first time with sets and costumes and lights and all that. They just start to get the hang of it with the second one. And then they don't do it again for three or four years. It's really cruel. But that's just actually the reality of the performing arts these days.

For broadcasters, Grace noted that niche marketing is now critically important. Supply and demand have changed within the industry:

> You better have something unique that is content-oriented, because having a great voice is not going to be enough anymore. Thanks to deregulation under President Reagan, we have a rapidly growing monopoly of broadcast companies. Fewer and fewer companies own all of the broadcast outlets in radio and TV. Manpower is very expensive. Opportunities are severely limited. They are switching to automation, because

human beings are notoriously unreliable. They are running satellite music services and satellite programming and replacing human beings with data coming out of outer space. They are so bloated with debt that they have to increase their operating profits. In a universe that is not limitless profit, you have to cut expense in order to keep growing that profit line.

REPORTED CHARACTERISTICS OF PERFORMERS

As with other domains, character generalizations have limitations and exceptions, and this is true among performing artists as well. It is useful for a consultant to have a sense of characteristics or attributes that apply generally to all performers but then approach each individual and situation as unique.

Among our consultants, Dr. Osborne was especially enthusiastic about working with performing artists, describing them as "wonderful people to work with. As a group, they have really faced themselves, they know things about themselves, and they're willing to go places which most people don't readily go to." We have found that performing artists, perhaps especially actors, are particularly interested in understanding themselves, seeing this self-exploration as useful to their art. One of the actors, Larry, described actors as "more mercurial than most people." Because of the constant demand for actors to take on different roles, he suggested that actors are especially adaptable and have changeable personalities.

The task of an actor is to take on a personality for a particular role, "becoming" someone else, albeit for a limited period of time. This can leave the actor less sure of his or her own personhood and personality. In working with one such actor recently, we encouraged him to notice and keep track of moments when he was most "himself," almost as if he were exploring and creating a new role, so that he could develop a clearer identity.

Being an actor requires some fluidity of personality, and this may be reflected in a certain tentativeness and fragility of ego. Some actors, Larry suggested, use cynicism to protect how much they care about the profession. Ian, with experience in both theatre and broadcasting, describes people in both arenas as displaying "enormous egos" to mask an underlying fragility.

> I used to go to these broadcast conventions when we were still playing phonograph records. I would be on the escalator from one floor to the next and I would be hearing all these people talk about how great their numbers were or "this great new format" and "I have a hit record here," and I thought, "This is all bullshit. This is just radio. You are playing records. All these

D.J.s with these enormous egos. You are just playing records.
Who do you think you are?" and it was because that is how
they got through their day. That is how they get the courage to
be in front of other people and walk that high wire.

Although it may be more of a "right" than "left" brain activity, music
is highly cerebral. There is the frequently noted connection between music
and mathematics. We also have noticed that musicians often like to play
with language in ways that would be more expected among linguists. At
times it seems as if there's a direct correlation between the obscurity of
the music played and the use of puns and double entendres. Having
worked with musicians in a variety of genres, Dr. Norris observed that
there seems to be a match between personality and type of music, as well
as the kind of issues likely to occur. For example, jazz musicians, whose
music may be improvised, enjoy extemporizing and engaging in the creative process, even though they may need assistance in understanding
when to lead and when to follow. Orchestral musicians, whose roles are
supportive and whose music is prescribed, may be more passive and may
need assistance in using the power or influence available to them.

Sport psychologists recently have been applying research on adaptive and maladaptive perfectionism to athletes (Gould, Dieffenbach, &
Moffett, 2002). Broader consideration of the dimensions of perfectionism has also begun with regard to performing artists (Gould & Pennisi,
2002; Hamilton, 2002; Hays, 2003; Krasnow, Mainwaring, & Kerr, 1999).
Among our consultants, Dr. Martin characterized musicians as primarily
desiring perfection and fearing making mistakes. Perfectionism is also
highly characteristic of dancers, especially in ballet. Dr. Desmond contrasted dancers with actors, describing the former as perfectionists and
introverted and the latter as "laid back, everything is just sort of out there,
and they're more extroverted than dancers tend to be."

Hesitant to generalize, former dancer Charlotte commented:

I don't know if this is just in dance—it probably isn't. I'm sure
in the acting profession it's kind of rampant too. Because of the
kind of world it is, there are huge issues of insecurity and lack
of confidence, and it's a very tricky balance to remain humble
and open and to have confidence in yourself at the same time.
You seem to get one extreme or another: the ones who think
they know it all and the others who are like little baby birds in
the nest, always so needy that you constantly have to tell them
they did well.

Musicians may be less likely than other performers to be aware of
the mind–body connection in relation to their art, and consequently they
may be less likely to care for their bodies. Dr. Martin commented that

many musicians are physically "under par," not paying attention to the importance and value of muscular, physical, or kinesthetic training. Similarly, they may not understand the impact of nutritional intake on their musicianship. An orchestral musician with whom we worked presented with borderline anorexia. As she began to eat more nutritious food and increased her caloric intake, she pleasantly discovered that she had more energy for the long hours of rehearsal and performance.

Our experience and interviewees' comments suggest that as a group, actors are more attuned to physical tension in their bodies and often have learned the importance of breathing techniques to help adjust physical tension. Instruction in basic relaxation and imagery techniques is common in actors' training. A consultant working within this domain can often build these foundational skills for application in broader areas, such as dealing with tension while auditioning or improving relationships with co-workers.

ROLE FUNCTION

As noted earlier, role function addresses the various expectations beyond the immediate performance, such as technical expectations, attending to business aspects including marketing and running a profitable enterprise, maintaining relationships with the public or "political structure," and dealing with relationships within a group or troupe of performers.

The technical aspects of performance differ between the various types of performers within this domain. A number of the performers commented that although a consultant need not actually *know* the technical specifics, it is important to know what the technical issues are and whether they are being appropriately addressed.

Each of the instrumental and vocal musicians spoke about specific elements of the technical aspects of being a musician. Because the musician either is the instrument or is using her or his body in conjunction with the instrument for performance, it is important to know about various practical, technical, and physical issues. For example, Faith pointed to the additional physical demands experienced by singers when they are required to use their full vocal range as compared with working within their comfortable or natural range. This physiological stressor may stem from the specific composition, the performer's interpretation, or others' demands (conductor, audience, or current fashion). Diane also described some of the technical challenges of specific instruments: "Most brass and wind players—especially brass players—find it's very, very difficult to play to age 65 because their 'chops' go." With age and overuse, the muscles around their face and their mouth may stop functioning effectively. Other musicians may be subject to repetitive strain injuries or hearing problems related to the bombardment of loud music—whether their own or others'.

Role functions also vary depending on whether performance can potentially improve or occurs only in the present moment. Grace spoke of the evanescence of talk radio. "Talk radio is live and it's immediate. It's intimate. Once you say it, it's out there and it's gone. In live talk radio, you can't do over. There is no filter in between your words and their ears. It's out there. That is what makes it exciting." Her comments are also relevant to live performance in music, dance, and theatre, in contrast to recordings, film, and video productions.

Not unlike psychotherapists' entrepreneurial knowledge, performers generally learn about the business of performing as they experience the profession, rather than during their training. The extent to which the business of the profession is central to the performer's role is in part a function of the particular performance area and one's role within it. To market themselves, actors and musicians must know how to make demonstration videos and CDs. As a conductor, the business aspect of his profession occupies a large proportion of Harold's time and energy. The demands are both complex and central to his role: "The management of people and programs and budgets and all of the sort of nonmusical things that never get covered in school ends up being probably 75 to 80% of my job."

Similarly, a ballet dancer who is a member of a company has very different business responsibilities than a dancer with administrative responsibilities. Charlotte, a retired dancer, is now an arts administrator. She compared the business world of dance to an orchestra full of talented, strong-willed musicians in which

> there's one person (the conductor) who's appointed because of his expertise to make decisions, and each one has to fall in line behind the leader; otherwise, it's chaos. And that's sort of how a ballet company is. You have all these strong personalities who work very hard and have very definite ideas about how they want to dance and how they see a role. And then you have somebody whose job it is to oversee that, stylistically, there's a cohesive production, and that things are all in the same line of thought.
>
> If everybody does what they think they should do with their own part, you have a production that has no cohesiveness. Artistic directors are more than just the CEO of a company. They have to get everybody on board to be approaching different productions with the same kind of through line. Everyone puts their own stamp on what they do, but to have a satisfying artistic experience from an audience's point of view—it's like a director with a bunch of actors: Actors all think that they're experts on every classic play that's ever

been written, how they see it and how they would do each role. A director is hired to harness all that energy and focus it.

In broadcasting, the business of running the business is particularly complex. In part, this is because the industry attracts young people and gives the appearance of high energy and liveliness. Grace explained that

> because it's a fun business, people enter it young and inexperienced. They may not focus on industry changes and dealing with the realities of the business world. My business attracts a lot of people who are: "Dude, you rock!" and that is super good, except when you have to negotiate a contract.

Similarly, Ian noted with some bitterness the power differential and antagonism between management and performers in broadcasting:

> The programming aspect of a commercial radio station or a commercial TV station is evil. Programming is seen as just being there to fill the time between the commercials. The commercials bring in the money; the talent spends it. So you are a necessary evil. They want to maximize the profit. They want to maximize what they get from you. They will drive you until you are dead.

> There are so many intangibles, because talk radio is an invisible product. You need to know oceans of stuff about the population—demographics and psychographics. You need to have an understanding of what radio is: We fill space between commercials. That is what we do. We're an advertising vehicle.
>
> —Grace (broadcaster)

Most artists function within an ensemble at least some of the time, and thus, group relationships are an important factor within the performing arts. For example, even musicians who are known as soloists often play or sing with groups of varying sizes. Similarly, although auditioning is a solo enterprise, among actors the cast that gets assembled is intensely, even if briefly, connected with one another. Other actors are members of a repertory company, changing roles from one play to another, but essentially working with the same people. These same variations of group involvement occur among dancers.

Larry suggested that actors are particularly attuned to nuances of interaction, and provided a developmental explanation for his statement:

> Actors have a particular sensitivity to the reactions of other people. Generally for actors, there's been some kind of breakdown or some kind of problem in childhood, some kind of disruptive pattern in the relationship with their family that then makes them more aware of what people are thinking and

feeling. Mine was that I was adopted and I didn't know till I was 26. And certainly for other actors, there was some kind of problem in the beginning and they have to find ways of coping, so their sensors became extra tuned, extra fine, in order to perceive what was happening, to avoid pain, to survive.

In many of the performing arts, an interesting paradox relates to the simultaneous need for connection among a group of artists, yet an implicit or explicit hierarchy of power. "Remember," commented a film producer recently, "film is a monarchy, not a democracy" (Abramowitz, 2000). Although conducting has been described as "this profoundly undemocratic activity" (Littler, 2003, p. E4), musical conductors are entirely dependent on the singers or instrumentalists for their success; as such, they are especially conscious of group dynamics. Michael elaborated: "Conducting is a unique profession within the world of music, because you have others work making music for you. And therefore the attitude one has, the viewpoint one has towards that relationship is probably the heart of the whole thing." He spoke of the types of relationship that can exist between conductor and members. The master and slave relationship of a dictatorship—"Do what I say or you're dead—solves all sorts of problems. You don't have to worry about anything because it's decided: you're right and they're wrong and that's that." Although that relationship has, historically, prevailed,

> if you actually care about the welfare of those who are working with you and adopt a more democratic style, it becomes infinitely more complicated, and much harder to achieve the same kind of results, the same kind of perfection that was attained sometimes under those other [dictatorial] conditions.

The conductor using a more democratic system struggles with a variety of questions:

> How do you get the respect of your players, freely, willingly without force or enforcement, instead of punishment? How do you gain control over the essential character of music you're doing with them? How do you create a frame and many of the details and achieve the organic unity that the work might have? Or put it all together in a certain direction without totally squelching the musical initiative of those that you are working with?

Michael concluded that it is not possible to make this shift entirely, "because in the end, the positions are controlled in many ways by your point of view, your attitude, personality, tempo selection and so on." The conductor's responsibility is also reflected in and reinforced by the audiences' expectations and perceptions: "How often do you hear the crowd go, 'Boy, look at what that conductor gets out of that orchestra,' instead of, 'Wow! Look at that orchestra play, look at that orchestra play.'"

Relationships are essential to theatrical performance, whether live or on camera. Larry, an actor, commented that actors tend to cloister, talk shop, and feel separate from the rest of society. As a consultant in this field, Dr. Osborne noted the rhythm of connection and engagement:

> The group process that happens in theatre is very intense. At the same time, it's surprisingly temporary. What happens is that a group of people—actors, directors, sometimes the writer— work together in a very concentrated way for a very limited amount of time. It's not just about getting the show up; it's really about the whole process of creating or re-creating the piece. People bond incredibly; they really become very involved with one another. And then the show is over. They strike the set, they have a cast party, and two weeks later, they can't remember each other's names.

THE NATURE OF PERFORMANCE

Aside from the setting (milieu and role functions) and the individual, as discussed above, the nature of performance in the performing arts involves memorization, the use of emotions, various physical demands, and, by definition, an interaction with an audience.

Memorization forms a crucial aspect of many types of artistic performances. One has not only to perform but also to know the performance exactly beforehand (and then, at the time of performance, be able to deviate from it if necessary). Memorization is a task and skill in itself, and for many it is a stressor. "The symbol system specific to the particular art form will determine what is remembered—notes for musicians, words for actors, movements for dancers, notes and words for singers" (Kogan, 2002, p. 3). Although the performer must be adept at rote memorization, a performance that can be considered *art* must also be transformed from mere technical mastery into physical, emotional, and expressive memory.

Each art form differs to some degree in terms of memory requirements and the manner in which it is reproduced in performance. An actor performing Shakespeare deals with arcane language but may find the known structure of the play easier to handle than the seeming lack of connection in Harold Pinter's dialogue. These experiences, in turn, are entirely different from those of a group conducting improvisational theatre.

Certain conventions in music dictate whether music should be memorized for performance, as well as how challenging that task is. A solo recital, for example, involves the greatest amount of memorization without the benefit of visible or meaningful cues. In contrast, even though memorization is needed when performing opera, the story line can serve as signal or anchor, used by the singer to hold the memory. When performing as part of a chamber music group, others have responsibility for part of the program, thus taking the unremitting spotlight off any one performer. This lightens the burden, even if the music is memorized (and often it is not).

As a pianist, Ilene found the memorization for a solo recital stressful, because of the time involved and the concern about remembering.

> It's basically a big commitment to studying. The way I memorize is away from the piano. I'm just looking at the score a lot and trying to think through the music a lot. And then I also have to practice so that my fingers move. So it's just a huge time commitment. And then I'm always worried that it's not going to work. With chamber music, I'm usually not ever worried that it's not going to work because I don't have that memory hurdle.

Because it is improvisational, jazz might appear to be entirely spontaneous. Instead, it is based on certain structural elements: The essential architecture of jazz form is known by the performer and the musician memorizes the fundamental structural elements of a specific piece of music. The resulting openness and improvisation have their own general design. This same mix of essential structural elements and flexibility within the moment occurs with improvisational theatre.

The appropriate use of emotion is a defining characteristic of the performing

I learn a piece of music bit by bit. If I'm learning a song I've never sung before, the very first thing I do is look at the language, look at the meaning of the text. First of all, I see if I like the text, because then it can go into the emotional part of my brain, and it's much easier to learn. I always pick a text that I can understand and one that I'm willing to portray. Tunes are very easy to learn—they go into your head, the third time around probably you've got the tune memorized, depending on the complexity of the rhythm. If it's a really modern piece, it may not ever really be memorized, but assuming it's something that I can memorize, I write out the text, particularly if it's in a foreign language. I may write those songs out ten times, each one of them. So I'm learning them minutely, every curve of each letter as I write longhand, and I carry them with me.

I just carry the words in my pocket when I go to run laps at the gym or in my neighborhood, and usually, I can memorize a song in half an hour, if the tune is already there at some level.

—Faith (singer)

arts. It is one of the ways in which performance moves from technical accuracy to full engagement of the audience. Using the image of Mary Shelley's monster, Frankenstein, a musician with whom we worked refers to music without emotion as *Frankenmusic*. The notes are there, it is technically alive, and it performs the duties of the printed music—but it's not the real thing. Similarly, actors sometimes describe a performance in which they're not engaged as "phoning in" the performance. "The artist's emotional self-expression must evoke the kind of emotional response in the audience that convinces it of the performer's authentic artistic talent" (Kogan, 2002, p. 4).

Charlotte (dancer) described the challenge and the beauty of the way in which dancers bring their entire emotional vulnerability to the dance. In discussing what is going on mentally as dancers are performing, Helena commented: "Some people literally don't think as they're performing. Their emotions are driving them or the music is driving them."

Particular art forms place different physical demands on the performer. Some musicians may be nearly static during performance; in contrast, the physical stresses on a dancer's body may be compared with those placed on athletes in contact sports (Hamilton & Hamilton, 1994).

Actors can be subject to higher risk of injury than one might expect. They are often called on to use a variety of skills for which they may have minimal training. Singing, dancing, or playing a musical instrument may all be integral to performing a particular role. Yet if they lack training in these areas, their risk of injury may be increased (Brandfonbrener, 1999). Keith recognized that "acting can be highly physically demanding and some actors get injured and are debilitated for months and months and months before they can work."

Another defining feature of the performing arts is the presence of an audience. Actors speak of "the fourth wall," an imaginary wall separating those on the stage from those in the audience. The performer simultaneously acts as if the stage is the real world and maintains utter awareness of the audience, the impact of his or her performance on the audience, and even, at some levels, the interaction with the audience. We discuss this aspect in greater detail in chapter 11.

Performing artists do not risk people's lives with their performance. In fact, performers at times use this lack of actual risk as a way to decrease their anxiety about performance. Self-talk, such as "This is not life and death," can help diminish the fears associated with being "on." At the same time, performing artists are among those with the most public vulnerability. Like professional athletes, the better known they are, the less privacy they have, with fewer opportunities to be their private selves. "When I was on television," commented Ian (now a radio talk show host), "I wouldn't go to the grocery store unless I had shaved or combed my hair. I had to be nice all the time."

Actors and broadcasters are especially aware of the public nature of their performance—and themselves. For example, Larry commented that, in contrast to a number of other professions, actors' failures and mistakes are public. Grace, a broadcaster, spoke of the ways in which a publicly known person ends up feeling insecure about how she is perceived. She wonders whether people are reacting to her or to her persona. "It's a horrible thing to go to a party where you don't know anybody. It's an awkward thing to go to a party and not be able to start at ground zero and mingle."

FAMILIARITY WITH CONSULTANTS

On the surface, it might seem that performing artists would be more receptive to consultation than performers in other domains. Unlike sports, for example, where athletes may view psychotherapy, psychologists, and counselors with a certain degree of wariness (e.g., Van Raalte, 1998), a long tradition, dating back at least to Freud, connects psychoanalysis and psychodynamic psychotherapy with the performing arts and artists (Obrecht & Telson, 1992; Ostwald, 1992). Recent research suggests that ballet dancers may feel comfortable with the idea of psychotherapy in which performance issues are discussed (Schoen & Estanol-Johnson, 2001). This straightforward acceptance is more complex than it appears, however. These same ballet dancers may be hesitant to seek "performance enhancement training." They may interpret these words as implying that their performance or abilities are lacking (Schoen & Estanol-Johnson, 2001).

More generally, the level of comfort with and sense of legitimacy about psychotherapy can lead potential clients to make some inaccurate assumptions that a consultant must address. For example, performing artists may assume that any "mental work" is psychotherapy, that it is long-term, and that a brief intervention would not be legitimate or relevant to central issues of concern. For these reasons, even though seemingly less skeptical than some athletes, potential clients among artists may need as much, albeit different, education concerning psychological skills training. To facilitate this shift in perspective, a consultant might provide information concerning performance enhancement as compared with pathology-focused approaches, the efficacy of mental skills training, the utility of briefer treatments, and a present or present–future focus.

Diaphragmatic breathing is a commonly prescribed mental skill used to decrease performance tension. Most musicians, whether instrumental or vocal, have received extensive training in diaphragmatic breathing. Often, however, they have learned breathing in relation to sound production. They may be entirely unaware of the arousal management or anxiolytic (anxiety-reducing) capabilities of this form of breathing. Furthermore, in the performance moment, if they do not make intentional use of this method, performance anxiety may override what they have learned and they may revert to shallow thoracic breathing.

With the increased popularity of mental skills training, many performers are familiar with various techniques. Yet even if they know about such techniques, they may not have learned how to use them, they may have learned them in ways that are not useful or effective, or they may not have truly understood their use or applicability. For example, as noted earlier, actors are often trained in various pre-performance routines in acting school. Although they have obtained this training, they may not use the routines they learned, or they may haphazardly and superstitiously try one and then another. They may not have settled on specific methods that are expressly useful for their own needs.

Recommendations to Consultants

- The performing arts domain is a highly competitive environment in which performers are routinely judged and evaluated, through the process of auditioning. This process is a major source of stress for many performers, and one that a consultant should be prepared to address.
- Many performers in this group begin their training at a very young age. This is especially the case in ballet, where early exercise and stretching is critical to developing the form and flexibility necessary for later success.
- The large number of performers vying for a relatively small number of paying positions results in extreme competition, often for low pay. A performer serious about a career in these areas often must be prepared to find supplemental means of support.
- Performing artists may have limited financial means. Consultants interested in working with performers in this domain may need to develop creative strategies for getting paid for such work.
- Training in these areas is heavily influenced by tradition, often within a rigid hierarchical context. A consultant should be aware of the traditions, customs, structure, and standards of a particular performance area and be prepared to work within its framework.
- The potential "closed" nature of many organizations and "us–them" mentality of individuals in the performing arts suggests that consultants also must legitimize their knowledge and experience in

these areas. In some areas, such as film, consultant access to artists may be limited by layers of protective personnel.

- Emotional vulnerability and public exposure are a central concern for performing artists. Significant success and recognition often occurs during their formative years. However, early success may be followed by later disappointments and rejections, which may prove particularly difficult for some performers. Consultants in these domains should be trained to deal with a wide range of emotional issues and expressivity, especially those related to the performer's ego, concerns about rejection, and multiple symbolic or real losses.

- To establish realistic goals with a performing artist, a credible assessment may need to distinguish between a performer's capabilities in their art and their mental or psychological skills regarding performance. This differentiation may require collaboration with other professionals who are qualified to evaluate talent.

- Memorization is a key skill for success in these areas. Consultants should have a basic grasp of learning theory and techniques.

- Success in the performing arts is not only contingent on talent and perseverance; often, luck or circumstance plays a major role. Consultants should be aware of the uncertainty inherent in these areas and the impact of that uncertainty on all aspects of the performer's life.

- The emphasis on the shape, form, and thinness of one's body creates special stresses for women performing in ballet. Consultants in this area are advised to be well-trained in the assessment and treatment of eating disorders. They are also advised to have a network of associated professionals in nutrition and health care with whom they can provide coordinated services.

- The management of perfectionism, injury, and career transition may also be an area in which consultants working with performing artists need expertise.

- Whereas performers in these areas may be receptive to psychotherapy, a consultant may encounter reluctance to address specific performance issues or engage in any process other than long-term therapy. Performance consultants should anticipate these issues and be prepared to educate performers and individuals within this domain as to the nature, process, and benefits of performance consultation.

- The ability to interact with others and function effectively within group settings is central to success in the performing arts. Consultants should be well versed in group dynamics, and should have a repertoire of methods to facilitate effective interpersonal interaction. If working with performers who have leadership roles, such as musical conductors, the consultant should also be familiar with the literature and techniques of motivation, leadership, and effective team functioning.

- Various aspects of the connection between mind and body are central to the performing arts:
    - Performance in many performing arts requires finely tuned physical functioning. Accordingly, the consultant should have training in addressing the physiological factors that affect performance. The more physically demanding the performance medium, the more important this knowledge becomes.
    - Because some aspects of performance do not require active physical movement and may be more cerebral, the importance of physical activity to mental well-being and performance may need to be emphasized or reiterated.
    - Some areas of performance, such as ballet, are actually anaerobic, even though they involve considerable physical activity. Thus, performers may need to understand the importance and value of ensuring aerobic exercise to their general functioning and well-being, as well as to their art.
- Performers in these areas may have training in many of the techniques common to performance enhancement; however, they may not apply these techniques in the most efficient or effective fashion. For instance, actors are traditionally well trained in relaxation techniques, but they may not transfer those skills to cope with the anxiety of auditioning. Musicians may be well trained in diaphragmatic breathing but not apply the technique to aid in relaxation. A consultant is advised to identify these skills that a performer may have and to broaden and build on them.
- There are several suggestions of gender inequities within the performing arts domain. Consultants should be aware of prevailing attitudes within a specific area and take them into consideration when deciding intervention options.
- The use and abuse of alcohol, prescription drugs, and illegal drugs are frequently encountered in this domain. Consultants must be qualified to discern the presence and to assess the impact of such substances and to ensure that appropriate treatment is obtained.

III

Key Factors in Performance

The Foundations of Excellent Performance 6

There's plenty of stuff that can drive you nuts, but there are things that are within your control that are definitely worth it. To me, it just makes sense to take care of myself.

—Faith (singer)

What are the key elements to performance? The performers we interviewed identified a number of them, which we then grouped in a mixed developmental–chronological sequence, representing the stages and processes of peak performance. These elements can be labeled *foundation*, *preparation*, and *performance*. In this section of the book, we explore the elements more fully. We present this information in a linear and static fashion, even though we recognize the essentially interactive and overlapping nature of this process.

Gould developed a unifying model of psychological preparation for peak performance in which he referred to the base of peak performance for athletes as fundamental foundation attributes. "These factors are important because they influence everything the performer does which in turn, either directly or indirectly, influences the degree to which the athlete achieves the desired task-specific ideal performance state" (Hardy et al., 1996, p. 241). Among these fundamental attributes, Gould included personality characteristics, motivational orientations, values, and philosophical beliefs.

From our interviews, three underlying factors emerged as essential for peak performance. These relate to basic abilities, such as intelligence and motor functioning, a coherent sense of self, and attention to self-care.

Basic Abilities

A basic level of inherited abilities or characteristics is generally considered necessary for excellence in each domain of performance. Gould's investigation of Olympic champions (Gould et al., 2002), for example, indicates that genetic attributes play a significant role in achieving excellence. Successful Olympic athletes have to work diligently to make the most of these natural gifts. The various studies and programs on giftedness or talent suggest that nature as well as nurture is intrinsic to optimally skilled performance.

> I first showed the desire to become a musician when I was 2. My father was a public school music teacher his whole professional life, and whenever classical music was played, I used to dance around and wave my arms. That's how I got started. My father was my first private teacher on the violin and trumpet.
>
> —Michael (conductor)

As psychologists, we consider that basic abilities are necessary, especially in laying the groundwork for other factors. However, it is worth noting that few performers or consultants referred to this area directly. Perhaps they considered basic abilities to be so obvious as not to require mention.

One performer who referred to these "obvious" basic abilities (David) commented that within the business world, one must have a "reasonable" level of intelligence. He qualified even this statement: "Everybody doesn't need to be a member of MENSA—I don't by any means think that the smartest people in the world are the most successful in business."

Grace, a successful radio personality, described her intellectual abilities as essential to her achievement. She characterized herself as a voracious reader, with strong comprehension and retention. At one time her sharp remarks were problematic but this same style now stands her in good stead:

> You always want the "closer" where there is no comeback. It's always been this way for me, but it's only recently that I've been getting paid for it. In school, it got me into a lot of trouble, because I always had a snappy comeback for the teacher.

Heredity is more critical to some performance domains than others. Physical requirements are set out for many high-risk performers. For example, the U.S. military has broad minimum specifications: Men must be 60–80" tall and weigh 100–255 pounds; women must be 58–80" and weigh 90–227 pounds (U.S. Army, 2002). To be a U.S. astronaut, the requirements are slightly more restrictive: a person must be 64–76", with vision no worse than 20–70, correctable to 20–20.

Still, these are fairly broad parameters in perhaps all of the domains, with the exception of ballet. As noted in chapter 5, rigid physical standards within ballet are entirely based on body type: the length of the torso and neck, the shape of the legs and feet, the dancer's weight, and the ever-elusive "line." As dance consultant and former ballet dancer Dr. Desmond pointed out, despite being incredibly dedicated and talented, some ballet dancers' careers are limited by the structure of their bodies.

Children first become aware of the differences between ability, effort, and luck around age 10 (Nicholls, 1992). Shortly thereafter, adolescents begin to drop out of sports in which they perceive themselves as having low ability. This is likely to be the case with performers in areas other than sports. As we note in the next chapter, the combination of innate ability and practice ultimately allows for optimal performance.

Coherent Sense of Self

A performer brings his or her fundamental identity to every task. Excellent performers exhibited a coherent sense of identity. They showed confidence in their abilities and expressed a sense of purpose and direction, self-knowledge, a clear sense of identity, and, for some, even a sense of destiny.

In recent years, sport psychologists have paid more attention to the importance of a coherent self-identity (Miller & Kerr, 2002). At times, the emphasis on performance excellence in athletes has seemed to be at odds with the typical developmental tasks of adolescence. For example, an athlete might show a strong identity as a performer but have no sense of self or self-worth out of the competition arena (Baillie & Danish, 1992). Within sport psychology, a recent shift in philosophy proposes that an athlete should ideally develop a sense of personal excellence—a strong personal identity with clear morals and character—simultaneously with performance excellence. Athletes with both personal excellence and performance excellence are better prepared to deal with challenges throughout the performance life cycle, including inevitable retirement from sport.

In sport psychology research, personal confidence is described, depending on the specific theoretical frame, as perceived ability, self-efficacy, or confidence (Duda, 1992). Confidence in oneself was mentioned by performers in all categories as vital for performance excellence. Consistent with Bandura's (1986) theories of self-efficacy, each performer noted confidence as a product of thorough preparation and cumulative experience.

As a conductor, Harold found that confidence derives from a combination of adequate study and experience:

Whether I am talking about a great high school baseball game or a particularly successful meeting, I would chalk up the truly successful experience to three things. First was a very strong belief that I could do it. Going into a baseball game, I knew after throwing the first pitch that the ice was broken. Similarly, if I felt intimidated going into a meeting, two minutes into the presentation when things were falling smoothly, I knew I had their attention. Before you know it, ten minutes have gone by and you just believe in yourself.

Second, you go in with a feeling of obligation, a sense that it's up to you. In the baseball game, I was in the starting rotation and it was my obligation to do a great job. With the company, I was a newly appointed president, the top person. I had to be good.

Third, you feel like you have a right to do well. You own that 15 inches of plate. If anybody gets too close, they are in your territory. That's yours and you are willing to defend it. Walking into that room, I had the feeling that I had the right to be there. I had the right to tell them what was right or wrong by virtue of the fact that I felt that I had more experience than anybody else in the room.

—Barry (advertising executive)

I can conduct anything, virtually anything, that I've studied. I can go on stage and I will not suffer from any stage fright. None. Zippo. I'm excited for the moment. I can hardly wait to do this. When I get on stage and I'm conducting, I know what I'm doing, and as time goes on and I get more experience, there's more confidence that I will be able to deal with anything that comes my way.

For musician Diane, the intertwining of preparation, practice, and performance reinforced self-knowledge:

[When you're performing] you know if you just settle down and do what you know how to do, nine times out of ten it comes out right, because your body knows what to do. You didn't start doing this yesterday. A lot of it is just trusting that you know what you're doing. And that's [the result of] preparation and practice. But it does help to remind yourself how long you've been doing something, and how well you know how to do it.

In addition to experience and preparation, an overall sense of purpose helps solidify one's sense of self-confidence, in an interactive loop. Conductor Michael stated the following:

I know what I'm about, I know why I'm out there. As long as I feel a reasonable expectation that I'll be able to fulfill my mission, I don't have any anxiety about walking out on stage in front of the public. This involves becoming more and more certain as an artist as to why it is that I'm an artist, and what

I'm trying to accomplish, knowing without any doubt what
that is, and then working toward being able to accomplish it. It
sort of goes hand in hand. When you see yourself
accomplishing a purpose, it gives you confidence and you can
just do it and in fact you just do it.

Advertising executive Barry also noted the importance of a sense of
purpose, even a sense of destiny. He characterized his peak performances
as experiences in which he had an unshakable belief in his abilities. Beyond that, he felt a sense of obligation and a sense of providence that
supported him in rising to the challenge before him: "I know it is going to
sound corny, but you are really knowing it. It is a feeling of destiny; it's
my day. Nobody is going to be this on at this moment the way I am."

Other attributes that spoke to a coherent sense of self covered a wide
range of elements. For example, in his role as police sniper, George described his ability to maintain an internal locus of control and vigilance,
regardless of the level of threat. David commented that as a banker, "It
takes drive, determination, fear of failure, competitiveness, and greed for
the wealth it will create for you and what you want to do with it. When
hiring, I look for somebody who has excelled in something—I hardly
care what. [This] shows they're competitive and can excel and that they
have some drive."

Physicians and attorneys routinely cite being drawn to their chosen
professions because of the desire to help others, a sense of purpose that is
sometimes frustrated by having also to manage the entrepreneurial aspects of their professions. George, the police sniper, perceived "saving an
innocent person" as the very foundation of his commitment to his work.
Larry's description of the actor's sense of self was more nebulous and less
incisive than that of the businessmen and the high-risk performer. Larry
thought that much of the sense of self

is intuitive. In the area that we are as performers, we live in the
realm of emotions. We live in the observation of people; we use
body language, vocal inflection, dress, whatever-colored hair,
eyes, the general look. We're constantly observing. I think it's
the same as a good psychiatrist or psychologist, you're looking
at everything. You're looking at the total package, what the
person is saying and more importantly, what they're not
saying. You learn to intuit.

Self-Care

The performers we interviewed were all professionals, earning their living by providing consistently high-quality performances on a routine basis.
Their methods of self-care were typically tailored to the unique demands

of their specific performance domain. In the business areas, performers count on their mental skills; in the high-risk areas, there is a high degree of reliance on tools and apparatus; and for performing artists, the body is the device most central to performance. Because performing artists must be able to depend on their physical abilities, self-care is another central element that forms the groundwork to performance.

For individuals whose bodies produce the sounds, gestures, and movements of performance, this is essentially "care of the instrument." Dance critic Deborah Jowitt (2001) used the metaphor of "instrument" to describe dancers' "own perishable bodies." She remarked that "dancers' instruments are often compromised by inadequate nutrition, lack of sleep, and performing while injured" (p. 4). As an aging dancer, self-care for Jerry involved limiting the amount of physical rehearsal: "As I got older, I did less preparation, because I realized that the fatigue that I was building up through over-preparing in effect was probably the largest factor preventing me from doing everything that I wanted to."

Musicians, more than any other group of performing artists with whom we spoke, seemed particularly attuned to this element as central to performance excellence. Singers, whose instruments are internal, are particularly conscious of the need for disciplined self-care. Faith described her own life:

> I really do a lot of self-protection, and I'm very disciplined about that. It's not worth it to me not to sing well. Everything that I do is influenced by that, whether it's being out late at night, or making a decision not to have wine, which I often do because it's too drying, too dehydrating. If I have a choice to take care of myself, it's not really a very hard choice.

> I don't like to have a lot of stress in other aspects of my life. It's important to make good decisions in taking care of myself mentally and emotionally. I like to feel more or less organized, keeping up with what I need to do at home. That means, for example, that financially I'm acting within reason. Having a good relationship is extremely important to being able to be trusting and at ease and calm, not having any extra emotional stresses going on. Those things affect my emotions.

Diane compared musicians to athletes in regard to the importance of physical well-being:

> Things have to work. You need to be in good physical condition and have your muscles and your nervous system in good working order. You need to make sure that you never drink or do recreational drugs and that you get enough sleep. We're

athletes—in a way we're athletes—and as such we have to take care of ourselves.

Some elements of self-care for performing artists are specific to one's role. Conductors are unique among musicians in that they are physically active throughout performance; broadcasters with early morning shows structure their lives to accommodate their working hours; and aging dancers need to regulate their amount of activity. Michael considers two types of exercise important, both general exercise and specific warm-ups before rehearsal:

> Nowadays, I do Pilates which is a really great regimen for toning the muscles and aligning the muscles with the spine. It's not a good idea for me to conduct without having warmed up. I usually stretch for about half an hour before I run any rehearsal. It's easy to pull your neck or hurt your shoulder muscles if you're not loose before you conduct.

Musicians emphasized physical self-care, mental stability, and relational calm. Granted, these respondents were all in their 40s or 50s, and they were classical rather than popular artists (among whom risky behaviors may be more the norm). Nonetheless, this prosaic recognition of the value and importance of ordinary care belies the image of the artist living on the edge.

Observations by our consultant to musicians, Dr. Norris, suggest that our sample was not representative of the music industry as a whole, however. He noted that substance abuse is widespread in the music business. He included pop and country musicians among those who may use alcohol, marijuana, and other recreational drugs and classical musicians who rely on beta-blockers and prescription medications to calm their nerves prior to performance. Professional musicians who play in traveling bands are particularly susceptible to drug use as a diversion from boredom.

Whereas the range of drugs may vary, Dr. Norris identified one in particular as significantly problematic: "The substance of choice is going to depend on whatever is 'hot,' whether they're dope smoking every day or whether they're doing cocaine, or whether they're speeding, or whether they're doing heroin—but alcohol is the one that has destroyed more musical careers in a wide range of genres than any other drug." The music industry recognizes this problem. At the Grammy Awards ceremonies, for example, a room without alcohol is designated as a special "safe room." The industry is aware of far too many situations like that of the drummer from a "top, top, top performing band" who stood up at one of Dr. Norris's conference presentations and shared, "You know, I started playing gigs at 16, where alcohol was always on the stage. And then I woke up a full-blown alcoholic at age 28."

Substance use and abuse is a major issue within the music industry, whether with classical players, pop, rock, or C&W. Alcohol is a part of the music industry. If you go to Symphony Hall, you're going to have alcohol available at intermissions. And if you go down to the club level, to the big pavilions, the sheds—alcohol is a part of that. Or you're playing in a bar and so you're working in a highly hazardous occupation. You can't work in the business without exposure to alcohol.

When you think about it, for a musician—a traveling musician, a full time musician—it's an hour or two of playing and a great deal of boredom. And so what do you do during this boredom time? Between the time that you pull into a bar and set up your stuff and do your sound check at 6 or 7, and go on at 11 or 12, what do you do? Well you sit around and wait. And it's a set up for "Oh hell, let's smoke a joint or drink a beer."

—Dr. Nick Norris (consultant, music)

The physical demands on dancer's bodies means that they need to engage in the same types of physical self-care as athletes. A further parallel relates to issues of weight. Just as athletes in some sports need to "make weight," dancers, in ballet in particular, need to meet specific weight requirements. The quest for perfection of body and form makes dancers particularly susceptible to eating disorders. Not infrequently, dancers also smoke cigarettes for the appetite suppressant qualities of nicotine. Dr. Desmond, herself a former professional ballet dancer, sees issues of body image and disordered eating as inevitably intertwined with the quest for performance excellence among dancers.

Self-care can be a challenge for a broadcaster with a morning drive program. Along with proper nutrition, including a protein breakfast that typically contained fish, Grace emphasized the need for sleep: "Sleep is the single biggest tool that I have. I need nine hours of sleep a night. Nine will get it. I get up at 4:00 a.m. I take a nap every afternoon and I go to bed early. On weekends, I log ten hours if I can."

For those with rotating schedules, such as Frederick, the emergency room physician, self-care means planning his schedule in accordance with circadian cycles and sleep patterns. Neurosurgeon Eric emphasized the importance of good sleep and diet in preparing for complex surgeries. For medic–sniper, George, constant physical training is required to be prepared for performance demands.

Somewhat whimsically, yet semi-seriously, banker David reflected on the balance between mental and physical activities:

Our business is kind of the opposite of the athlete: They spend at least 95% of their time and effort on the physical side of things and then for the kick they need, the 5% is the mental. If we spend 95% on the mental, what difference would it make if everybody were in top physical shape and didn't have that dragging on them? Should we have athletic trainers making sure we're physically fit? In the last few years, I've been in better physical shape than in the previous few years. I don't know whether the physical has helped me, but the mental sense of feeling in better shape has helped me. When you feel like you have more energy, then you have more energy.

Recommendations to Consultants

- Heredity provides a basic level of ability that is necessary to become an "elite" performer. Skilled performers may focus less on their natural gifts and more on the work involved in achieving excellence.
- Optimal performance and optimal satisfaction occur when performers have a sense of purpose (at times described as one's "dream"; Newburg et al., 2002) and identity.
- A sense of confidence or self-confidence in performance is built on a foundation of thorough preparation and cumulative experience.
- Physical self-care is necessary for optimal performance. Although this observation may seem obvious, both performers and consultants may be more accustomed to operating from a "Cartesian" framework that separates body and mind.
- Consultants working with performers must be aware of the norms and hazards pertaining to self-care in particular domains and areas of performance.
- Consulting in certain performance areas require knowledge of clinical, as well as performance techniques. For example, consultants working with dancers should be knowledgeable about eating disorders so as to screen and refer affected people to appropriate treatment resources. Consultants in the music industry should be knowledgeable about alcohol abuse and other substances in order to ensure the availability of treatment options.

Getting It Right: Preparation 7

We are what we repeatedly do. Excellence, then, is not an act, but a habit.
—Aristotle

An excellent performance is like the tip of an iceberg. What is seen is only a fraction of the underlying process. Although some propose that heredity is a foundation of excellence, innate talent is of limited value unless it is coupled with extensive preparation.

The relative importance of innate ability as compared with learned skill has been extensively debated. Focus on talent detection and talent selection within sports in the 1970s proved frustratingly elusive (Durand-Bush & Salmela, 2001). A swing in the opposite direction, toward pure practice, has more recently dominated the field of expertise development.

Bloom (1985) was one of the first to study exceptional performers in a wide variety of domains. He concluded that talent development involves three stages: the early years or Romance phase, during which the child develops a love for the activity through play and exploration; the middle or Precision phase, during which the child typically works with coaches or teachers to achieve technical mastery; and the Integration phase, in which the person works with "master" coaches or teachers to blend technical excellence into exceptional performance.

For centuries, practice has been recognized as essential for developing excellence. Scientific verification of this precept has only occurred within the past ten years. K. Anders Ericsson (1996b; Ericsson, Krampe, & Tesch-Römer, 1993) has been a leading researcher and proponent of this perspective. He presented a compelling argument that years of "deliberate practice," rather than any innate ability, are critical in leading to excellence in performance. Deliberate practice differs from fun and play in that it is not inherently motivating or enjoyable. It differs from work in that it allows "for repeated experiences in which the individual can attend to the critical aspects of the situation and incrementally improve her or his performance in response to knowledge of results, feedback, or both from a teacher" (Ericsson et al., 1993, p. 368). From his extensive investigations of exceptional performers, in domains as diverse as typists who produce more than 147 words per minute, Grand Master chess players, violinists, physicians, and ballet dancers, Ericsson (1996a) concluded that "elite performance is attained gradually and around ten years of intensive preparation are necessary to attain international-level performance" (p. 12). These ten years, or 10,000 hours, are applied to a "well-defined task with an appropriate difficulty level for the particular individual, informative feedback, and opportunities for repetition and corrections of errors" (Ericsson, 1996a, pp. 20–21). The feedback and explicit instructions of qualified teachers are essential, because they lead to "more and better organized knowledge" (Ericsson et al., 1993, p. 397).

Ericsson offered one concession to the popular belief in the importance of innate abilities. He acknowledged that genetics may be a factor in a person's ability to engage in the hard work (deliberate practice) that is required to achieve excellence.

We take a somewhat more interactionist perspective, recognizing the multiple, complementary, and interweaving functions of (minimally) heredity, systemic supports, and practice that allow for the full development of individuals' capabilities (e.g., Csikszentmihalyi, Rathunde, & Whalen, 1993; Durand-Bush & Salmela, 2001; Kogan, 2002; Winner, 1996). Csikszentmihalyi and colleagues, for example, suggested that talent consists essentially of

> individual traits, which are partly inherited and partly developed as a person grows up; cultural domains, which refer to systems of rules that define certain ranges of performance as meaningful and valuable; and social fields, made up of people and institutions whose task is to decide whether a certain performance is to be considered valuable or not. (1993, p. 23)

Our participants noted four essential elements in preparing for peak performance: knowledge, active intentional learning, practice, and the purposeful development of mental skills. All four elements are consistent with Ericsson's findings. In this chapter we discuss the first three elements. The following chapter is devoted to discussion of the development of mental skills.

Knowledge

As noted above, Ericsson and colleagues (1993) postulated that expert performers are distinguished by more and better organized knowledge. It is particularly critical that a performer know the most effective strategies and methods for performing a given task. Prochaska and DiClemente (1983) suggested that in altering habits, one needs knowledge of both *what* needs to change and the process of *how* to approach change. In Stephen Covey's (1989) best selling book, *The Seven Habits of Highly Effective People*, knowledge of *what* to do and *why* to do it is also recognized as essential to developing excellence. Jackson and Csikszentmihalyi (1999) emphasized clear knowledge of one's goals as a necessary component of achieving flow.

Our interviews, as well as our own professional experience, attest that knowledge is a foundation of preparation. Essentially, one needs to know what the "givens" are before embarking on learning or practicing for a specific performance. All groups recognized the value of this awareness; musicians spoke in especially great detail on its importance. We considered three broad categories of knowledge: knowledge of the product, the audience, and oneself.

The first category, knowledge of the product, refers to what one is attempting to produce through performance. It includes clarity about the overall goal as well as comprehension of the technical skills, techniques, and information necessary to achieve that goal. For a surgeon or high-risk performer, foundational knowledge entails all the information associated with assessing a given situation as well as the technical skills to deal with it. In the world of business, knowledge of the literal "product" has always been considered essential to effective sales and marketing. For Barry, the advertising executive, there is no doubt regarding the importance of such information: "From a business standpoint, you have to have more knowledge than anybody. You have to have a memory for that and the ability to use it."

Our conductors were eloquent in conveying the complexities of knowing a piece of music. Much of a conductor's preparation involves steeping himself or herself in the music well ahead of any actual rehearsal. Harold described his initial process:

> For a conductor, everything is in the head. The conducting end of things is all about analysis. Before I program a new piece of music, I will have studied the piece for a year and lived with it and found out whether I have something to say or not. One analyzes the score, reads about the history of the piece, reviews

the different movements, key structure, and orchestration. I live with it and then when I'm virtually ready to go on stage, that's the point at which I put it into maybe what we're going to do the next year.

Michael started a bit differently:

The first thing I usually do—especially if it's a piece that's new to me—is to get lots of recordings and listen to them all. I'm interested in what the great conductors of the past and present have done and are doing with these works. Then I begin my own study process of the works. Once that's done in a general sense, I get involved with making the notes themselves more personal. In other words, then I start digesting them thoroughly, by repetition and by singing and by playing the piano. Or sitting on the dock at the lake in the sun, looking at the score.

Once I've decided basic issues about things like the speed, the tempo, and what's significant about the music itself in terms of the details of it and what's expressing moods and concepts and ideas, then if it's a new piece I'll do some physical work with it, getting my arms moving and communicating things with my hands. With works I've done many times before I don't do very much of that. Beyond that, I'll give some thought to the sequence of rehearsals. Depending on the rehearsal process and the flow of events at rehearsal, I'll give some thought to how much time I have to rehearse each work I'm conducting.

Both radio show hosts spoke of the immense amount of background reading that they do. Ian emphasized the importance of sufficient preparation for each show. Thorough preparation allowed him to relax and be free-wheeling:

A lot of people don't need specific preparation. Larry King does not do any homework at all. He does not even want to know much more than the guest's title. But I have to feel comfortable. I have to feel like I have a foundation to stand on. I do a lot of homework. I do a lot of reading. I want to know everything I can about the subject. Partly it is my own insecurity. It's like walking a tight wire. I don't particularly want a safety net while I am out there; but I want to know that I don't need the safety net because I'm going to be okay. I want to be clear that I am going to be able to pull it off no matter what happens. That is part of the challenge.

> You can't just simply throw something of great complexity to a public that is unprepared to receive it. That's not good. The audience feels stupid, they feel like they didn't get the message, they get angry about it, the ticket sales drop, the whole organization suffers for it. The way to do it is to prepare your audience for it, and gradually educate them and bring them along to increasing levels of appreciation and understanding of the possibilities inherent in contemporary music.
>
> —Michael (conductor)

Most performances involve a process in which the actions are either perceived or received by one or more individuals. We have labeled these individuals *the audience*. As peak performance in music, theatre, and dance is often intertwined with audience interaction (discussed more fully in chap. 11, this volume), understanding the characteristics and preferences of a given audience becomes an important aspect in the choice of what is to be presented.

Knowing one's audience is essential to effective business presentations. For decades, the applied knowledge gained from social psychologists' study of the science of persuasion has guided the actions of persons in sales and business (Aronson, 1994; Aronson, Wilson & Alpert, 1994; Mandel, 1993).

In the world of business, market research is a critical component of any company's success. Vast amounts of money are devoted to understanding consumer demographics. For radio host Grace, attending to the psychological characteristics of her audience takes on greater importance than the more obvious demographics of income and education: "You've got to figure out who your target audience is and how to talk to that person. Psychographics versus demographics. What does the 18–24-year-old woman who eats, drives, lives here—what does she care about?"

For a trial attorney, successful performance often hinges on knowledge of the audience. Trial litigation is one of the few performance domains in which a person has input regarding "audience" participants. During the jury selection process, attorneys have the right to interview prospective jurors and "strike" or dismiss individuals from the pool of applicants. Many attorneys believe that this selection process is the most important part of any trial (Stapp, 1996), and this has in turn given rise to an entire field of consultants who specialize in the jury selection process. How vital is it to know and even choose the audience? A recent study indicated that when a jury consultant was used, a death sentence was recommended in only 33.3% of cases; without a consultant, the death sentence recommendation occurred in 61.1% of the cases (Horowitz, 1980).

In our paradigm, knowledge of oneself differs from a coherent sense of self. As we described in the last chapter, a coherent sense of self refers to a gestalt about oneself, a general sense of identity. Knowledge of one-

Find your unique ability, what it is that you do best, and delegate everything else. Find competent people to delegate to, and then do what you do best.

—Charles (insurance broker)

self, on the other hand, pertains to performance-specific data, such as knowing the emotions associated with an ideal performance state and the specifics of how an individual best achieves that state. It also involves knowing explicitly one's strengths and weaknesses, which is critical in devising effective performance strategies.

George, a Special Forces medic, pointed out the importance of having both technical knowledge and knowledge of oneself. In an emergency medical situation, a medic needs diagnostic and treatment skills. Equally important, he needs to know how he is likely to react in such a situation, so that he will be able to perform his task optimally. He is aware of the importance of regulating his level of arousal and the direction of his attention (Nideffer, 1976):

> You need to be able to look at signs and symptoms [in the patient] and recognize what you have and then go ahead and treat it. If you can't recognize [the signs], then you're not treating the person properly. For myself, I know it is very important for me to be able to keep my heart rate down so I can think clearly. I also need to have an awareness of the situation around me. If I'm being shot at or things are happening around me, I can't just stay focused on this patient or else I become a casualty.

As a musician, Faith points to the importance of knowing one's own capabilities and preferences, "making sure, vocally, that you've chosen music that's appropriate for your skills, your range. It's very hard to sing things you don't like. It's just hard to learn it, to get beyond."

Knowing how to go about preparing—knowing how to rehearse and all the facets that are involved—can be considered a general skill that is learned by the performer over time. Norman (musician) commented:

> The strength of your technique rests on the fact that you know how to prepare. And I feel that about myself. I feel like I know how to prepare, I know how to get ready to go on stage, and I know how to sit in my chair, regardless of other factors in the moment.

Norman's perception of himself supported Ericsson's research: He had a world-class reputation, which he attributed to practice rather than natural talent:

> I don't feel myself to be an overly talented player. If I have success, it's due to my practice habits. I spend a certain amount

of time doing rudimentary exercises every day. Some people say "rudiments are the key" and some people say, "I never practice rudiments. I don't even care about quarter notes. I don't care about scales and circle of fifths and seventh chords." And I say "Well, that's all I care about."

At the same time, Norman suggested that there is a specific relationship between each piece of music and each artist. This in turn affects how one practices a particular piece of music:

> Playing every piece of music is specific, so you have to see [practice behaviors] as specific behavior to each individual person and each individual piece. One thing that I feel is of extreme importance among performing musicians is this: What is the material, and how does the performer relate to the material? Is it new, is it old, is it partially improvised, is it not improvised? What is the exact nature of the task: Is it a solo piece, is it an ensemble, is it a concerto with orchestra? These are often the determining factors as to why things go a certain way.

Active Intentional Learning

Ericsson argued that deliberate practice—the process by which a person engages in a highly structured activity with the explicit goal of improving performance—is the very foundation of performance excellence. As we have indicated, this process involves deliberate, intentional practice, with gradual improvement "in response to knowledge of results, feedback or both" (Ericsson et al., 1993, p. 9).

A number of performers from various domains described technical preparation as important both in and of itself and as a key element in bolstering self-confidence. Charlotte used overlearning and overpreparation to cope with low self-confidence. She also deliberately tired herself out through extensive practice. "If I danced all day, I would be too tired and too nervous to destroy my own performance."

Technical preparation for actors involves learning and memorizing a script. Ian commented, "You have to know your lines and where you are supposed to be." Brenda observed that "some people are sort of casual about rehearsal, counting on some great spark of something or other to hit them when they get out there. That's a very dangerous way to proceed." As a veteran actor, Brenda remarked, "I don't even believe in acting. I believe in being, you become the character, that's all." *Being*, however, takes work: "You rehearse until you know what you're doing."

In dance, Jerry described the thorough preparation that was essential for his peak performance. The more that he knew about his body in dance, the more he could plan the performance:

> Certainly, the more you repeat something correctly, the more likely it is to be correct the next time. I've seen people who never, never had a 100% correct run-through in the studio and yet they would walk on stage like, "Okay, curtain's up, time to do it, let's go." I personally would be more nervous if I hadn't gone from the beginning to the end without missing a lift. Not that it was ever 100% correct, but I would want to have done that before I went on stage.

This knowledge about himself and the particular dance was important not just in terms of self-efficacy, but also for appropriate planning:

> I wanted to know how tired I was going to be. I wanted to know where I was going to have trouble focusing. I wanted to know what it was going to feel like. The difficult thing for me about preparing for ballet was always that the tool I used, the body, felt so different from minute to minute. And physically finding a way to prepare the body to be ready—that was always the tricky bit.

Norman (musician) emphasized the importance of practicing in such a way that the music becomes one's own. Varying what one does, in terms of speed and improvisation, brings the music into oneself:

> It really comes down to the speed of your reflexes to hear and respond. I try to cultivate that by practicing slow and practicing fast. You play loud, you play soft, you play fast, you play slow.
>
> I sprinkle a lot of my practice time with improvisation. The difference between playing classical music and improvising is whether you're playing notes that are your own. With classical music, you make the notes your own through practice.

This same kind of pattern variation is described by Michael (conductor):

> I don't like to become too routine in the rehearsal process. For example, if I have four rehearsals and they're all two and a half hours long with a break in the middle, I don't necessarily go to the wire. If I'm happy with what I've accomplished for the day and it's 20 minutes before a rehearsal is supposed to end, I just end it. I also mix it up: I may have a day where I'm just really fussy and I'm stopping the rehearsal a lot. I'm saying "Do this, do that, do this, do that, I want it this way, I want it that way,

shorter longer louder softer, more trombone." What I'll do, though, is the next time or the next moment or maybe after the break, I'll let 'em run, just let 'em run. I'll open the corral and let the horses run. Take a piece, let them go without stopping. I do it for several reasons. One is because being stopped a lot is a tedious thing. You've got to do it sometimes, but I try to balance that off by giving them a chance just to be expressive for a while and not be stopped. But I also do it for variety at rehearsals, so that every day doesn't seem to be the same for the players.

Diane compared and contrasted the physical sensations of playing the violin with playing golf.

[If you make an error] a lot of the time you know immediately what went wrong. It's weird. You know exactly, for instance, that your hand didn't feel quite right. It's like with a golf swing: When you step up to the ball, you can sense whether your stance is right. If you don't feel perfect, you don't swing. You should put your club down, step back, and walk back up to it, because you know you're not going to do it right. It's hard, though, to get yourself to step away from the ball. When you're performing, you don't have a whole lot of opportunity to re-set up, so you know you've got to be practiced enough to remember what it feels like in the first place.

Sufficient rehearsal has a constant and interactive relationship with the prevention or management of performance anxiety. Even Faith (singer) who describes herself as not experiencing stage fright, says: "The only time I have been nervous is if I feel a piece is under-rehearsed."

Thorough preparation allows the performance to become sufficiently part of oneself such that the response becomes automatic, regardless of what happens. One does not have time to think; one simply does that which they have trained their body and mind to do. This type of over-learning is also stressed by coaches who work with athletes (Gould et al., 1993; Hardy, 1990; Hardy et al., 1996). For those performing in high-risk situations, overlearning is especially critical in that it prevents "performance from being disrupted by anxiety and pressure" and can keep one's "timing sharp even when you are injured" (Nideffer, 1985, p. 83). For the performing artist, the overlearning allows music or dance to become sufficiently part of oneself to make possible the emotional communication that is essential to art.

Thorough preparation becomes a key element for crisis management as well. Harold commented: "You *cannot* prepare enough. There is no such thing as over-preparation. Every performing artist who really knows

There are the kinds of moments where something horrendous happens, and your instinct has to take over. I know my way around the podium. I know where the edge is. Once, in the midst of conducting "Messiah," when I stepped, the platform wasn't there. I lurched forward, trying to save myself. I pushed into the music stand that my score sits on. The stand went crashing towards the harpsichord. I retained my balance. An orchestra member got the music stand. My score hit the floor. It got handed back to me—upside down. I didn't know until the end of the movement, because I just switched into conducting from memory. And I didn't lose a beat.

It's a critical moment. Your mind totally shuts, you go into shock, and that triggers you to go into a different level of reacting. The conscious is cut off and you go into subconscious. Suddenly, survival is the important thing. Not interrupting the performance was the first thing on my mind. I was also really concerned about the music stand doing damage to the instruments. There were violins and violas and cellos right there whose value was higher than my house.

—Harold (conductor)

what they are doing over-prepares. If something [negative] happens, your subconscious just will take over."

In addition to active learning focused on technical preparation, some of our participants also commented on the importance of time between learning and performance. Creating a break between practice and performance allows a critical, but often overlooked, aspect of the learning process, for two separate reasons: (a) performers require an opportunity for recovery and rest, and (b) the interval is a kind of "incubation" period.

The intensity of concentration for practice is such that it cannot be sustained for long periods of time (Ericsson et al., 1993). Seashore (1967), a pioneer in music psychology, concluded that "the command to rest is fully as important as to work in effective learning" (pp. 154–155). Mental and physical recovery are vital.

When performers quest perfection, the risk of overtraining increases. If practice improves performance, more practice, one would think, improves performance even more. However, performance decrements—psychosocial as well as physical—begin to occur with too much training (Raglin, 1993). In a recent study that compared athletes who exceeded expectations with those who did not perform up to expectations in the Atlanta and Nagano Olympic Games, overtraining was identified as a key factor associated with negative performance (Greenleaf, Gould, & Dieffenbach, 2001).

Some remedies to overtraining in sports have been identified, including taking breaks, cross-training in another sport, and allowing time for personal and social relationships (Greenleaf et al., 2001; McCann, 1995). The best antidotes are those that involve prevention. Just as in sports performance, "tapering" of activities may be recommended prior to a major event. In music and dance, performers may "mark" their performance, thus decreasing the physical stress on their bodies. A singer minimizes vocal strain by singing more quietly; a dancer may learn some dance patterns by moving her hands to represent the physical placement and movements of her legs or reserve energy by not dancing "full-out."

For some performers, rest involves a physical respite to allow muscle recovery. For others, rest allows for a period of "incubation," a time during which performance memory sinks in more deeply and becomes more thoroughly absorbed.

A violinist, Diane, described this important function:

> Preparation is mental as much as physical, and so if you sort of have the piece rolling around in your head, I find that that really helps. I've actually thought of solutions for technical problems just from doing that. I've heard other performers say that there's always some music in their head, no matter what. There's always something there. We always say that it's good to live with a piece. That means if you're going to perform it Wednesday it's not a good idea to first see it only on Monday.

As a banker, David also valued the opportunity to let ideas percolate. Thinking issues through out loud with others was another means to more complete and effective planning and decision making:

> I like to have some time so that I can work on something and put it aside, be it a presentation or a memo. I might think about it when I'm [doing household projects] and have a great idea— or I might not—but then I like to come back to it and see what I think of it, as opposed to just whipping something out and then going and doing it. I try to allow time to make a first cut at something and then put it aside. And then, I love to talk to people about things, to bounce ideas off of people. I love to get input. We've got a philosophy around here that we don't have a corner on brains and that we love other people's opinions and we love to think through our own ideas out loud. A lot of staff come in who want to tell me about a deal. They will tell me about it and just by talking about it, and before I can even give them my thoughts, they've reached some conclusions. I think that it's helpful to have the time and opportunity to do that on things. That's actually the way we reach investment decisions—a lot of conversations over a period of weeks. Small groups, or one on one, just talking about issues and about deals and reaching conclusions.

Practice the Delivery

Knowing oneself, one's audience, and the product one is delivering is critical, as is technical preparation. In addition, the process needs to be rehearsed in conditions that replicate the actual performance context as closely as possible. One needs to attend to both the broad sweep and the details of a performance or an event. A classic example of practicing the delivery was relayed by Dr. Martin (consultant, music):

> This is the best example I know of, of full pre-performance preparation: Itzak Perlman was preparing for a Carnegie Hall recital, and he was nervous about how he was going to get on and off stage, because of needing to use crutches. The recital date was May 1. In his mind, he set his recital date for March 15. He told his family "It's not just a little thing like I'm going to run through the recital in the living room. I'm going to prepare for it and present the recital, in the living room and alone." He needed to have an imaginary audience—the audience was going to be his Carnegie Hall audience.
>
> He started working toward this goal, and the closer he got to it, the more he had to consider things like his weight and eating and sleep and getting to bed earlier at night. He cut down his social life. He did all this in this way coming right into this mock performance event. A couple of days before it, he turns his wife and son out of the house, because he wants to be absolutely alone.
>
> The day of the "recital," he puts on the new tux, the whole thing. The recital is at 8 p.m., let's say, and so he needs to factor in when he has to be at Carnegie. He gets dressed and goes downstairs in the elevator, out on the street on Central Park West. He turns around and he walks back into his apartment building. He goes upstairs in the elevator, and now in his mind this is Carnegie Hall. The living room was the performance place, and the den was the green room. He goes into the green room and starts to warm up. He imagines the stage manager saying: ten minutes, five minutes. He even imagined the stage manager saying: "We're going to wait a couple of minutes," as they often do, especially in New York. So you're primed for 8:00 p.m. and there you are and they hold you.
>
> Then he goes out and he starts the recital. He comes out and he bows, in the living room, he plays the first piece, he leaves the stage. Comes back for the second piece—three big pieces—intermission. He still does not evaluate, he just does

what he's going to do. He drinks some water, sits back, whatever. He goes out and plays the second half of the program, he bows, does a couple of encores, and leaves. And then he takes off his tie. It's over. He's done his Carnegie Hall recital. He sits there and he reviews the whole recital: What could have been better, what did he need, and so on. Now he has a chance to appraise directly.

Sport psychology consultants know the importance of preparing for the first few minutes of competition, as this time often sets the tone for one's entire performance. Attorney Anna became systematic in rehearsing for these crucial moments. "I would make a list of every conceivable question the court might ask, and think about what my answer would be. I would then practice my oral argument—excessively probably—over and over. For me typically it's getting through the first three minutes, two minutes even. If I am off to a good start, then I'm fine."

Advertising executive Barry, provided an example of overlearning during *in vivo* rehearsal in business settings: "I have been most successful when I have taken the time to use the knowledge I have and the preparation and just practice until it becomes kind of second nature." He uses the natural opportunities for "audience" and feedback that occur while developing a project: "There is working with the team to develop the actual work for the pitch. There is overseeing the team as they go through their rehearsals and offering feedback to them and having the guts to rehearse in front of them and making sure you get their feedback."

Equally important, Barry learned to generalize, understanding the ways in which many aspects of his life could be designated "performance" and therefore became opportunities for practice:

> There is some solo preparation and practice and then there is some group-oriented stuff, but also—I must be getting old or something—there are so many opportunities to practice during the course of the day. Every interaction is like a little bit of a sales pitch. It's not that I am constantly trying to sell, but every interaction is a learning opportunity. When you are having a meeting with three people in your office, you have to be knowledgeable and you have to be prepared. You have to come off very polished and very professional so that they will believe you and so that they will follow you.

In medicine, the importance of practice is reflected in the growing body of research documenting the increased success rates of surgeons who routinely perform specific procedures over those who only occasionally perform the same surgery. One study estimated that "up to 13 out of every 100 surgical deaths could have been prevented in the hands of high-volume surgeons" (Mishra, 2003, p. A1).

We end this chapter with the classic performance story: A man was walking down the street in New York when a stranger stopped him and asked, "How do I get to Carnegie Hall?"

His reply: "Practice, practice, practice."

Recommendations to Consultants

■ Performance consultants must understand the central role that practice plays in developing and maintaining competence and confidence.

■ Performers need to have different types of knowledge—knowledge of their product, audience, and selves. These types of information and understanding often interact with each other.

■ Knowledge of what to do is different from practicing what needs to be done. Both are vital.

■ Whenever possible, performers are encouraged to make practice conditions replicate those of actual performance. This process facilitates comfort with and competence in performing under those same conditions.

■ Overlearning involves knowing the material thoroughly—different performance areas require different types of overlearning. It is important to differentiate overlearning from overtraining or overuse. The latter involves working on the material to such an extent that physiological and psychological decrements occur.

■ Overlearning is critical in order not only to thoroughly know one's product but also (a) to be able to shift into an automatic mode at times of high stress, such as when one encounters unexpected circumstances in performance and (b) to develop and incorporate the level of emotion and emotional expression appropriate to that performance.

■ Attention to the need for rest is important for (a) incubation of material, (b) recovery from the intensity of training, and (c) prevention of overtraining or overuse.

Keeping Your Head: Mental Skills 8

If I were able to do it the way I would like to, I would be locked in my dressing room and I would be just relaxing, sitting down, eyes closed, as if I were getting ready to go into meditation.

—Harold (conductor)

port psychologists working with athletes have developed a number of classification systems to describe the mental skills necessary for peak performance. For example, Nideffer (1985) recommended that athletes develop expertise in concentration, mental rehearsal (imagery), relaxation (tension control), the management of distracting and negative thoughts, and the regulation of attention and focus. Orlick's (1986) model emphasized goal setting, regulating tension through relaxation, self-talk, having clear plans for competition, precompetition plans for achieving the ideal state of preparation, refocusing plans, and effective communication with coach and teammates. Williams and Krane (1997) clustered seven key mental skills that distinguish successful elite athletes: goal setting, imagery, managing physical activation or tension, thought management techniques, well-developed performance plans, well-developed coping strategies (contingency planning), and pre-performance mental readying plans. These mental skills need to be intentionally learned and practiced in order to be effective and available to the performer.

Although the majority of the performers that we interviewed had no formal training in mental skills, they consistently demonstrated the interweaving of these various skills in their performance preparation. Using the information available from the sport psychology literature, we clustered the responses into the following psychological skills training categories: (a) goal setting, (b) activation management, (c) imagery, (d) thought management, (e) attention management, (f) pre-performance mental preparation plans, (g) well-developed performance focus plans, and (h) refocusing or contingency plans. In this chapter we look at each of these skills and the ways in which it contributes to peak performance.

Goal Setting

One may not typically think of goal setting as a mental skill; however, it is often the first step toward performance excellence. A goal is essentially "what an individual is trying to accomplish; it is the object or aim of an action" (Locke, Shaw, Saari, & Latham, 1981, p. 126). Research by industrial–organizational psychologists has documented that effective and efficient goal setting has a significant impact on motivation (Locke & Latham, 1990). Goals are critical to performance in that they direct a person's attention, influence effort and perseverance, and serve as stimulus for developing new learning and performance strategies. Whether one accomplishes his or her goals has a tremendous impact on self-confidence and efficacy (Bandura, 1977).

Applied sport psychologists (Burton, 1989; Hardy et al., 1996) have distinguished among three types of goals: outcome, performance, and process. An *outcome* goal compares one's performance with that of another person. For example, a runner may want to beat all others and win a race; an actor may want to win an audition; or a business person may want to win a contract. Outcome goals can have a great motivational effect on performers; however, focusing solely on outcome goals can actually hinder performance. Research with athletes has indicated that exclusive focus on outcome goals increases anxiety during performance (Burton, 1989). Relying solely on outcome as a reflection of a performer's abilities can needlessly shatter one's confidence. In a competitive situation, individuals may complete the best performance of their careers, only to lose to someone who happens to perform even better. Numerous factors—in this case, the behavior of another person—are entirely totally beyond the performer's control. Thus, even under seemingly positive circumstances, serious disappointment can result if the performer focuses only on the outcome.

Performance goals measure one's performance by a certain standard, independent of other performers. For example, a runner may want to complete a race in a specified time; a dancer may want to successfully execute a complex and demanding move; a businessman may want to have a certain volume of sales during a year; a musician may want to master a particular solo piece. These goals are typically more efficient than outcome goals, as goal achievement is under the control of the performer. A major pitfall with performance goals, however, involves set-

> If they want to show off, then forget it.
> If they're competitive, forget it. All these
> are destructive. The one thing you learn
> in the theatre . . . if you don't work
> together, you've got nothing at all.
>
> —Brenda (actor)

ting "perfection" as the standard. When this occurs, the performer is inevitably doomed to fall short of the goal. Performers' struggles in regard to perfection seeking are woven throughout this book, notably in regard to stress and stress management, as well as performance itself.

Process goals refer to moment-to-moment goals during one's performance. For example, the runner may attend to lengthening his or her stride; a musician may focus on articulating a soft, but clear entrance; a dancer might focus on a particular turn of the hand; and a surgeon may focus on keeping his shoulders relaxed. These goals are extremely efficient: If process goals are achieved, one will have done the very best possible for a given situation. Our interviews consistently indicated that focus on the immediate process of the moment (i.e., process goals) was central to performance excellence.

Goal setting is reflected in the way each performer approaches active intentional learning (discussed in chap. 7, this volume). Acquiring knowledge, mastering technique, and practicing the delivery are all examples of clear, efficient goals that prepare one for the moment of performance. In the following section we share examples of the ways in which our performers used the skill of goal setting in their quest for excellence.

Goal setting was a central concern and framework for Michael (conductor), an issue to which he continually returned. Throughout the interview, it was apparent that clarity of purpose guided his approach to music. Michael inquired:

> What is your purpose for doing what are you doing? If you haven't decided the philosophy, the reason, the mission when you walk out on stage, of course you're going to be in a very unstable condition, and that itself is cause to be nervous.
>
> People have all kinds of reasons why they do what they do. Some [reasons] are based on social concerns; some [people] are more concerned for themselves. If your purpose is to get a stamp of approval from somebody else, if your purpose is to be perfect, if your purpose is to get a good review or to be thought of as being more gifted than somebody else, if that's what you're all about, you're going to be a mess your whole life. You're never going to have a moment's peace.
>
> And it will all be suffering for you one way or the other, because I think you're not really fulfilling the purpose of art anyway. I think the main purpose of art is to be dramatic.

That's it. To be dramatic and then beyond that, to stimulate people's thought processes and emotions and get their ideas going, to make them feel ultimately much more in love with life because of having contacted whatever it is you've intended for them.

I think that, over time, art has been one of the major civilizing influences that we have. I have a belief that art doesn't exist in a vacuum. It exists to serve humanity. It's fundamental to existence.

For many, life in the arts doesn't follow a straight-line trajectory that the term goal setting might imply. "Unlike the business world, the amount of effort and time put in to master your craft in the arts does not pay off with predictable success" (Dunkel, 1989, p. 51). Among actors in particular, long-term goal setting is challenging, if not impossible. Keith commented:

We tend to get lost in the increments of success in this profession. So many people skip the queue—and in weird ways. A kid can pack his suitcase and go to L.A. and be doing a $20 million movie in six months. Other people work in the industry for 25 years and then suddenly they're in every other television series. We all have sort of a lottery feeling about it, the Lana-Turner-in-the-drug-store image. But it's not like that for 99.9% of us.

Keith contrasted long- and short-term planning:

In a lot of ways, there's no such thing as planning a career in acting, unless you're independently wealthy and willing to sit on your behind for a long time and just wait for what you're wanting to come up. Very often you have to take what work arrives, so you find yourself in a circuitous route that wasn't really planned. But you can look a step ahead rather than 20 steps ahead and set a goal and reach it or revise it.

As a dancer, Jerry differentiated between the value of specific external goal-

> At any one time, 85% of actors are unemployed. Almost nobody really can be told with any assurance that they are going to work, but some people obviously have fewer chances than others. In the acting world, a very wise thing that I heard said was that there are three things that can make your career. One is luck, one is talent, and one is perseverance. If you have two out of three, you have a good chance at making it.
>
> —Dr. Owen Osborne
> (consultant, theatre)

setting relevant in some fields and the appropriateness of personally framed goals in others. He distinguished between athlete and artist, external and internal—but described process goals in either instance:

> If we're talking about a runner, in some stages of the training it might be useful to say "today all I care about is shaving a tenth of a second off the time." But for an artist, the only goals that I would really be comfortable with trying to achieve would be things like: "Today I'm going to listen to my body, that's my goal"; "Today I'm not going to fight somebody else's expectations." It's important that you have that kind of internally measured goal, that you get to say whether it happened or not. It's up to you to know what your mental state was when you did a certain action.

Having taken a motivational course, Larry thought that goal clarification would be useful for actors. He understood the ways in which "it allowed me to understand that if you have objectives, you can work toward your objectives and realize what the outcome is, both negative and positive."

Not surprisingly, businesspeople are very comfortable with goal setting. Charles (insurance broker) described the importance of differentiating between two primary motivators or goals in business: "Either you want to make more money or you want more time off." He was also well versed in breaking goals down into small, achievable steps and being accountable to someone for those goals. As an example, he described a long-term insurance case that required continual adjustment of goals:

> I just kept focusing on that case: What do I need to do to move it forward? What's the next step? Where are we roadblocked? How can we get around the roadblock? What are the impediments? How can I get around them? What do I see as the next impediment, and how can I get around that one?

For David (banker):

> I hate the phrase "win–win" but I don't have a better one. I think you are trying to create "win–win" situations. Business is not a contest to see if you can beat down the other guy. It's preferable that you don't just crush somebody. Maybe it's just the heart of negotiating that you try to figure out what's important and not important for you and what's important and not important to them, and see how those match up. You see if you can accommodate them on some things first of all that aren't important to you, that are easy. And you try to do that— try to do that as opposed to being willing to—so that you can

come out with some benefit. Obviously before you do anything, you figure out who's got the negotiating leverage and who's sitting in the higher chair—figuratively and not literally—those kind of games.

David concluded by emphasizing performance rather than outcome goals: "You worry mostly about yourself. You don't get caught up in how well this person is going to do, what they deserve, what they're getting. You worry about yourself and don't worry about the other guy."

Eric described clear process goals for a successful performance in the emergency room. He summed them up:

The most important thing is to see the patients as soon as possible after they come in the door. Second, when patients are ready to go, discharge them and keep the flow going. And above all you must always maintain self control; you can absolutely never lose your temper.

Activation Management

Activation refers to "a complex multi-dimensional state which reflects the organism's anticipatory readiness to respond" (Hardy et al., 1996, p. 135). Activation includes both physiological and psychological factors and ranges along a continuum from a comatose low to a frenzied peak. The physical hallmarks of high activation include rapid heart rate, increased blood pressure, quickened breathing, and sweating—all physical symptoms associated with the activation of the sympathetic nervous system and the release of adrenaline. The psychological components of high activation typically include feelings of nervousness, worry, and anxiety. At higher levels of activation, fine motor skills tend to suffer and a person has difficulty with memory, concentration, and the ability to shift attention.

For each individual, there is an optimal level of arousal for performing a given task (Hanin, 2000). If arousal is too low, the performance or effort is "flat"; if it is too high, a person "chokes" or experiences panic. The ability to regulate one's level of activation—to either "psych up" or "chill out"—is a skill associated with performance excellence.

George, the Special Forces medic, used traditional relaxation techniques, such as slowing his breathing and relaxing unnecessary muscle tension, to consciously lower his heart rate in combat situations. Other performers used creative techniques for activation management. Faith (singer) typically marked her music in specific ways:

I write some positive cues around difficult passages in the music. The music usually becomes easier the more you do it.

Over time, I erase these reminders. But I might just write [my husband's name] in there if I need to think of something really positive in a particularly difficult section. If you get too tied up worrying about spots, then anxiety starts to creep in earlier and earlier in a piece, so I try to make sure I really separate them out. Maybe three-fourths of the piece is really comfortable and easy and one bar is hard. I try to make sure I color that section uniquely only in its own place so that tension doesn't start at the very beginning of the piece. Usually I try to go with the emotion of the text, but if it's a repetitive piece—and by that point you're simply singing the music—I will do something that's totally abstract, think of roses or eating or shopping or something. I'll just put some crazy word in there to catch my mind and trick it a bit to not think only technical tension.

Norman spoke of the dynamic balance that a musician needs: to be totally aware yet not overreact. "What you really have to do is practice the feeling that you are not going to respond or react to what you perceive you did, although of course half of the battle is being able to hear yourself."

Sometimes performers do not need to change their level of physiological activation. As we discuss more fully in chapter 10, the performer can achieve a greater sense of calm by altering the interpretation of the experience. Physician Eric reframed anxiety as attentiveness in surgery:

The more complicated the procedure, the more fearful I am of the procedure and the risks of it when I'm starting out. I focus on what I need to do and how I am going to do it. You don't find a lot of people who are casually relaxed in some of these procedures. There is a little more anxiety but you can control it and just convert it into more attentiveness rather than anxiety.

Imagery

Imagery is the technique most commonly associated with mental skills training for athletes (Gould, Tammen, Murphy, & May, 1989). In addition to using imagery for mental rehearsal of a performance, it can be used to develop new skills, practice coping strategies, build confidence, control emotions, and regulate physical and emotional response to stressful situations. Effective imagery is more inclusive than mere visualization; as a mental experience, any or all the senses and emotions can be involved. Performers in each of the domains described the use of imagery in their own field.

The multiple and frequent opportunities for imagery are incorporated into all aspects of advertising executive Barry's life:

For me, it is in front of the bathroom mirror in the morning; it's the whole morning before the pitch. You are rehearsing in your head, visualizing what success will look like, and you are visualizing what failure might look like and trying to prevent it.

Anna (lawyer) described preparation for a trial presentation:

If I was going to be saying something that I felt hesitant about, I would try to imagine somebody who I admired saying what I was planning on saying. If it seemed reasonable in my head that this person might say this, then I was okay with it. I would try it out through this other person's speech. I would imagine if he were standing up and saying this—and it was almost always a man, because there were almost no women [attorneys] who were older than me—how would it sound? Would it be a reasonable argument, or a reasonable statement? Frankly, I can never think of a time when I didn't think that it was okay; but it just was a way to test it out.

Using a similar process, insurance salesman Charles described imagery in his work:

A lot of times when I'm going to go out on a call, I visualize what's going to happen. I visualize where people are going to sit. I visualize what they're going to say, I visualize what I'm going to say. I visualize what the objections are going to be. It really has helped. When I don't visualize it and go on an appointment, it's like I shouldn't even be there.

Musicians commonly use various forms of mental rehearsal and review. Diane spoke of images rolling around in her head, music that is present throughout. Faith memorized the text of songs while working out: exercise deepened the learning and associated images.

By contrast, Harold (conductor) used imagery to rehearse tempos for himself but refrained from suggesting images to others. He was adamant about the abstract nature of music and considered it important for him as a conductor not to interfere with his musicians' own interpretation:

Music is abstract communication and imagery interferes when you're trying to express the abstract. I think imagery would be counterproductive, and in fact would make the person less creative. At my best, I'm a leader in some ways; but what I like to hear and what I like to do is give all the musicians that are on the stage—and I'm thinking most specifically of my instrumentalists and my soloists—as much room to express their musicality and their understanding as possible, rather than impose my understanding or my interpretation on them. On the other hand, if someone is in an opera, for example, maybe imagery is beneficial for going into character. But not for me as a conductor.

As an administrator and emergency room physician, Frederick described his use of two different kinds of imagery, one retrospective and the other prospective:

When I've had a negative encounter, I do retrospective fantasy role-playing. I go back to what I refer to as "the Count of Monte Cristo fantasy." The Count of Monte Cristo was deeply wronged, bashed on, treated like shit by bad, bad people and he came back and got them. So I think: "You have really done something that is odious. You have harmed me; you have stabbed me in the back, you scum." I abstract the fantasy and I exaggerate what they did so that it is absolutely blatantly obvious that it was totally wrong, as black and white as you can get it. Then, at the end, I come back and conquer. I work through all that anxiety and work through all of that meanness. When I actually have my second encounter with this person, all of that is gone—unless they fulfill my fantasy, unless they come out and do the worst possible thing they could do, which they virtually never do. I'm okay. I have role-played that out.

I do the same thing every morning. I wake up at about 4 a.m., and I get out of bed at 6 a.m. My wife says, "You have an amazing clock in your mind because you get out of bed at exactly the same time every morning." But that is because I have been staring at the clock and when it turns 6 a.m., I get out of bed. I've been awake and all that time, if I'm going to give a lecture, I've been rehearsing the lecture. If I'm going to have some meeting with somebody, I go over that. Reviewing everything allays my anxiety.

Some performers use imagery to control their level of arousal. T'ai chi is a form of martial arts that, unlike fighting styles that accentuate speed and physical strength, emphasizes a "centered calmness" and movements that are slow and flowing in nature. Special Forces medic George has applied the philosophy and style of t'ai chi to his preparation for combat situations. He calls his own process "medic t'ai chi":

I have a friend who is a jump master. He's the guy who runs through all the parachute inspections before we jump. I'd see him sitting over there, rehearsing, going through the inspection with his eyes closed and his hands moving. He calls this process "jump master t'ai chi." I adopted that for myself as a medic: Whenever I had a moment and was just thinking about my role as a medic, I would try to sit down and get into a very relaxed state and then run through these things. I'm basically doing "medic t'ai chi."

Similarly, radio celebrity Grace described a particular image that she developed and used over the years for activation management: "When I'm dealing with unpleasant things that interfere with being able to perform, I breathe, relax, and imagine a green handi-wipe passing across my face and brain, simply wiping the unpleasant thing away."

Thought Management

There is ample evidence that negative, self-defeating statements and thoughts have a negative effect on performance (Hardy et al., 1996). Being able to stop nonproductive thoughts and develop an internal dialogue, involving positive counters to negative thought, has been repeatedly demonstrated to improve performance (Mahoney & Avener, 1977; Van Raalte, Brewer, Rivera, & Petipas, 1994).

Jerry (dancer) spelled out the ways in which through self-talk, or a mental conversation, he practiced thought management:

I've always found for myself that once the problem is identified, the solution is obvious. For instance, I was nervous, and I thought this was just a part of my makeup. But I just realized that I didn't have to be this nervous; that I really wasn't helping myself. I asked myself: "What do I want to do? What do I have to do next to improve?" And the response was: "You have to do on stage what you do in the studio." The next question was: "Why don't you do on stage what you do in the studio?" "Because I'm nervous and I'm not well focused, and I project things that might go wrong." "So change that."

It certainly didn't stop me being nervous, but it stopped being inevitable; it stopped being destructive. The first symptom would appear, but the rest wouldn't. I wouldn't go from feeling nervous in my stomach to throwing up. I would go from feeling nervous in my stomach to feeling "oh, now I feel nauseous; this is part of getting ready to go. Let's not throw away however many hours of rehearsal on indulging the fact that I'm nervous." It sounds like it was some kind of mental discipline, but it wasn't, it was just being aware of it, just putting a name to it.

This kind of self-talk, in which the person actively reframes negative thoughts into constructive alternatives, was used by singer Faith. She reflected on her past experience to give her confidence in the present: "I've never walked off stage. [Remembering that] always builds your confidence. It's like, 'Look, this may seem scary, but you've never fallen apart, you're not going to fall apart now.'

Attention Management

In addition to managing one's internal dialogue through thought management, a critical mental element involves the control of one's attention, to enhance concentration and focus. Attention management addresses problems of both concentration and attention. Concentration is the ability to focus "the mind on one source of information, often to the exclusion of others" (Hardy et al., 1996, p. 174). However, concentration alone is not sufficient. The performer may focus on aspects that could hinder performance, such as fear, a mistake that has been made in the recent past, or future events, such as the eventual outcome of the performance. Ideal attention management entails the ability to focus on elements or "cues" that are relevant to performance while ignoring nonessential factors. Research has indicated that the ability to manage attention in this fashion is one of the features distinguishing successful athletes from those less successful (Gould et al., 2002; Gould, Weiss & Weinberg, 1981; Mahoney, Gabriel, & Perkins, 1987; Williams & Krane, 1997).

The ideal focus of attention may shift as circumstances change during the course of an event or performance. One can direct attention either externally to events and circumstances in the environment or internally to events and experiences within oneself. Focus can be broad to encompass a wide range of information, or very narrow, directed to an isolated event (Nideffer, 1985). For example, a physician may need to pay broad attention to external matters during the initial assessment of a patient coming into the emergency room. The physician may then direct broad attention inwardly, recognizing muscle tension and feelings of unease in anticipation of performing a difficult procedure. He or she may then direct attention narrowly and internally, taking slow deep breaths to gain a sense of calm, and then direct attention externally in a narrow focus, as the first incision is made.

All performers noted the importance of focus during performance. As we indicate in subsequent sections, the primary objective of planning and preparation is to facilitate proper focus and attention during performance. Concentration and focus, however, are not automatic by-products of practice. They are skills in and of themselves. Several performers, notably the dancers and musicians interviewed, seemed particularly attuned to practicing and developing these skills.

In her role as both a musician and a conductor, Ellen commented on her responsibilities:

> I think the way rehearsals are is the way concerts are. As the person who leads the rehearsals, I have to make sure that there's a good, congenial working atmosphere, but also one where attention is very concentrated. If you're not concentrating and people's minds are wandering in rehearsals, you can't expect them to be focused in the concert—it won't happen.

Ilene also had a dual focus. During much of her workday, she was an arts administrator. She used her music skills in this situation, and this in turn reinforced her approach to music playing:

> My job is basically a business job. I manage staff, and I fund raise, and I do budgets, and I talk on the phone. When I'm doing my [administrative] job well, what I'm taking from my music is that kind of intense focus of the moment and holding the line all the way through the 30 minutes. To me it's all about focus.

Ilene cultivated the skill through practice and intentional learning:

> Even when I'm going to be reading the music in a chamber music situation, I do a lot of just trying to sit alone, still, think the music through from beginning to end, and concentrate. I try to pay attention to whether I've had a mental breakdown in time, whether I had a distracted moment that made me break the line. If I were to play a solo recital now, I would spend a lot of time on the couch just seeing if I could mentally play the piece and not break my concentration, even if it was 30 minutes long.

Charlotte (dancer) described the interaction of tension management and focus, as well as the conscious development of her skills of concentration:

One of the most important mental elements is the ability to concentrate. It sounds so obvious, but there are so many people who when they really get down to the moment of pressure, can't focus their mind on the task at hand and block out all the distractions around them. Each person is different, but I learned over the years that if I could get myself relaxed, I could focus. If I was tense, thinking I was being really serious and really concentrated but with tension, I couldn't really achieve it. In rehearsals, I was relaxed because I knew that I could try something again if it didn't work. But I would also use the rehearsal to find that inner pinpoint of concentration, to be able to do certain things and to create an atmosphere around me. I would find that atmosphere in a rehearsal, find that concentration, and then recreate it for myself. That meant that I could be relaxed in the wings, laugh and be open to comments from people and kind of easy about it. But then when the music for my entrance started to come, I could immediately go into that concentration and that place.

Pre-Performance Mental Preparation Plan

Williams and Krane (1997) reported that successful athletes achieve an optimal mental state just prior to beginning an athletic performance. This is often accomplished through a combination of rituals or predictable pre-performance routines. Hanin (2000) emphasized that this involves more than physical preparation. He suggested that every athlete has an Individual Zone of Optimal Functioning (IZOF) that includes a unique recipe of emotions leading to peak performance. For one person, an ideal performance state might involve a combination of feeling relaxed, thrilled, and a bit apprehensive. Another might perform best when angry, determined, and invigorated. A popular misconception and misinterpretation suggests that being totally relaxed is the ideal performance state. Although it is true that many athletes perform worse if they become over-activated, some performers do their best work when they feel nervous, jittery, angry, or annoyed. For example, one of us (CB) knew a professional basketball player who confessed to being nervous before every game. If he wasn't nervous, he tended to be "flat" and have an off night. Some years ago, television host David Frost interviewed composer–conductor Leonard Bernstein. Frost *had* to become icily calm before interviewing people; Bernstein *had* to throw up in order to feel ready to perform.

The performers we interviewed also use specific physical, mental, or emotional routines to effect a certain state of being. These activities are designed to assist in accessing an optimal state of functioning for the performance. Some performers focus on the routine, some on the state itself. Participants from each of the domains commented on this aspect of performance.

As singer Faith stated:

It's those moments before you go out there that can be nerve-wracking. One of my colleagues says, about five minutes before time to go on is when the shit hits the fan. That's when the adrenaline usually kicks right in and you have those five minutes to get yourself organized, go to the bathroom one more time, and breathe deeply if you need to. If you need to concentrate, you'll go away. Some of the stuff I do with colleagues is that we just tell jokes before we go out; that is part of our silliness and usually we go on stage laughing or smiling.

Performers appear to achieve their optimal pre-performance state in a way similar to that of athletes. They focus on the key factors of predictability, ritual, or routine. The specific management of interaction with others is one element of this process. Neurosurgeon Eric gave a classic example of the active process he uses in the five minutes before beginning to operate:

Typically what you do is position the patient, prep the wound, look at the angiogram films—the dye study that shows the aneurysm and the anatomy around it—and kind of imprint them in your mind. And then just go out into the scrub sink where you are by yourself. You've got five minutes there. All you're doing is just scrubbing your hands. It's just a time of rote activity. You are not really talking to anybody; you're not doing anything different except just standing there. That's the time I'll try to piece together the anatomy with what I am about to do. I try to picture what I am going to see when I get there, because the x-rays are taken at a couple of fixed angles straight on or from the side and we are coming in at a 20° angle to that. We don't have any way to visualize pre-operatively what we are going to see when we get there. It's this two-dimensional view from straight up or the side and it's up to us to kind of figure out how to transfer it to three. We try to transpose those two views in two dimensions to make it three-dimensional and rotate into the view that you'll be looking at when you come down.

Physician Frederick described emergency medicine as shift work:

The ritual is that you set a period of time when you start being anxious. Otherwise, you ruin too much of your day. You say, "Okay, I'm going to start thinking about going to work two or three hours before I go to work." And then you take a shower. You methodically get dressed and you remember to take this and take that and then you get in your car. It is real simple.

I try to make it absolutely routine. Get in the car at the same time. Get there the same ten minutes early. I go around to all the different parts of the emergency department to figure out just how bad it is, how good it is, and then I go into one of two modes. Either things are caught up and you can move forward, or you just plug along and plug along and keep one foot in front of the other and try to be as efficient as possible when you know you are going to be so far behind, you will never catch up.

As a lawyer meeting with people, Arthur approaches his performance through gentle physical activity and quiet time to himself:

I like to be relatively clearheaded. If the weather is halfway decent when I commute, I'll walk. That's like 35 minutes of not focusing on anything in particular. I think it helps overcome the natural inclination to go in and talk. I call it "having two antennas." Clearing my mind allows me to be a little more open to walk in and be half balanced about it, really listening and watching, as opposed to walking in and thinking, "I am going to do five things and I am going to start right now!"

If I were preparing a presentation to a jury or that sort of thing, that would be more of a performance. I would prepare differently. I would have to know what I was going to say and be ready to go.

Advertising executive Barry similarly used time and solitude as a tool for optimal performance:

At my best, I always leave about a 15–30 minute buffer between meetings. I try to take about 15 minutes before every meeting to think about who I am meeting with; why am I meeting with them; what will make this a successful meeting; and what are the one, two, or three things I need to gain from this. I need that time to become fully focused and attentive.

Like many athletes, Barry also deliberately used music to set an optimal level of activation for any specific performance:

I like solitude beforehand. If it's a big presentation, I like to get about an hour of quiet time or alone time beforehand. I might play Jimi Hendrix to get my heart going and to get excited about it. Crusader songs will just take me to a different place. It is very relaxing. I have Pearl Jam on there when things are at their hardest. I like to start out with a really high level of energy and confidence, with my heart pounding and then kind of settle into a groove . . . . It just heightens everything, especially, for whatever reason, my sense of humor.

Dancer Helena detailed the individual differences inherent in pre-performance preparation, as well as the effects of both time (personal development) and varying circumstances (dancing with others in a company vs. solo work). She identified ritual, centering, and solitude as key elements:

In a company situation, I had one or two little rituals that I would always do: I'd go onto the stage before the curtain went up and do a deep plié [knee bend] on the stage. That was my one little talisman thing. I always had to do that. And in my makeup case, I always had one of those tiny little bottles of Metaxa brandy, and I always had a sip of Metaxa before, just one sip. I didn't want to have the whole bottle—I mean we're talking about one of those little mini bottles. Those two little actions, one sip of brandy and one deep plié on the stage before the curtain went up. ·

Some people need rock music and adrenaline pumping and that kind of energy before the performance. And some people need a more interior focus. For me, if there was a choice between two dressing rooms, and one had a Walkman playing rock music and the other didn't have any music, I liked to be in the quiet one.

When I've prepared solos or duets, it is usually important for me to get myself to a very calm and very centered state. Usually I try and find a space where I can be alone. I put on my makeup and I try and listen to the music for the performance, either literally if I have a little cassette with me, or just sing it through in my head. I'll either go through the dance if I have a space to mark through it or just do it in my head.

I almost have to put myself into a meditative state, where I can close myself away from any distracting people or noises. I try to go to the place in myself where I am most grounded, I'm most at peace, am most myself. I'm most able to speak from that center. If I can get in touch with that center, that's the place I need to start from to speak in terms of performing as a dancer.

Dancer Jerry emphasized the physical warm-up, the sense of routine, and community:

> I always did a barre [practice routine] before performance, half
> an hour or 40 minutes of repetitive physical activity in a
> predictable sequence. And there were some others who always
> did that as well, so you had time for a little community of
> people who prepared that way.

Likewise, Charlotte (dancer) spoke about her own pre-performance methods that changed developmentally as a function of age and intention. Ultimately, learning to make adjustments and to focus on the present were key elements in sustaining a high and satisfying level of performance:

> When I was too fresh and too nervous, I would do
> performances and have no idea what I had done. I'd come off
> stage and I'd try to run the film back. I knew I hadn't done
> anything horrendous because I would have remembered if I'd
> fallen down, but I had no idea what I had done. I was totally
> unconscious [of my own actions], because there was so much
> adrenaline surging through me. I was so revved up, I'd feel like
> somebody who's just shot out of a cannon and goes through
> the motions in super high speed. Sometimes when you have
> too much adrenaline you just look manic; you look like you're
> on speed or something, and that's how I danced. Fortunately I
> had good instincts and I was talented enough to get away with
> that for a while.
>
> Of course, that was something that people loved about my
> dancing. That was exhilarating for the audience, it wasn't
> boring for them, but ultimately it became kind of unsatisfying
> for me.
>
> It worked when I was 21, 22, 23, but then I started to want
> to be in control of myself a little better. As I became more
> mature, that wasn't the kind of performance I wanted to do. I
> had done all this work in the studio and I had no idea if I had
> accomplished anything that I had set out to accomplish. I
> wanted to be conscious, not unconscious. You want to grow;
> you want to be doing the sort of performance that you've
> developed, and you're wanting to put it forward in an
> intelligent way, rather than just wild crazy.
>
> I realized that one of the ways that I could control that was
> to be tired—tired physically and very, very, very warm. When I
> was tired, I didn't have the extra energy to be so nervous, and I
> could control my reactions much better.

> Just before the performance, it's almost like you're entering into a time of meditation. You are really focusing so that you live entirely in the moment. You shut out everything else, you shut out everything that is extraneous. You become superbly focused on your task at hand. And there's only one task and that is performing the work that evening.
>
> —Harold (conductor)

The integration of active intentional learning and incubation, described earlier, was important to Harold's (conductor) achievement of an optimal performance state. Feeling fully prepared, he could then interpret the pre-performance increased adrenaline as excitement rather than stage fright.

> Tension is necessary, because tension can actually make a performance, if it's good. That's one of those things that you work at for a lifetime. What is good for someone isn't necessarily good for another person. Some of my colleagues are procrastinators, and somehow they find that energy, that crisis energy, invigorating. For me, it's anything but invigorating. I find it overwhelming, and I can't deal with it. I learned, fortunately fairly early on, that what was going to make for a comfortable performing situation for me involved adequate and early preparation.

For Larry (actor), an optimal pre-performance state could be developed through relaxed breathing and affirmations. He recognized, "There's a duality to that moment. I'm still an actor and yet I'm always trying to lose myself in the character." He has developed a consistent routine.

> There usually are some physical warm-ups, just shaking the limbs, lying on the floor, yoga positions. Breathing exercises are very important. When you breathe, you become calm. The one thing I usually do, especially before a difficult show, is simply say "I can do it. I am doing it. I will do it." I'm signaling to myself that I can handle it, that I will deal. The repetition of the words is also important. And it feels natural. It creates a stillness, a reinforced positiveness, that allows me to achieve full peace.

Faith used systematic breathing, as well, to regulate the amount of tension she experiences before going on stage to sing.

> I've never had nerves that have taken me anywhere I didn't want to go. The adrenaline is real important—getting excited and really feeling like you've got that power, that little extra energy to take onto the stage, but I've never had it be out of

control. Breathing is *extremely* important. I take in some deep breaths, and if I feel at all like the adrenaline is going crazy, or if I'm waiting longer than I was hoping to wait, then I just take deep breaths and make sure my abdomen is really extended. It's a fairly basic thing. If for any reason I've gotten a little more excited than I want to be, I just make my heart slow down.

Ilene refocused attention from herself to the music:

When you can be conscious of the music and not conscious of yourself, a lot of the performance anxiety problems go away. What playing new music has taught me is that you need to look at all music as if it's freshly composed.

Radio personality Grace used the early morning drive into work as a time for transition to her show. Talk show host Ian found it important not to have contact with his guests before the show:

I don't go to the studio until the very last possible minute. I don't want to talk to the guests. I don't want to meet them. I don't want to chitchat with them before the show, because it makes the conversation on the air stale or it allows an opportunity for a dynamic to be set up where I am not in control, I am not the Supreme Being. I don't want to be in a situation where they could say something to me that would take me down a peg or knock my self-confidence. I do my best to put them at ease, because it is not a good show if they are not at ease, but it's my forum and my platform.

Although most of the performers with whom we spoke had settled on a routine that worked for them, Keith was still struggling 10 years after he began his acting career, to find the best way to prepare himself mentally, especially for auditions:

Sometimes, I'll get to an audition and I'll sit quietly and just try and breathe slowly, try and get my body relaxed and alleviate some tension. Other times, I'll just be really active and I'll think, "This is feeling good, it's keeping me loose, it's not allowing the rigidity to set into my body." And this is it: There's no consistency, it's sort of a crapshoot. One time I'll try to prepare my material, then I'm ready to go in and another time I'll think, "Well, maybe you'll just be better if you don't even open the book, if you think to yourself: I've already worked on it enough, so don't even look at the script while I'm here in the waiting room, look at the paintings on the wall" and then my name will get called and I'll just launch into it.

Performance Focus Plan

Several studies indicate that successful elite athletes have well-developed plans and strategies for performance (Hardy et al., 1996; Orlick & Partington, 1987; Williams & Krane, 1997). These plans are generally "designed to facilitate attentional focus on the process of performance as opposed to factors over which they had no direct control, such as other competitors or outcome . . . . These competition plans usually have process-oriented goals as their central feature" (Hardy et al., 1996, pp. 191–192).

Our interviews and our own consulting experiences suggest that successful performers in all domains are aware of the importance of maintaining moment-to-moment focus on process goals. A recent client who had incorporated mental skills training into his role as principal player with a major orchestra provided an eloquent description of his performance focus: "There's a great feeling of being alive where risking fully and committing fully meet; here everything is at stake and everything stands to be won. I feel driven to seek this state. I want this to be my 'trademark'."

A successful performance plan involves achieving the optimal performance state, anticipating what one will encounter, and being clear as to the relevant cues and points of focus that one has to maintain. Not all performers articulate an explicit performance plan, but the plan can be inferred from the images they rehearse, the process goals they describe, and the importance they attribute to focus and concentration. We discuss this in greater detail in chapter 11.

Dr. Nick Norris (consultant, music) proposed that the ideal performance plan for a musician is not directed toward the technical aspects of performance. Instead it is designed to emphasize what the musician wants to communicate through his or her music: "They need to convey, 'I have something to *say*, and I have confidence in what I'm saying'."

For Helena (dancer), it was the physical demand of long performances that necessitated performance planning:

> This focusing on and trying to draw on all of my resources and my strength probably [began] when I started to do solo performances. I really had to build up my stamina mentally and physically for this experience because it involved two hours of performance on stage. I was on stage through the whole show. I had various guests doing duets with me, but basically I was dancing for two hours. And that was a whole other dimension to performing from what I had been doing with companies until then.

In many respects the neurosurgeon, the thoracic surgeon, and the automobile mechanic are very similar. They can't see what they're working on, so they need to visualize it. The auto mechanic reaches behind your engine, looking for a particular shape. It might be a five-sided bolt, or a half-inch as opposed to an inch-and-a-quarter bolt. It may be something with a little tube coming out of it, like a fuel pump. He knows what he's looking for, he's visualizing. Once he gets there, he's essentially performing the operation in his head, because he can't see it.

By and large, neurosurgeons or thoracic surgeons are doing many of the same kinds of things. They have to have a very clear image in their mind of what the ideal version of something looks like, whether it's the cortex or the left ventricle. They need to know where there is a vein or an artery that they're liable to nick, because they can't see it. So, when a surgeon says he prepares himself, he focuses, he gets grounded, he gets centered. One of the things he's doing is reproducing some figures that came from a neuroanatomy text or autopsies or other things that he's done. And that's what he learned from another neurosurgeon: Before you get in there, make sure you remember where the "fuel pump" is and remember where the "gas gauge" is.

—Dr. Irving Ingram (consultant, high-risk)

Refocusing Plan

In addition to having strategies for achieving the ideal performance state and plans for maintaining focus and attention during performance, successful athletes have detailed plans and strategies for maintaining focus in the face of distractions and disruptions (Williams & Krane, 1997). By practicing for situations that deviate from the ideal, an athlete develops the skill of refocusing to maintain the ideal performance state. The importance of contingency planning and preparation for the unexpected was noted by performers in all of the domains. Those in the high-risk areas were particularly explicit in their preparations for maintaining focus.

Coping imagery, in which the performer mentally constructs a difficult scene and then develops methods for handling the situation, may be used as an active aspect of contingency planning. George (medic–sniper) used imagery along with relaxed breathing to practice mentally how he would respond to traumatic situations. Rather than passively hoping that a threatening or unexpected event wouldn't happen, he actively anticipated various possibilities:

> As a police officer as well as a medic, I try to prepare myself with the attitude that it is going to happen to me, not that it happens to the other guys. That's a mental trap. I'll be perfectly happy if I go through my entire police and professional soldier careers not having fired a shot, not ever

getting shot. I'm not out to get a Purple Heart. But I want to be mentally prepared to take on whatever is dished out.

I actually close my eyes and work my hands as I would for specific injuries or ailments. I need to really stay relaxed when it comes to the medical scenario. I do deep breathing and create a tactical scenario where bad things are happening around me. I try to bring in all my other senses, like the smell of blood, screaming. Things like that, that really can just overwhelm a person.

I try to take care of the "what ifs" in my training, so that when I see something in actuality, it [won't be] a shock to me, because I've seen it in my mind several times before. If I get shot and I'm the casualty, am I just going to sit there and stare at my wound, or am I going to treat myself and take care of the problem?

I design my training plan so I'm doing as many things as I can foresee that I would be doing on a real operation, so it's not new to me. I don't want to get into a trap where I'm just going out on the range doing marksmanship training and packing it in. I try to put myself under physical and emotional stress on the range through a variety of exercises that will elicit stress responses. Now that's difficult to do when you're just shooting paper or mannequins, so I try to create stress by setting time limitations, by having people trying to break my concentration, yelling at me, throwing things, spraying me with water, whatever they want to come up with. Training might involve running, so my heart rate gets up and I have to recover quickly.

Performing surgery, similarly, requires attentive anticipation of problem situations. Eric said:

When I am thinking about a difficult case that I am on edge about, I will tend to pull up the worst-case scenario. That's what I want to have ready. When all hell breaks loose, you have reflex movement and memory. You can be working around an aneurysm and you've got this thing 95% dissected out and you know exactly where you are going and you've been working around it for 20 minutes and you know visually where it is and kind of what the anatomy is; but there may be one component you have not seen clearly and all of a sudden it goes, and you've lost your visualization. The field is just full of blood. You can't see. In those cases, if you can keep a memory of where the aneurysm was, you can often just slide a clip

A half hour before the curtain was to rise at the last performance of the school show, they discovered that the lighting board didn't work. The students were going to have to do the whole show on a wing and a prayer with basically no lights. They had no other option. The dancers who were in the first piece had to wait through one announcement saying, "Ladies and gentlemen, I'm sorry we're having a bit of trouble due to the lightning storm last night blah blah blah." They had gotten themselves ready, and then they had to wait, and they had to wait, and they had to wait until 8:20 for an 8 p.m. show. It finally started, and then they had to come bursting on, to do this very lively dance. It was very difficult for some of them to hold on to the readiness that they had prepared themselves with, through 15 or 20 minutes of extra distraction. Some kind of technique to re-focus would probably have been really helpful to them.

—Helena (dancer; dance instructor)

down and put it across what you knew was there. And take what could be a life-threatening problem and just end it.

The natural reaction until you get comfortable doing aneurysm surgery is to panic and pull back. Then what was potentially very salvageable is gone. And that's a weird step to overcome. To go from that panic, that "Oh my god, the field is full of blood," to staying where you are and getting the clip from the nurse and putting it on.

It's truly the highest anxiety case we do, that minute-to-minute potential for change. In most of what we do, there is not this risk of something that's going to uncork and turn into a life-threatening situation; but the aneurysm truly is.

Many musicians face the challenge of dealing with last-minute distractions. Diane commented:

We (orchestra members) were just talking about this the other day. There was an issue of people coming through backstage before concerts. And the cleaners always seem to be coming in. Right when we're going on stage, they're picking up bags of trash. It's just little intrusions like that. We all agreed that we really wouldn't like to have anybody but orchestra people backstage before a performance and at intermission too. Because you really have to focus on what you're doing. The mental preparation is important. You have to be *in* the element before you go out there and be thinking about what you're going to play.

As a musician, Norman used rehearsal as a deliberate and intentional method of contingency planning. Being in charge of the notes during practice gives him sufficient preparation for handling errors that might occur.

I try to cultivate in my practice the idea that I can stop and start anywhere. Many performers of music stop and start their practice in the same place too often, which is a mistake. While practicing, if I'm going to decide to stop, I decide to stop on an unpredictable note. It's deep concentration to be able to stop when you command yourself to stop, rather than when you break down. When I'm practicing, if I make a mistake I try not to stop. I always go forward and then I stop at some other note, at a place that I determine, just to say "Oh, that's it, this is the note on which I wish to stop."

Similarly, Harold (conductor) recalled how, as a child, he had created a game of contingency planning for himself:

I used to practice it as a kid, not knowing that I was practicing it. It was just a stupid little game that I used to play for myself. In my practicing, I would consciously make mistakes, or purposefully do something wrong that was going to make me react to a situation. Being able to get yourself out of any situation seemed to me to be an important thing. Now it was a very surface thing at that time, but in fact it was very valuable for me in some of my keyboard playing. The whole thing with some performers is if you make one mistake then everything falls apart. If you have the ability to carry on, even though something goes wrong, whether it's a note mistake or you make a wrong turn, like a memory problem, there's more confidence that you will be able to deal with anything that comes your way.

Recommendations to Consultants

- The array of mental skills or psychological skills techniques have undergone extensive investigation, especially in sport psychology. Many of these techniques are applicable to other areas of performance.
- The direct application of mental skills should not be done wholesale to a specific performance population without taking into account the particulars of that area of performance.
- Because of the popularization of psychological skills techniques, many performers know about them but not what they actually

are. They may have an inaccurate understanding of the techniques or may be dismissive, in part because of that very popularization.

■ Even if performers know psychological skills techniques, they may need direct training to be able to apply them to their own situations.

■ Total relaxation is not necessarily the optimal pre-performance state.

■ For any one individual, an array or mix of mental skills may be appropriate. The skills need not operate in isolation.

■ Performers should learn how to incorporate practice of mental skills into their ongoing practice, in order fully to make use of these techniques.

The Microscopic Nightmare of Infinity: The Experience of Stress

9

> The microscopic nightmare of infinity is the sense that, in the space of a very tiny moment—a split part of a second, less than an eighth of a second—you can experience infinity between two notes. It is the feeling that you can fall into the black hole at that point. And that's scary. That is deeply frightening.
>
> —Norman (musician)

To be alive is to experience stress. Stress is not a static condition, but, rather, a process. Stress has been described as "a substantial imbalance between demand and response capability, under conditions where failure to meet that demand has important consequences" (McGrath, 1970, p. 20). There is an interaction between the demands of the physical and psychological environment, the individual's perception of those demands, the person's physical and psychological response to stress, and the behavioral consequences.

In addition to the ordinary stress of human existence, performers experience stress that arises from the practice of their profession. The way in which a performer manages stress is a crucial factor in achieving performance excellence (Poczwardowski & Conroy, 2002). What types of stresses do performers experience? We have already detailed some that are particular to each of the three domains. In this chapter and the one that follows, we focus on stresses that appear related to the more generic aspects of performance. We review stresses and methods of stress-coping described by our performer interviewees in more than one domain.

Researchers have found that McGrath's stress sequence, described above, serves as a useful model to understand the stress experienced by athletes (Weinberg & Gould, 1995). The model appears appropriate for performers in general. Performance naturally entails physical and technical demands that, together with situational factors and the performer's expectations and perceptions of them, can intensify the experience of stress. Research identifies two major situational sources of stress for athletes: (a) the importance of an event and (b) uncertainty (Weinberg & Gould, 1995). The performers we interviewed also described these as sources of stress. Perceived importance of the performance event was reflected in discussions of competition for limited resources, the potential impact of mistakes, the sense of personal responsibility, and the expectations and standards to which one is held when performing for a living. Uncertainty is experienced by performers in a number of ways. These include the unpredictability of some types of performance, the variability that occurs within a group of performers, and a recognition of the limits of human performance.

We have organized this information by first looking at the physical activation or arousal associated with the stress of performance, and then we explore the demands that performers experience. Situational factors that contribute to the experience of stress are described, noting both the perceived importance of each situation and the impact of perceived uncertainty. Each performer strives for excellence yet must come to terms with the inevitability of imperfection. Finally, we look at the impact of stress and the toll that it can take—physically, mentally, and interpersonally.

Physical Activation

The physiological activation necessary for performing typically produces a surge of adrenaline, one that can be experienced either positively or negatively. Hans Selye, who coined the terms *eustress* and *distress* to describe these two extremes, also called stress the "spice of life" (Selye, 1975, p. 83). Anna, a lawyer, described these two stress elements: "I tend to need stress to work. So good stress is a motivator to perform. Bad stress for me is worrying about the things that you can't really control." Our other attorney, Arthur, also spoke of the "adrenaline-inducing" element of stress. "The stress component of it (work) is either trying to satisfy your own expectations or hopes, or somebody else's."

Csikszentmihalyi (1990) described the experience of "flow" as the balance between skill and challenge. The excitement of maintaining this equilibrium is experienced by Eric in some types of complex neurosurgeries: "The more difficult the case, the more stress you put on yourself; subconsciously, the more exciting it becomes. Your anxiety is up, but you are also charged for it in a lot bigger fashion, so you're ready for it."

The simultaneous tension and excitement of working at one's ultimate capacity was experienced by Faith as a singer. Music that demands the full range of the singer's skills is both a stressor and a source of deep satisfaction. In this same manner, Norman, a cellist, called stress "exhilarating." Performers' habituation to stress can also mean that sometimes one is so wrapped up in it that one is only aware of the presence of stress by its absence: Norman described the beginning of a two-week free period as "the most depressing day of my life." He knew that he would settle down after a few more days, "but I don't like that feeling that I'm not going to be gearing up and getting out there. I *like* to be gearing up and getting out there."

Barry (advertising executive) dichotomized performance: "Really good performance is euphoric and really bad performance is depressing. A lot of times, the half hour before performance is very stressful. Once you are into it, it is either euphoric or depressing."

The absence of stress can, ironically, be a source of stress. Using Csikszentmihalyi's (1990) model, if challenge exceeds skill, an uncomfortable level of stress is felt. If skill outpaces challenge, one experiences the lack of an adrenaline rush, the lack of stimulation, or boredom. Illustrating this point, Diane (musician) commented on the stress of having played a particular piece of music many times previously, being bored or turned off, yet in performance still needing to have the music sound new and exciting.

Demands of Performance

By its nature, performance is inherently demanding. Any type of performance involves technical and, often, physical demands. As noted earlier, some types of performance involve memorization of specific performance material. Time stresses can add to a sense of pressure. Because performing involves being "on," the sense of exposure or vulnerability can be experienced as a stressor. And the weight of history provides a further "demand" in many areas of performance, that of expectations or standards.

PHYSICAL AND TECHNICAL DEMANDS OF PERFORMANCE

A number of performers highlighted the physical and technical demands of their work. Eric, the neurosurgeon, described the level of endurance imposed by an eight- to ten-hour surgery; the emergency room physician, Frederick, spoke of the demands of continuous changes of pace as well as rotating shifts.

Dance stresses the body both presently and cumulatively. As Jerry aged as a dancer, he increasingly needed to limit his physical practice in order to maintain his performance abilities.

Ilene, a pianist now studying voice for pleasure, was in awe of the demands experienced by singers.

> As a pianist supporting singers, I'm just daunted by the fact that for singers, your body is your instrument. And it's very physical; it can get derailed by all the physical things that happen to you that you don't plan. And that seems to me to be *so* stressful.

MEMORIZATION

Performers in some domains must deal with a distinctive demand: memorization. The performing arts are in part defined by presentation of specific memorized content. We have described the role of memorization for performing artists in chapter 5. We mention it here, again, because it is not only an element of performance but a stressor as well.

TIME STRESSES

Time stress is specific to and inherent in some aspects of performance. Music and dance are structured in relation to time. In business, life often moves at Internet speed. In high-risk occupations, time and timing are often matters of life and death.

"Broadcasting," Ian commented, "is a business of deadlines. It is a time-consuming business. There are no holidays or weekends. How can you manage time in your personal life? How can you make sure your career does not eat up your entire personal life?" Attention to time may be a central element framing one's entire life: To be functional during her early morning radio show, Grace spoke of the rigid daily time pressures she experiences, including the need to get to bed early.

Although time is for the most part irrelevant in neurosurgery, it is critical at two specific moments: (a) if one is on call and another surgery is waiting for the first to be completed, and (b) with some surgeries, if things go wrong. Eric elaborated:

> Time is almost of no consequence in the operating room. There is no stress to time. It just does not exist. You start and you finish and that is it. There is nonlinear time in between. But if you are on call and you are the only guy covering the whole service and you are in the operating room and you're finishing up one head problem and there is another downstairs that you are not quite sure of—there is stuff brewing that you need to

Every musician has his or her own paranoia. It can be fear of carpal tunnel syndrome for a string player or a brain aneurysm for an oboe player. Singers have the reputation of being much more paranoid than other musicians, but there are reasons for these stereotypes about divas and prima donnas. All singers worry about their voice at some level. We get obsessed with it.

It's not so natural to develop the voice to be a beautiful instrument. There's something very fragile about it. To actually practice, and get it warmed up, and to be the instrument that is beautiful, is not so natural.

There's always worry that you're going to get sick, or that you'll inhale something. This time of year, pollen is a real issue, so I don't go running outside. We don't like to deal with any kind of [postnasal] drips, because it really affects the voice very, very quickly.

I'm aware of my voice the very first second that I wake up. The first thing I think is: "Well, how does it feel today?" "Is it going to be a hard warm-up or an easy warm-up?" or "Darn, I wish I didn't have to sing at 10 a.m. Yuck!" because it's always much harder to get it cranked up in the morning.

—Faith (singer)

get in to look at—that is the only time I have ever worried about time in the operating room.

The critical elements of time and speed in certain neurosurgeries add to the combination of stress and accomplishment. Eric described surgery on an aneurysm on the basal artery. It is a complex procedure and, additionally, is conducted while looking through a microscope.

As a neurosurgeon, probably one of the peak procedures that people can do from a technically challenging standpoint is aneurysm surgery on the basal artery. It is challenging because it is very deep seated and it is surrounded by literally "no man's land." There is a lot of room for really devastating consequences to occur just from little errors or little problems with technique. When done successfully and smoothly, that procedure probably is still the one that leaves you with the strongest sense of accomplishment. It's also the one that has the greatest angst associated with trying to get through it. It's one of the procedures with the greatest risk of catastrophe. There is no in-between where one can have "a little bit of a complication" or problem, yet recover from the operation. Typically, if there is a problem, it's life-threatening or nearly life-threatening.

It's probably the consequences and the rarity combined that make it pretty challenging. You are working around a time bomb. Most of the time the issue is they (the arteries) have ruptured and you have to repair them or else the risk stays and it's pretty significant. Some people talk about it as being like walking through a snake pit. You have to get in to the aneurysm and you have to identify and surround it before it bleeds or before anything happens to it. Not only is it the mental element of the slow methodical dissection, but at any minute it can just go BOOM and the whole operating field is visually gone. And then it turns into a fire drill to try to regain control and get back into position to do something.

EXPOSURE–VULNERABILITY

The sense of exposure and vulnerability is most intense among people who literally put themselves in physical danger. George, the medic–sniper, has an acute awareness of the physical risks to himself as well as, at times, the sense of being alone against the world. He began his study of mental skills training following an incident in which, as a Special Forces medic, he was attempting to treat the victim of a sniper. When an untrained coworker shone a bright light on him, George became an obvious target. Not knowing whether the sniper was still present, he found his hands shaking, his movements hesitant. He assessed his overall performance as far below that in situations where his life was clearly not in danger.

Exposure and vulnerability can also be experienced metaphorically. Although there is certainly huge physical danger associated with being a sniper, George focused instead on his sense of vulnerability about his role responsibility: He struggled with the potential challenge of deciding the fate of another human being.

The sense of exposure is particularly profound when one is being judged. The audition process, for example, is not a matter of actual life and death. It could in some ways be compared to a job interview. Yet this particular "job interview," with its repeated, often unexplained, rejections is one that is experienced at frequent intervals throughout many performing artists' careers. Kogan (2002) explained the stress of a life of auditioning:

> An analogous situation for most of us would be one in which we send a succession of manuscripts to referred [sic] journals, all turned down without a word of justification. How many of us would remain in a field with that kind of reward and punishment system? (p. 10)

Dunkel (1989) further elaborated on the stress of auditioning, highlighting differences between live concert performances and auditions. In a live concert, "the performer, in a sense, has invited the listener to enjoy the music . . . the audience is, so to speak, on the side of the performer.

. . . In an audition, however, the atmosphere can be one of hostile competition" (p. xxi). In a survey of musicians, Dunkel found that approximately 70% were more likely to experience nervousness and anxiety during auditioning as compared with performing.

Our performing artists spoke of the sense of vulnerability, or exposure, and a sense of personal nakedness around auditioning and performing. Keith (actor), who was especially forthcoming about his audition discomfort, said:

> I don't think it's just me. You always get directors joking, "I
> wish there was a better way to do it. I know it's awful but . . . ."
> It's important to understand auditioning in that context, when
> all of those very tangible judgmental things are so present and
> so immediate. If nothing else than the physical space, you just
> really feel like you're in a fishbowl. In contrast, there's
> something so liberating about being on a stage in performance.
> You could be in front of 15,000 people, but when there's a
> "fourth wall" (audience), it's sort of a sea. It's entirely different
> than having two people six feet away from you watching you
> work. Give me the 15,000 any day of the week.

Charlotte (dancer) reflected on the sense of vulnerability of an artist who loves the art—and recognizes that performing in front of others is a condition for creating her art:

> I wasn't a natural performer. I wasn't somebody who went into
> dance because they just love to get up in front of people and do
> stuff. I loved to dance, but I would have done it by myself, or
> for my mom and dad; not for the whole world, in front of
> thousands of people, and not doing steps that I wasn't sure I
> could accomplish in front of thousands of people. I was just
> very highly strung. If I had a show, I didn't sleep for weeks
> before it. I'd obsess about it, go over every detail in my mind,
> and worry about everything. Even if I could do it perfectly
> twice in a row in rehearsal, I would never just assume that I
> could pull it off in front of thousands of people. Somehow
> when you do the simplest thing by yourself, it becomes much
> more treacherous when you have all those eyes on you and it's
> very quiet.

At the same time, it may in part be the sense of vulnerability that becomes an element of the art and its expression. Charlotte also commented on the interaction between beauty and vulnerability in dance:

> Students and young dancers bring all of themselves and how
> they feel about the music to their work. They're creating

characters from their own feelings, and they really are very vulnerable. And you want them to be that way because that's what makes them so beautiful to watch.

EXPECTATIONS AND STANDARDS

The pressure of having to deal with others' expectations and anticipations, or the ways in which tradition holds sway, also can be stressful. These can include audience and media expectations, the expectations arising from one's reputation, and the standards and traditions of one's field of endeavor.

Norman described the contrast between what an audience expects, because it has become accustomed to perfect recordings, and what a classical musician can actually produce in a concert:

> With the standard repertoire, you're always living up to a particular recording. Everybody has an ear for what that piece should sound like. It was such a release to know that this was a premier of a piece which nobody had a preconceived idea about (at a concert in which she played a new composition). And it wasn't that joke that everybody says, "Oh you can play wrong notes and nobody knows," because the composer's there, you can't play wrong notes, it doesn't sound good. It's more that you don't have to live up to the great traditions of the past about a particular sound.
>
> —Ilene (musician)

Some classical musicians lose a lot of confidence in the realization that the audience has an exact feeling about what the music should sound like. That's a confidence sucker. You go out to play the Brahms Violin Concerto and you better believe that a lot of people in the audience know that piece, and they have their favorite recording. And you know that you're definitely not going to sound as good in their ears, because nothing could sound as good as having the earphones on, listening to their favorite performer play it.

Another musician, Michael, told a story from his first professional "gig." It is easy to imagine performers in any field having similar experiences, especially at the start of their careers:

> As a young conductor, I had a post with an orchestra composed of college-aged musicians. It always had a young conductor; that was what made it unique. I was assigned an advisor, someone who came from "on high." He was a pretty sour person. He would come to my rehearsals and he would sit in a

corner shaking his head and muttering "Oh, my god." Then I'd go to his house for lessons, and he would tell me that the conductor had to be perfect and couldn't make any mistakes. This went on for a couple of months. I hadn't really thought things through for myself at the time. And because he was an important authority, there was a tendency to simply swallow what he was saying without thinking about it. This was a big mistake. After about two months, I found that I couldn't conduct. The ability—where did the ability go?—it just went away.

One day I went to a rehearsal and I couldn't conduct, I simply could not conduct. I thought "I have no idea what I am doing. I am incompetent. What am I doing on the podium?" I said, "I'm going off for a little while," and I left. That night I sat in my apartment with my wife. I couldn't have been in a blacker mood, I couldn't have been more depressed. I had no idea, not a clue. All I knew was that I had no talent.

And then all of a sudden it was like somebody turned on a light. The room flooded with light, figuratively speaking. And I went, "It's *him*!" Boom! And that was the end of that. I threw off his influence immediately. I had had no idea where it was coming from. I had assumed it as my own viewpoint for myself, but it really wasn't. It was his, not mine. That was all it took. By the next rehearsal, not only had I recovered all of my ability, but actually I was better. I think that I was able during that same time period to shed other situations from the past as well, other experiences of undue influence.

The experience of stress, however, does not end with achievement and acclaim. In fact, like the novelist whose first book was a best-seller, the pressure of living up to one's reputation can become an additional source of stress. In one particular role, Charlotte (dancer) commented, "I already had quite a reputation for doing [this role] well, and that caused more pressure because you're not sure you can pull it off again as well as you did it last time." She described the unnerving spotlight of the media:

> In my early years, I had the sort of success that was just astounding, and especially astounding to me. For the longest time, I ignored it that people were writing about me and talking about me and excited about me. I pretended it was about somebody else. And then eventually I started not to be able to pretend it was about somebody else and couldn't cope with the fact that people were expecting great things from me all the time.

The two broadcasters commented on the stress of various expectations within the industry. Ian observed that people expect broadcasters to make live special appearances without pay. Despite her "celebrity" status, Grace noted the stress of an ever-present double standard: intelligent, verbally articulate women in broadcasting are perceived as aggressive. It is still not socially acceptable for a woman to demonstrate such competence.

As mentioned previously, cultural anthropologist Pearl Katz (1999) studied the culture of surgeons, describing the intersection of military and medicine, surgery in particular. Beyond the historical links and linguistic metaphors, surgeons have been held to the tradition of "surgeon as hero," men who are able to counter patients' fears of "invasion" with their power and confidence.

Our physicians found three aspects of the standards and expectations within the medical domain particularly challenging: the mismatch between personality and role expectations (Frederick), the level of technical demand, and the military-style tradition of silently toughing it out (Eric). Self-described as an "internal" person, Frederick was uncomfortable with the expectation of extensive interaction with others:

> I don't think the "weight of responsibility" is a significant
> factor. You are trained to do something. It's a job. But I am not
> an extrovert, so for me, it is work to have social interaction.
> That tires me out.

Eric commented on the military tradition involved in training and, thus, medical practice. Doctors are expected to be "tough enough" to do their work without attention to the emotions or stress experienced

The Perceived Importance of the Situation

In addition to the demands of performance, the perceived importance of a situation has been identified as a major source of stress for athletes (Weinberg & Gould, 1995). The performers in our project reflected this process in their discussions of competition for limited resources, the pragmatic limitations of certain areas of performance, and their strong sense of personal responsibility.

COMPETITIVENESS

Performers in all domains strive to achieve optimal performance. The Latin root of the word "compete," *competere*, means "to strive with." At times, this determination is directed toward oneself. At other times, it is experienced as pitting oneself against another.

Competitiveness in the business world is often described as a zero-sum game, one in which someone wins and someone loses. Charles, an insurance agent, spoke with frustration about the increased level of interorganizational competition. Within the field of law, the one-up, one-down perspective often is not experienced as fulfilling. Arthur (lawyer) said:

> If it's just kind of a zero-sum game, you're not going to be satisfied and the other party is not going to be satisfied either. The hard part is to try to find a place where it is not just zero sums.

Anna, also a lawyer, described this win–lose perspective as Darwinian, the epitome of a life and death struggle. Becoming inured to the struggle seems connected to the lack of pleasure in their profession that many lawyers experience over time: "Lawyers win and lose a lot, and it goes so bad when you lose. You do become somewhat immune to it."

Although competitiveness is clearly endemic to the world of business and the masculinized high-risk professions, it is experienced equally within the performing arts. At times, competitiveness is intrinsic, involving systems that are designed to pit people against one another. As we noted in chapter 5, Diane (musician) described a system that starts early and becomes relentless. From an early age, music students compete for specific orchestral positions, annual performance competitions, and auditions. This same type of competition, also beginning early, is experienced within the world of dance.

The adult world of broadcasting involves a continual awareness of positional instability. Ian described a dualistic but constant anticipation of getting fired: "There are two kinds of people in broadcasting: the people who have been fired and the people who are waiting to be fired." Grace spoke of the competitive atmosphere of industry functions. Brought in to give a keynote address to industry colleagues, she described the audience as "people who want to dislike you. They want to be cynical. They want to be a hard laugh and a tough nut to crack."

In some situations, the competitiveness derives from either a scarcity or an abundance of resources. This is in part a function of supply and demand. In ballet, as we noted, an over-supply of female dancers means that they need to be more competent than their male counterparts to obtain a role. Consultant Dr. Owen Osborne routinely worked with performers seeking a career in the world of the theatre. For those who are talented and fortunate enough to land paying roles, other competitive challenges are also present: meager pay or performances that run for a finite length of time.

Both broadcasters described these stresses within their field as well. For Ian, it involved a low level of pay; for Grace, it was the limited time frame available for one's career. Grace said:

> I can't do this forever. I have a longer career than an athlete, because I don't need my knees, and eventually I can do something else in this industry. But even though my show is very lucrative and popular, the clock is running on it.

SENSE OF PERSONAL RESPONSIBILITY

Although personal responsibility is one of the cornerstones of functional teams and team building, this issue is not a typical focus in descriptions of stress in performance. We were intrigued to notice that performers in each of the domains mentioned a sense of personal responsibility as a stressor. This sense of responsibility was described in relation both to oneself and to others. It was reflected not only by those who were actively involved in group efforts in which the success of the group depends on each individual, but also by successful performers who manifest the biblical injunction, "To whom much is given, much is expected."

Whereas lawyers are stereotypically portrayed as being amoral, in reality a sense of personal responsibility not only is expected but also is often demanded by clients. Anna explained:

> There's an aspect of the relationship between a lawyer and the client where you are the parent. You are the person they expect to be their advocate. And a lot goes with that. They really want you to know everything. They want you to be super-capable. Whether in litigation or in corporate deals, they want you to beat the other side. They want you to prevail on their behalf.

Great athletes often personalize responses to a competitive challenge (Clarkson, 1999). The sense of personal responsibility was also reported as stressful by some of the performers we interviewed. Keith (actor) experienced this as an internal pressure, his responsibility to himself: "The pressures are so internal; they're not brought on so much from the performance aspect. They're from me facing me, not me facing 2,000 people."

Helena (dancer) commented on the sense of responsibility in relation to personal injury:

> Dealing with injuries is very difficult, very demanding, very draining, very stressful. You feel frustrated and disappointed with yourself. You also feel that you're letting down your colleagues and your public. You failed, you're not good

enough. You feel like you might as well go jump off a bridge. You just come down with so many harsh judgments on yourself.

This sense of personal responsibility, as Helena noted, also carries with it an implicit sense of responsibility to others, whether fellow performers or audience. Jerry, also a dancer, elaborated on this point in relation to injury and injury management:

> You can always find at least one person who says, "You know, you brought this on yourself; this isn't a disease." Sometimes that's true; sometimes it is a technical fault. But five people can have the same technical fault and two of them will get injured, so it's not entirely your fault. For dancers, that's a major source of stress and a major source of guilt.

In both of his roles—one as a Special Forces medic and the other as a police sniper—George experienced a strong sense of responsibility to others. He was more concerned about letting teammates down than even losing his own life. As a police sniper, the sense of personal responsibility was multilayered. He must be a lone decision-maker; he risked not saving an innocent person; and here, too, he was concerned about letting his teammates down. Although he had not yet been required to "take the shot" (actually fire on a human target), he anticipated complex reactions: In such an activity, he expected a shifting perspective that would weigh heavily on him. The perpetrator would shift from being an object to being seen as a person who must then be transformed and depersonalized to the category of "target." George talked about being in a potential sniping situation: He might be the only person to see a particular event and thus would be placed in the simultaneous roles of "judge, jury, and executioner."

> I may be shooting to kill somebody, but I'm doing it to save an innocent person and that's what keeps me motivated. At the same time, I may be watching that person (the target) through my telescopic sight for hours on end. That person becomes not just a target; he can become a real, live, breathing person. You see him doing things that you can relate to.

The Uncertainty of the Situation

Uncertainty—whether involving the unknown, aspects of the performance that are out of one's control, or dependence on others' performance—is a major situational source of stress for athletes (Weinberg & Gould, 1995). It is no different for the performers that we interviewed, although each experiences it slightly differently in relation to their own field of performance.

For a surgeon, uncertainty is a salient stressor. Eric spoke of two types of stress in surgery: one related to more difficult surgeries and the other related to uncontrollable factors that can occur even with routine operations. He commented that for complex surgeries, the combination of life-threatening consequences and rarely performed procedures made such operations "pretty challenging."

> [Ironically,] the operating room is many times the most controllable part of our day. We know what to expect there. The potential for problems does not surface until several days later or down the road. Probably the harder stress to deal with is the patient management stress, where you are not sure and you don't have the same control. Most of the time those are deals when you have to sit and wait and watch to see what is going to happen.

Self-efficacy, the confidence that one can successfully perform a task, is situation-specific with athletes (Weinberg & Gould, 1995). The same appears to hold true for nonathletic performers. For example, Harold felt entirely comfortable in his role as a conductor but said that he experienced "debilitating stage fright" when he had to perform on piano. Although an accomplished pianist, he focused on and became concerned about physical technique. Paradoxically, conducting, which he described as being "all about analysis" and quintessentially mental, did not frighten him.

Ian described acting, especially the first night, as involving the uncertainty of whether one can get through the whole show. As we noted in chapter 5, the question of sufficient memorization adds its own frisson or edge:

> I am always a little tense before it starts, even on the opening night. I always ask myself, "What the hell are you doing this for?" It's the first time you've done it in front of an audience and you don't know if you can do a whole show, recall all those words.

Because David (banker) worked in an environment with long-term rather than immediate outcomes, his stress came from "making decisions and not knowing if you're right or wrong, whether you were doing the right thing, whether it's going to work. The long-term nature [of the decision] kind of eats at you."

For some people, the interaction with others is stressful, in part because of the dynamics of the group. Differentiating between anxiety and stress, Barry (advertising executive) commented almost dismissively that "there is a terror that goes with speaking at conferences, but that's mostly stage fright." He found the fear of the unknown to be stressful. That unknown increases when working as a team: "The more people you add, the less known it is how well they will perform."

In a management position, along with the stress of uncertainty, David (banker) found that dealing with people and their issues—whether compensation or the processes of hiring and firing—was stressful. "Dealing with people and what they think the issues are, dealing with compensation issues with people, and dealing with hiring people and letting people go—all that can get pretty sensitive."

Although all performers strive for perfection in one way or another, they are confronted with the inevitability of *im*perfection. Attention to imperfection can be another stressor, yet another manifestation of uncertainty.

Imperfection is a constant aspect of uncertainty with which surgeons must deal. Eric recognized that for certain medical conditions, there will be a poor outcome regardless of what one does. The surgeon must come to terms with this frustrating reality.

A number of the musicians spoke to this issue—the inevitability of imperfection. Michael, a conductor, wisely noted that the individual who focuses on perfection as the goal burdens himself or herself with stress. Diane (musician) described the ways in which expectations of perfection can interfere directly with performing well:

> Just before you go out on stage, you can't be thinking "Now I better make sure I get my third finger just a little bit higher on that string or I'll never make that shift." You can't move as quickly or as easily when you're tense. That means all your fifths (intervals between notes) are going to be under (pitched flat), or if you realize that and try to overcompensate, then they're going to be over (pitched too sharp).

Norman reflected on this inevitable dilemma:

> The truly great classical composers—Bach, Mozart, Beethoven, Monteverdi, some of the really antique composers like Josquin DesPres, and the modern masters Arnold Shoenberg and Stravinsky—wrote the most perfect music on the planet. The idea of one of these composers staring over your shoulder, saying "You're never going to play it as well as I wrote it," is daunting. You can't play it as well as they wrote it because, like the Heisenberg principle, by playing it, you spoil it or you

change too much of it. But if you change it, you have to be comfortable that you've made it enough your own that you at least feel okay about whatever changes you made.

Consequences of Stress

Stress has consequences on oneself and on relations with others. Although the mind and body are inextricably linked (and perhaps this is nowhere more apparent than in stress reactions), for clarity of presentation, we have separated out the consequences in a general way, dividing them into physical, mental, and interpersonal.

> I hate doing taped interviews, because they have to be right and they have to be perfect. You have no excuse. I will sometimes start over twice to three times. I like live better, because you can't start over.
>
> —Ian (broadcaster)

David (banker) gave a classic description of his physiological experience of stress: "If I'm making a presentation, especially by myself, the stress level goes up. I may not sleep as well the night before, and the next morning I wake up earlier, begin fidgeting." Also typical was his initial reluctance to consider stress as the source of his physical difficulties. People often require a great deal of convincing before they accept the interaction of stress and physiological response. David learned about his stress reactions:

> Ten or 15 years ago, I was getting terrible headaches every day and feeling kind of dizzy. I thought I was dying. I went to see a doctor and I said, "Something's wrong." He was very smooth in the way he did it, but basically he said, "Well, we can do lots of tests and we can do brain scans and we can do all this kind of stuff; but let me ask you: How are things going at work?" And I said, "Well they're going fine." I really thought they were. And he said, "Well, it just might be stress."

Arthur (lawyer) recognized some of the common physical effects of stress, the ebbs and flows of adrenaline: "Physically you are either energized by stress and go high or you're sort of wiped out by it and you have to try to get yourself back up to keep going." Physical stress is not isolated. Its impact on one's thought processes and affect can be profound. Larry (actor) ascribed a recent panic attack to the buildup of physical fatigue.

The mental consequences of stress are experienced through one's thoughts and feelings. Charlotte (dancer) commented: "I'm dramatizing a bit, but every performance to me was life and death. For me it was the most important thing that could possibly be happening." Sleep was interrupted as she mentally reviewed all aspects of her performance. We have described (chap. 3, this volume) the ways in which for Barry, in advertising, cumulative stress resulted in problems with concentration and memory. Arthur (lawyer) also described the impact of stress on his ability to focus: "Some of what I have to do is very technical. It's very hard to be really stressed and technical at the same time."

For the physicians, various stressors were mentioned. Frederick (emergency room physician) noted the ways in which constant change is itself tiring, especially having to relate differently to different patients.

Stress serves to narrow one's attention and heighten one's sensations. Intriguingly, this vividness can be a challenge in surgeries that involve magnification of one's visual field. Eric described the mental and physical stress on all of one's senses as a function of changes to a single sense organ:

> Microsurgery produces a very strange sensation. Along with vision, I guess all of your senses are magnified. You are working through this operative microscope that is incredibly bright and well lit—that's what allows us to do these procedures—but you are working at ten times normal power. You don't realize it but the acuteness of your hearing is turned way up at the same time. That's why, even though music is pretty common in the operating room, almost no microsurgeon in stressful cases can have any kind of music on. Just about everybody will have music playing for most things, but when you get to a difficult procedure, any noise is too much noise.

Microsurgeries can last as long as eight to ten hours, and physical and mental stress results from the sheer duration of the procedure:

> We rely a lot on teamwork when we are doing cases that are very complicated or very long. You want that extra set of eyes there with you, from both the complexity standpoint and also to spell you. I think a surgeon under the microscope has probably reached the peak of effectiveness at about four hours. Some types of cases, though, routinely will be eight or ten hours long. The guy whose case it is will typically start and run for about four hours. Once you have done that, somebody spells you for an hour or two. But then it's not like you're good for four more hours. From then on, typically you trade off every hour or hour and a half, because you can't focus. It's not

the visual but the mental focus. You begin to wander a little bit too much. And of course the cases that take that long are not cases where you can [afford to] lose focus. You are usually doing something that is fairly slow and tedious. That equates with something that is usually intimately associated with structures that you cannot mess with.

Stress can have marked consequences for one's primary as well as social relationships. Eric, a surgeon, commented that the stress of dealing with unpredictable outcomes can take a toll on one's family and other relationships. This awareness of the difficulties of integrating the personal and professional among performers has been more typically expressed by women professionals. In a detailed qualitative study of eight successful middle-aged lawyers, one of the primary themes of the women, but not the men, was this issue of balance (O'Donovan-Polten, 2001).

> Since I have been doing this job, I have not made very many friends. I have a million acquaintances, but have not made very many friends, because you don't know the difference between, "Are we having a conversation or are you gathering an anecdote? Which one is it? It's fine for you to gather an anecdote, but we can't have a friendship simultaneously." I've decided that it's best to dance with the one that "brung" you. I have the friends that I had before I began working as a public figure.
>
> —Grace (broadcaster)

Both broadcasters also commented on the challenges that their professions pose for their personal lives. Grace spoke about the impact for her in terms of both friendships and her primary relationship. Grace also described the impact of her success and visibility on the ways in which her husband is perceived: "You are literally invisible as a man. It's hard for a guy. He is just completely marginalized." She said that this spousal invisibility adds "another layer of responsibility for me that I do not see [my co-anchor] or other men having to deal with."

Yet this stress may not be entirely gender related. Ian commented:

If you are successful, you are in the spotlight, whether you want it or not. At first it can be pretty charming for your spouse. Then it can become damn annoying, not just because it is an intrusion, but because they never get noticed.

More generally, Grace commented on the challenge to the work–life balance:

The hardest thing is the work–life balance. This is a very selfish career. It is really hard in this business: You get up so early and go to bed so early. And then, you are the center of attention. You get used to being the center of attention and it gets real crowded for other people to come into your precious world where your head is the size of the earth.

The more of yourself you pour into the job, the more you feel like you need the adulation and feedback of strangers. But the more full and rich my own life is, the less those people can puff me up and the less those slams hurt my feelings. If I'm being a bitch around the house, if my husband and stepson do not love me, then it does not matter that some yahoo in Kentucky loves me. Conversely, if these people adore me and I love them *and* I have a good relationship with all the people that matter and some jerk thinks I should kill myself, the less it matters to me.

Recommendations to Consultants

- Performers experience stress similar to athletes: Stress occurs when perceived demands exceed perceived resources and the outcome is deemed important. The situational factors of uncertainty and perceived importance of an event tend to increase the experience of stress.
- Stress can be a positive experience, described by some as exhilarating, exciting, motivating, and as a catalyst for attaining optimal intensity for performance.
- Although there are common elements of stress in each domain and across domains, stress is an extremely personal, idiosyncratic experience. It is crucial for a consultant to determine what the client perceives as stressful. If the stresses commonly identified by others are not mentioned, the client may have coping skills in these areas that can be helpful in addressing those areas where stress is experienced.
- For some people who are acclimated to functioning habitually under high stress conditions, the absence of stress itself can be experienced as stressful or at least somewhat disorienting.
- Performers experience varying degrees of both physical stress and mental stress. Those most likely to experience physical stress include performers in the high-risk domain and performing artists. Performers in the high-risk domain may undergo high physical demand in relation to their work or may experience direct threat of harm. As with athletes, performing artists' bodies may be central to the performance itself.

- Where performance and practice make exceptional demands on the body (e.g., ballet), stress is typically cumulative over time. This can have significant implications for the duration of a performer's career. Consultants in these domains are advised to have knowledge of physiological functioning, recovery from injury, and career transition.

- Cumulative stress may result in a variety of difficulties: somatic reactions and physical or mental exhaustion. Consultants should be aware that performers in all domains are at risk for negative effects from prolonged stress.

- The requirement of memorization is a common stress factor for performers who are expected to follow a predetermined pattern, as in theatre and dance.

- In several domains, time can be a source of significant stress. This is particularly true in any domain that involves deadlines; when changes occur at lightning speed (e.g., in many aspects of business); and in high-risk performances where both speed and accuracy are critical.

- Some performers' sense of exposure or vulnerability may manifest itself in physical or emotional ways.

- The expectations and anticipations of others can be a source of stress for performers in all domains. This can be especially true when, because of tradition or individual personality, there are rigid expectations of what constitutes an excellent performance.

- Competition frequently increases the sense of stress by making the outcome more important.

- Performers frequently place additional stress on themselves by virtue of their own sense of personal responsibility.

- An omnipresent source of stress for many performers is the inevitability of imperfection.

- Stress can take its toll on performers physically through fatigue, injury, or somatic illnesses, such as headaches, backaches, ulcers, and sleep disturbance. In assessing physical symptoms, consultants should be mindful of stress as a potential cause.

- Establishing a work–life balance may be exceedingly challenging for successful performers. Consultants are advised to be mindful of interpersonal relationships as both a tremendous source of support and a possible source of stress.

Reframe and Relax: Coping With Stress 10

My great mantra is: "No matter how good or bad it is, 60 seconds is still a minute, and there are only 60 of them in an hour. This may be really fun right now, but it's passing. This may be really bad right now, but it will pass." When something is really heinous and I absolutely can't get it together, I just take a deep breath and I look at the clock. "This will not last, because nothing does." It is kind of a morbid way of looking at it. My other mantra is: "There's a rock in the river. The water can't flow through it, it can't jump over it, and it can't go under it. The water comes to the rock and separates and goes around it. I am the rock and it (all the stress" is the river—all of it.)

—Grace (broadcaster)

n the previous chapter, we described some of the stresses associated with being a performer and performing. Here, we discuss methods that performers use to cope with those stresses. We begin with a brief description of some of the schemas researchers have developed to characterize methods of stress coping; we then cluster our interviewees' responses. As other researchers have observed, we note that it is easier to name types of stress than to find an entirely functional taxonomy to describe stress coping.

Theoretical Perspectives on Coping With Stress

Coping has been defined as "constantly changing cognitive and behavioral efforts to manage specific external and/or internal demands that are appraised as taxing or exceeding the resources of the person" (Lazarus & Folkman, 1984, p. 141). Coping begins by assessing a situation. An individual first makes a judgment on whether the demands of the situation are stressful, a process that researchers Lazarus and Folkman called primary appraisal. They referred to the next step as secondary appraisal, the assessment of one's ability to handle the situation by evaluating available resources and possible outcomes. The combined primary and secondary appraisals determine the intensity of stress that one experiences; this in turn influences the choice of coping responses. Whereas the range of possible coping responses may be limitless, strategies can be generally classified as either problem-focused or emotion-focused (Hardy et al., 1996; Lazarus & Folkman, 1984). Problem-focused strategies attempt to change, alter, or modify the actual conditions that cause the stress. This may involve gathering more information, goal-setting, problem-solving, and time-management techniques, all of which are designed to change the basic conditions that give rise to stress. Emotion-focused strategies target changing one's emotional response to the stressful event. This may involve learning relaxation techniques to cope with a situation that must be endured or cognitive techniques to change the meaning or perceptions of the event.

Based on the initial work by Lazarus and Folkman, a more elaborated theoretical framework (Cox & Ferguson, 1991; Endler & Parker, 1990) categorized coping into four elements: problem-focused, emotion-focused, appraisal-focused, or avoidance-focused. This schema has been used in a number of studies of athletes, and various coping inventories, using this schema, have been developed for use with athletes.

Even though researchers may debate the merits of differing and complex classification schemas, performers are well aware that successful coping forms a central element in optimal performance. In a recent qualitative study of methods of coping used by athletes and performing artists, Poczwardowski and Conroy (2002) found that 15 of their 16 interviewees "viewed coping as a major part of their performance: Effective coping with emotions was an essential and inherent part of the performing craft" (p. 324). Although "universal patterns of coping might not exist, and . . . most commonly used taxonomies of coping behavior . . . may oversimplify the issue" (p. 325), Poczwardowski and Conroy concluded that "excellence in coping precedes excellence in performance" (p. 313).

The various models of stress coping remind us of Haley's (1987) guidance that whereas researchers need detailed and elaborate theories, practitioners need simple models from which to make decisions. We have found McGrath's (1970) model a useful overall guide to application. This model is influenced by Lazarus's concepts of primary and secondary appraisals. In McGrath's framework, stress occurs when the experience in which the *perceived demands* of a situation are greater than the *perceived resources*, and the *outcome* of the situation is considered important. From this model, managing stress is accomplished by intervening in one of these three areas: decreasing demands, increasing resources, or reducing the importance of the outcome.

To illustrate the application of this model: Although one might not be able to reduce the technical demands of a particular type of performance, it might be possible to reduce the frequency of performance. Likewise, one may reduce the self-imposed or *perceived* demands of a performance by changing one's standard from the attempt at perfection to sustained excellence over time. One can reduce stress by increasing perceived resources, such as having adequate rest and energy and ensuring that physical abilities are functioning at optimum level. Stress can likewise be handled by changing one's perspective on the importance of the outcome of a performance. If a person holds the belief that his or her entire self-worth hinges on a single performance, the stress can be insurmountable. The feeling of stress can be altered by shifting perspective on the importance of the outcome. For example, this reframing might involve recognizing that whereas it would be truly wonderful if one's audition performance had been flawless and the role had been won, there will be other opportunities and one's family and friends will remain, regardless of the outcome.

The vast majority of information shared by our interviewees described positive methods of coping; we detail these in the remainder of the chapter. However, performers, like the rest of us, sometimes use less than optimally healthy methods for coping with stress, and we would be remiss not to at least acknowledge that fact. We didn't ask directly, nor did we ask performers to differentiate between constructive and nonconstructive or less-than-healthful methods. We heard very little about these methods, and, thus, we can't generalize about frequency, type, or rationale, let alone make comparisons between individuals or across domains.

It is commonly understood that certain less optimal methods are endemic to specific performance cultures. Dr. Norris described the ways in which overuse of alcohol and other substances is ubiquitous within the music industry. Ballet dancers frequently turn to cigarette smoking for both weight control and stress management. Jerry (dancer) spoke about smoking as a way of stress coping:

> I smoked, even though I knew how bad it was for me. I would go through long periods of not choosing that response to stress, but occasionally, when I most needed to have every ounce of oomph, I would smoke anyway.
>
> When I say smoke I don't mean packs a day, I mean two or three cigarettes. But whether it's a mental or physical effect, I knew that smoking meant that I was going to have to work harder. The minute I put that thing in my mouth, I knew, "Okay, today you're going to feel physically less capable. Nothing extraordinary is going to happen to you today. You're not going to pull out that unexpected pirouette. You're going to have to work for every step." If I gave in and smoked, then I knew I wasn't handling my stress, and that took away some of the spontaneous pleasure in the performance. I don't like the

idea that ballet is so stressful that you have to resort to demonstrably unhealthy solutions. It's better than a nervous breakdown, but not a good solution.

We clustered performers' responses in terms of efforts to decrease the demands, increase the resources, or diminish the importance of the outcome.

Decrease the Demands

In most performance settings, certain explicit requirements may not be alterable. A performer's self-imposed or perceived demands can often be changed by adjusting his or her goals, reframing the task, or reinterpreting the experience of stress.

REDEFINE THE GOAL

If one reframes the goal or the focus of a performing experience, perceived demands may be reduced and stress thereby diminished. This can be accomplished in a number of different ways, such as shifting the demand from an outcome goal to a process goal. For example, the goal for a demanding situation may become the refinement of certain skills rather than the achievement of a particular outcome. Attorney Arthur noted that he often redefines the goal of a negotiation by focusing on the process. He said that he becomes "curious about how things work and why they work the way they do." This in turn changes his sense of demand in the situation.

Through a realistic appraisal of their goals, performers may reduce stress by limiting their expectations or demands on themselves. Arthur admitted his own limits:

> You have to bring different talents to the game, and you can't do it all. You might be able to do different aspects of the thing at different times, but you can't do it all at once. Or you can't do it all at once and be particularly effective.

ALTER OR REFRAME THE TASK

Another closely related method for diminishing demands involves redefining or altering one's perception of a task. Keith (actor) spoke of this process as a means of coping with the stress of auditioning. By changing his perception of the situation and its inherent demands, he was able to perform with greater ease and confidence.

> A woman who had stopped dancing, but who I had danced with previously, happened to be in Munich when I was performing there. She was going to start working with the company the next day. And she said, "Oh well, of course I'm coming to the performance," and I just turned white. I was like: "Oh man, it's going to be awful, don't come." And she said, "I'm not coming to see how you dance, I'm coming to see you." It just made me feel so good. I say that now to my students all the time: "I don't care what you do, I care about you; I want to see you."
>
> —Jerry (dancer)

It helps to view the audition as people wanting you to do well because they have a problem that they want to solve. They're not sitting back there saying, "Show me"; they're praying that whoever they desperately want is going to walk through the doors and they can say, "Ah! We found this person; this is fantastic! We have what we need. We have what we want." If you come in there with a real—not a false—sense of bravado, if you come with a real unshakable sense that you absolutely have what it takes to give them what they need, people are willing and eager to latch onto that.

REFRAME THE INTERPRETATION OR EXPERIENCE OF STRESS

Another method of changing the demand is by active relabeling or reinterpretation of the experience of stress. The Chinese symbol for *crisis* combines two characters, one depicting "danger," the other, "opportunity." Ian (broadcaster) viewed something going wrong during a broadcast as an opportunity to rise to the challenge.

This act of re-attribution can be intentional and can in turn strengthen one's self-efficacy, or "sense of self." Michael (conductor) commented that "there are obstacles and problems that come up and you solve them. I think it's the process of attempting to solve them which leads one to feel good."

As one feels a stronger sense of self, challenges that had previously been stressors can be viewed differently. This synergistic experience builds on itself. The former stressor becomes the learning experience that in turn allows other learning opportunities to become interesting and intriguing. In the last chapter, we spoke about musician Ilene's satisfaction with performing contemporary music. In the context of playing "new music," she experienced an epiphany regarding the weight of tradition. She was then able to take this sense of performance capacity and apply it to music she had performed for years:

I am committed to playing new music and working with composers. It's a perfect performance feeling, in terms of my body sensations and my concentration. I feel I can learn from that, and maybe go backwards and transfer those sensations and that knowledge to performance of the traditional repertoire.

Increase the Resources

As mentioned earlier, stress is experienced when the perceived demands of a situation are greater than the perceived resources and the outcome of the situation is considered important. Stress can then be alleviated when the demands are decreased, when the importance is decreased, or when the resources are increased.

> Most of the time, just by being conscious of the problem I can make it go away. It actually doesn't hit me very often, but about three weeks ago, I started to feel bad. I had a little bit of dizziness, a headache. I started thinking, "This feels the same way (as when his physician first suggested that he was experiencing stress)," but nothing's going on.' There was nothing particular going on at work, nothing exceptionally stressful. I couldn't figure it out, but I decided that's what it still had to be. I thought: "I must subconsciously be worried about stuff— and I'm not going to do that." It really did take two or three days to go away.
>
> —David (banker)

Most of the methods for coping with stress that performers described involved some aspect of resources (or perceived resources), whether mental or physical, intrapsychic or interpersonal. The primary categories involved aspects of physical care, attention to pacing, thorough preparation and minimization of uncertainty, the engagement of others, specific mental or psychological skills, and, as with demands, alteration or reframing of resources. *Physical self-care* recognizes that, as in a Maslowian hierarchy (Maslow, 1968), such fundamentals as sleep, exercise, and general attention to one's own well-being can minimize stress or its effects. *Preparation* and the *minimization of uncertainty* allow the performer to exercise control through moving toward and taking action, rather than avoiding the stressful situation. *Pacing* recognizes that the performer must balance his or her energy and focus. Increasing one's resources can be achieved in various ways. Increasing one's support system is a vital aspect of stress management. Important mental skills in stress management include imagery, thought management, and attention management.

PHYSICAL SELF-CARE

At the most basic level, stress coping occurs through physical self-care, taking care of the resources that one has. Often this method serves a preventative function. As we noted in chapter 6, one of the foundational elements that performers recognize is the imperative to take care of their "instrument," that is, themselves.

Across professions, a number of performers mentioned the use of physical activity as a way of managing stress. Some described specific types of exercise, including walking, bike riding, and yoga; others spoke more generically. The importance of adequate rest and sleep was also described by various performers. Radio host Grace called sleep "the single biggest tool I have." She considered it to be the primary factor in determining peak experiences where she is "in the zone."

The vagaries of performance schedules and demands often determine the ways in which these self-care activities are actually conducted. Because of her early morning drive show, Grace napped in the afternoon and went to bed in the early evening. Those who do shift work with rotating schedules have different challenges. Working in emergency medicine, Frederick figured out:

> If you are going to work seven consecutive days or six consecutive days, it is better that you cycle through, sequencing two days, two evenings, two nights and then you are off. Other than that, I don't know anything about how to make those times more manageable. I just dread those rotations. I hate working nights.

Self-care can involve a number of interacting functions. In preparing for a surgery of many hours, for example, Eric needed to attend more to his physical than mental state. "I definitely worry about making sure I get an extra half hour or 45 minutes of sleep the night before. And I will go out of my way to have a significant breakfast with protein to hold me over."

PREPARATION AND MINIMIZING UNCERTAINTY

Research with athletes has indicated that uncertainty is one of the primary situational factors contributing to stress (Weinberg & Gould, 1995). Thorough preparation and accurate knowledge add to one's resources.

Among the high-risk professions, inadequate preparation resulting in poor performance can have the ultimate adverse effect: loss of life. Without thorough preparation, businesspeople can lose the case or the sale. As a lawyer, for example, Anna reflected:

I needed to overcome anxiety about public speaking, presenting an oral argument, let's say before the Court of Appeals. In addition to practice, more general preparation has been important, in other words, sitting there and asking myself: What are the conceivable questions that could come up?

In business, knowledge is often power. Having more information than others is a way in which one can be competitive, decrease uncertainty, and increase self-confidence. Illustrating this point, Barry (advertising executive) reflected:

It's the unknown that is most stressful. I cope with it by doing my homework. For instance, I am going to be speaking at a conference in ___ next Monday. It is a conference on [a particular type of] advertising. Our company doesn't do a lot of it, but I have very strong opinions about it. I am passionate about it. I read everything I can find on it and while I don't do as much of it as many people at the conference, I think I probably have stronger opinions about what it (this type of advertising) can do. And that reduces stress for me. I know that while a lot of people who have done a lot more work will be there, I will be able to match them with passion and knowledge and a vision of where it is going to go two or three years from now.

Each surgery is unique, when performed on any particular individual at any one time. As a surgeon, Eric recognized that certainty about procedure was one way to decrease the stress of working on complex cases:

The more I can make it repetitious—the same pattern—the more comfortable I feel about it. It may be nothing more than to say I did the same thing the same way and I know that there are going to be a certain number of people that do not do well.

Performers rarely act in isolation. Even with thorough preparation, apprehension about the adequacy of others whose functioning is vital to one's own performance can also increase stress. Barry mentioned the added stress of some group presentations where the abilities of others on the team are uncertain. Similarly, a soloist may wonder whether the piano accompanist truly understands the complex rhythms. Dealing with emergency surgeries, Eric sometimes dealt with health systems in which he did not know the other medical personnel:

Many times we will be notified about an emergency situation coming from one of the surrounding communities. It may be just lack of familiarity with the health care system in those areas, but you do not trust what you are being told until you can see it with your own eyes. It is that unknown that is probably the bigger stress. There is a definite stress reliever when you find out that they have arrived at an emergency facility where you know the people and then you get a phone call from one of them saying: "This is what we've got." That familiarity [with the facility and personnel] is a great calming force. You may still have to deal with a difficult situation when the patient arrives, but the stress may be reduced because you do not have that unknown anymore. You know that you have to finish this current surgery and get on to the next as quickly as you can.

PACING

Performance, as our book title indicates, entails being "on." It is impossible to be "on" all the time and taxing to attempt to do so. In business, Arthur described the alternate potential for exhilaration and exhaustion that comes with stress. It can energize, but it can also debilitate. One aspect of stress management, then, involves knowing how to be "off." Another includes understanding what forms of being "off" work best. Fine-tuning is needed, such as figuring out the best balance of performance and respite, as well as the most effective timing of this pacing. This type of stress management often involves some changes in level of physical arousal—whether more, less, or merely different. At times, it means developing an alternate focus, or diversion.

For performers in all categories, finding some way to take "time out" can be a useful means of managing energy. Jerry (dancer), for example, would nap before a performance, less because of tiredness than as a means of getting away. Larry (actor) would literally move from his current space, either by walking or going driving: "It's called retreating; it's a reassessment, it's a recharging, restoring. I come back twice as strong after that."

Similarly, Arthur used movement as a method of energy management. During intensive meetings, he might take a walking break. Alternatively, during a meeting he might move within the room or decrease his own energy expenditure by involving others in conducting the meeting:

> Sometimes it helps just to walk away for a half-hour break and catch your breath and then go back in. At other times, I just walk around the room. I might try to see if I can get somebody else to carry the ball for a little while so I could kick back just a little bit and get more energy by not trying to push it all myself.

Within the surgery suite, Eric deliberately used time out to re-energize himself:

For me personally, to do nothing—to just vegetate—is by far the most helpful. To put your feet up on something and just sit, and not really be bothered by anything. That's not a time you want to get inundated with phone calls about this question or that question. You are not operating but you do not want to be bothered. You are recharging a little bit. The surgeon's lounge often isn't the quietest place; but it has several alcoves there to sit down, put your feet up, and get away from everything.

Across domains, different performers mentioned a variety of diversions. Diversions can be viewed as an energizing resource, a "time out" from the demands of performance. Some are prototypical, involving reading or gardening, for example. Jerry (dancer) used reading as a means of understanding more about the world:

> For me, handling stress is a matter of just going home and having down time. I come home and basically I just want to be by myself. I can just be by myself, listen to music, stay up as long as I want, go to bed when I want.
>
> My definition of down time is an evening or an entire day in which there is absolutely nothing planned, from the time you wake up in the morning until you go to bed at night. There is nothing planned. Nothing. If you are going out to dinner with friends, that is not a down time day because now you have to plan in relation to that. I have to have a down time day once a week—though sometimes I can't do that. Going on a vacation usually isn't down time—it's too scheduled.
>
> My car's license plate says "Down time." The name on my boat says "Down time." Down time is just literally that. It's sacred. That's the key.
>
> —Frederick (emergency room physician)

I read a lot of science fiction fantasy. For some reason I mostly enjoy authors with a very strong philosophical or sociological bent. Something that really gives you a hook to think about how society is organized, or what you should spend your life on.

Anna, a lawyer, commented: "I gardened for about ten hours this weekend. It was very hard work physically, and yet I felt so relaxed. It's just that it's so concrete; you're in there ripping away. And you get immediate results."

Larry may have described the most atypical diversion for an actor. In addition to driving his car and thereby changing settings, he has found that flying an airplane gives him a change of focus:

I'm a pilot. To me that's a wonderful source of relaxation. It's a challenge because it's not necessarily something I'm gifted at. Facing the sense of panic that I was feeling on stage is the same reason that I started flying: I was terrified of it, but I wanted to work through it.

For some, diversion can provide productive incubation. David, a banker, said:

> I try to mentally leave the office at the office. I don't need to go off somewhere necessarily, like go to the mountains for the weekend. Some of my best work happens when I'm doing projects around the house, painting and thinking about nothing. I can just void my mind. And sometimes I can figure out what I want to do on Monday.

INCREASING PERCEPTION OF RESOURCES

Increasing available resources may involve tangible resources, whether objects or people. It can also involve more intangible or cognitive aspects, such as one's perceptions or attributions regarding the available resources.

Increasing resources sometimes involves increasing one's awareness of self-attributes. As a method of combating performance stress, Faith (singer) spoke of confidence, while Keith (actor) described his "unshakable belief" in his own talent. Recognizing a strategy that heretofore was neglected or overlooked may also increase one's sense of resources. For example, Ian (broadcaster) discovered the relief of simply acknowledging a problem and accepting responsibility if an interview is not going well: "If things really aren't going well, I'll be honest about it on the air. I will take the heat. I will be self-deprecating."

In contrast to the static nature of visual arts, to which the observer can return again and again, the performing arts exist in a temporal mode. Music, in which the only sense that must be engaged is sound, may be the most evanescent of all. The musician cultivates a special relationship with sound in space and time. The possibility of altering time is thus, for a musician, a particular way of enriching one's resources.

Norman (musician) shared this particular perspective with us. He used a phrase he had first heard from Canadian pianist William Tritt to describe this relationship of the musician to an exquisite sense of the moment: "the microscopic nightmares of infinity." These are the moments when time seems to stand still and be utterly filled, in Tritt's phrase, with that most awful sense that error is everlasting. Norman spoke about the challenge of coping with this nightmare.

> If you fall into that jagged nightmare world of the microscopic nightmares, you've lost the battle.
> How do you get over it? One way is you just laugh about it. Another way is that you find your calm center. The microscopic nightmares can disappear in a second if you have that calm space. And that doesn't have to be only when I'm actually

performing. I cultivate it while I'm practicing—that's what practice to me is about. I chant to myself, "You can create time, as a musician you can create time."

Nobody can actually create time; time goes on its own way in various spots in the universe and in a special way when music is going on. But you can create time in those microscopic milliseconds. And if you can create it to your advantage, then you have given the audience and yourself the sense that everything is going to be fine, even when you totally screw up.

INCREASING SUPPORT SYSTEM

The high-risk and medical performers described support as an important resource. George (medic–sniper) spoke of the importance of having the opportunity to discuss situations with others in order to normalize reactions to stressful events. Similarly, Eric (neurosurgeon) commented:

> The only thing that really makes much difference, beyond time, is talking to other people who have been through similar situations. That is where having an age range in a practice like we have—it goes from 30 to 65—is so very helpful because we realize that everybody has been through something similar. They can explain what they went through and it alleviates some of the stress.

MENTAL SKILLS

A final resource available to performers involves the mental skills and techniques of psychological skills training. All of the mental skills discussed in chapter 8 can serve as resources; the ones specifically described by performers as methods for coping with stress included diaphragmatic breathing, imagery, thought management, and attention management.

The importance of breathing, involving some form of relaxation or deep, diaphragmatic inhalation and exhalation, was recognized and mentioned by a number of interviewees, especially performing artists. This technique is sometimes used singly or in combination with other mental skills. Some people use breathing as a technique to manage stress just prior to performance; others use it more generally as a method of handling the daily stresses of life.

In our interviews, Larry (actor) said that he meditated, whereas Keith (actor) described taking calming breaths to reduce tension just before auditioning. In broadcasting, Grace used both breathing and imagery. Combining breathing and self-talk, Charlotte (dancer) described the dressing room scene: "I used to sit in the dressing room and talk myself into confidence. 'You can do this. You just have to calm down and breathe deeply.'" Faith (singer) reported that she checked her tension "pulse." As she prepared to go on stage, she took deep breaths, assessed the level of adrenaline, and if she felt that she was too tense, continued to breathe slowly and deeply.

Ilene (musician) recognized the benefits of deep breathing in all aspects of life. She recently had started taking voice lessons as a way more fully to understand singers for whom she was an accompanist:

> Being outside, singing, and exercising, are all breathing-related. When I started singing I realized that it was the only hour—because I wasn't practicing, just going to my voice lessons—it was the only hour all week that I breathed. I went "My-y-y this feels so good! I feel so good afterward; I think better. Why don't I breathe all day?" Or at least, why don't I practice on breathing once a day? And then when I started going to yoga I thought, "Oh good, now I'm breathing twice a week." You just don't consciously breathe in your life nowadays.

Imagery can serve several functions, including stress management. Radio host Grace uses imagery extensively, particularly when facing unpleasant situations that interfere with her performance. She has developed a sequence in which she breathes, relaxes, and then imagines a "green handi-wipe" passing across her face and brain, simply wiping the stress away. Her image of herself as a rock in a river and stressors as water, quoted at the opening of this chapter, helps to stabilize her.

A number of performers across domains described methods of thought management to handle stress. These include deliberate countering, self-talk, affirmations, and thought stopping.

Keith (actor) described a situation in which he was worrying about his next line and then was able to counter his concern: "I'm already thinking of the end and I'm thinking 'I don't know it! I don't know it! I don't know it!' I can also say 'just relax, it will come; it will come; it will come.'"

Diane (musician) used affirmations for reassurance. The reverberation of her teacher's voice added power to these words:

> One big strategy I use is [self-talk]: "You know how to do this, you've been doing it since you were four years old. You know what you're doing. You know where that note is." One of my teachers used to say that, and to hear a really great teacher like her say that gives you the go ahead to just go out there and do what you know how to do.

Diane also pointed to the importance of cognitive methods to redirect attention from a narrow focus on technique to a broader focus on performance:

At the moment of performance, I think the only strategy I would use would be: "I'm doing what I know how to do." That's the one last thing you can tell yourself before you go out on stage. You can't be thinking "Now I better make sure I get my third finger just a little bit higher on that string or I'll never make that shift." You know that; you have to have that practiced into your system already so you know what it feels like and know that your kinesthetic sense can take over.

Refocusing and concentrating is especially important in some performance areas. Because the brass instruments are among the loudest in an orchestra, any errors brass players make can be especially audible. Consequently, brass players can become particularly self-conscious. The onomatopoeic term brass players use to describe their errors is, descriptively, kacking. In addition to her own mental methods used for violin, Diane spoke of those developed by her husband, a brass player:

My husband says everybody kacks and that you've just got to get right by it. He's a very logical person and he's able to just say, "That's done, I can't take it back, it's gone." It's just: "Let's focus on doing the next one better."

David (banker) actively organized his life to increase the likelihood of thought stopping. He deliberately did not talk about work at home, so that mentally he could leave the office.

It's important to go to the football game and stand beside another parent and not think about work, to think [only] about the football game, as opposed to trying to do both at the same time. If you start thinking about work, you need to say, "This is crazy! I want to watch the football game. My son's out there!"

David also used self-talk as a method of behavioral correction:

When I'm not proud of the way I act, I kind of mentally lecture myself about it. Unfortunately, rather than go apologize to somebody, I'll lecture myself not to do it again. What I should do is first go apologize to somebody and then lecture myself. I'd have a hard time doing that—but at least I do the second part.

Attention management is another mental skill, one that includes concentrating, focusing, and refocusing. Larry (actor) intentionally reassessed his performance, concentrating on the parts that are right. George (medic–sniper) described keeping his emotions suppressed until after the task is completed, handling the stress of the activity by focusing on the task at hand. Ian (broadcaster) deliberately focused on the present during performance, maintaining the zest of performance: "The hour that I am on the air is the best hour of the day for me. It does not matter what hour it is, it could be any hour." The other broadcaster, Grace, also found it critical to segment her personal and professional life, giving priority to the immediate tasks at hand.

Diane, who performed in a professional orchestra, has given the issue of attention management considerable thought. She used two utterly divergent methods to handle attention: distraction and intensification:

> I'm afraid to tell you that a lot of people do this whether or not they admit it to outsiders: If you've played something enough times, you can sort of put yourself on auto pilot and think about something else. I haven't really talked to men about whether they do this, but when we talk about it backstage I know that the women spend a lot of time doing things [while performing] like planning meals or where you're going to plant your flowers. Mundane things that you can just sort of think about while you're playing something that you already know. There is an ability to multitask; and in fact, if you've been doing music for a really long time, it's a big part of you. You basically can't escape the music, you always have it in your head. So you can also think about something else altogether.

More proactively, performers may focus their attention on engagement or meaning making. This alternative strategy has also been applied by Diane:

> Sometimes you'll get to a performance where you're bored or you've done this thing a million times before. If the conductor is terrible and I just don't like what he's doing to the music, I can look out and find people in the audience enjoying it and remember why I'm there. I might not be having a great time; I might do this three or four times a week; but those people are here and it's special for them. That's a good attitude to take on when you need to. It's always a good attitude anyway; but if you're not going to enjoy it (performing) for the music, then at least you can do that.

Diane also structured her musicianship by what she had learned from others. Her father played at a piano bar:

> Six nights a week he'd have to go and entertain these people in the piano bar. He was always in an upscale place, but I'm sure there were nights when he really didn't want to do it, when he was just not in the mood to be on. But he felt that if he could

take those people somewhere that was good for them to be for a couple of hours, then he had done something useful.

Decrease the Importance of Outcome

Some types of performance are intrinsically important. Life and death often hinges on the performance of those working in high-risk and medical areas. For all other performers, however, changing one's perspective on the importance of the performance can serve to reduce stress. As we've noted, Grace (broadcaster) made extensive use of this reframe. The other broadcaster, Ian, developed a mantra that incorporated this view. To defuse his anxiety about performance, he minimized the central significance of his job in comparison to life itself: "It's just television; it's just radio."

> I cope with stress by having a clear idea of what it is I'm trying to accomplish in life. The thing that keeps the stress down is the love I have for what I do and the ambition that I have for what I do and the sense of direction.
>
> —Michael (conductor)

The businesspeople also found it helpful to re-assess the importance of the situation when experiencing stress. Charles chose to put events in perspective. His father-in-law told him the following:

"I learned that the things that I thought were important at the time that they happened really weren't important." It's a way of basically saying "You're under a lot of stress, you created it yourself. Whatever is going on now will ultimately end one way or the other. When you look back on it, you'll recognize that it's probably not as big a deal as you think it is right now."

One way to diminish the importance of an outcome is to contain it rather than let it expand and override one's other experiences and understandings. For example, Keith (actor) commented: "Even if I 'blow it' in an audition . . . I view that as my psychological fear. It's not about my gifts; it's not about my talents. It's simply about my willingness to crack open, to put myself on display."

Humor is often used to put the importance of an outcome in a different perspective. When times were tense and a case had been lost, Anna (lawyer) commented that she and others in her law firm would joke to ease the stress. David (banker) was deliberate about the atmosphere that he wished to set in an office where millions of dollars rode on a single deal: "Around here, I try to keep a fairly light attitude, a sense of 'let's don't take ourselves too seriously.' A lot of joking and kidding people goes on around here."

At times, the importance of a performance is not merely reframed; it is *lived* by demonstrating the importance of other aspects of a performer's life. David (banker) described the expectations in his office:

> Everybody here is expected to work very hard but not to be consumed by this. I have told many of the guys here: "Don't miss the soccer games. You can come back to the office; [the work is] not that important. But don't miss the soccer games." Part of that is so they wouldn't not like it when I went to my kids' games. My only regret is that I missed any of my kids' sports events. I made about 90% of them. Of course, I told many lies. I think I've had 17 aunts that died.

Grace (broadcaster) reflected on many aspects of relationship-tending that keep the importance of performance in perspective:

> It is just very hard to maintain that balance between work and home. What's worked has been the ability to say "no" and mean no. To make the personal stuff as important a priority. It's not like I'll do everything I need to do professionally and with the time left over I will be giving you my 100%—no, that does not work. It's "I'm going to give this what I can and give you what I can and weigh them equally." That is what works. I wish there was something else that was easier that worked.

As we noted, Keith (actor) finds auditions especially stressful and has altered his perception of audition demand. He also has found that recognizing the realities of casting helps diminish his discomfort:

> I understand what's entailed in casting. I know that it's not a reflection or a judgment on my soul. At an audition, a director

> The very first time I ever performed, I was eight, and was playing the accordion for the Daughters of the American Revolution. I had been playing for a year and a half. I had never performed and I'm sure I was terrible—but I was eight years old. I was supposed to say what I was going to play before every song. I played my first song and it was okay and they applauded. I was then supposed to say, "Thank you, and now I am going to play such and such." I opened my mouth. My mouth moved, but nothing came out. I was petrified, sure that I was going to die. My father was in the back of the room and he said, "This is his first performance. He is going to play such and such." And I played and I was fine. I realized that I did not die.
>
> —Ian (broadcaster)

The Rose Adagio is the Swan's first entrance in Sleeping Beauty. It's very, very difficult. You have to balance on one leg for ages and it requires tremendous stamina. It's what we call "naked": You're either in balance or you're not. There's no in-between, and there's nothing you can do dramatically to cover up your technical flaws. It's really an either/or situation at every step: You either do it perfectly or you fall over. I was absolutely terrified about this.

In order to make your entrance you come down this huge staircase, but to get to the top of the staircase backstage, you have to climb up the staircase. I remember that moment backstage, at the Metropolitan Opera House in New York. I already had quite a reputation for doing it well—which caused more pressure, because you're not sure you can pull it off again as well as you did it last time. I felt like I was going to the guillotine when I walked up the staircase. I tried to think about things I'd seen in the newspaper that morning— the wars that were going on, and the really dramatic world events. I tried to remind myself that this was just a performance, this was just ballet.

—Charlotte (dancer)

or a casting person may see a number of people who are perfectly capable. That gives them the luxury to be as picky as they want, to pick someone with the earring and the purple eyes.

Reframing the importance involves something of a balancing act. Although decreasing the significance of the activity can lessen the performer's concern about it, there is a slippery slope in which the imputed decreased importance may imply devaluing of the activity or the performer. Both in her own performance career and as a teacher, Charlotte (dancer) decreased the sense of pressure she experienced by comparing dancing to other situations and professions that truly involve critical life issues. Although she recognized the accuracy of this perspective, she also expressed the need for utter devotion to one's work, in order to develop and maintain performance passion and skill.

I want dancers to feel that their work is the most important thing on the planet when they're in the studio— otherwise there's no point in doing it. It's got to be done with that kind of dedication. I also want them to be healthy people. When they step away from it they can think, "It's just ballet, it's not brain surgery, it's not curing cancer, it's not what some people are having to go through in their lives."

Recommendations to Consultants

- It is important and useful for the consultant to be aware of nonhealthful stress coping methods used within particular domains.
- The model of stress proposed in this chapter—an experience in which the perceived demands of a situation are greater than the perceived resources, and the outcome of the situation is considered important—can be a useful overall framework from which consultants and performers can adapt stress coping methods. Within this model, coping may involve reducing demands, increasing resources, or diminishing the importance of outcome.
- One can alter demand by adjusting one's goals, reframing the task, or reinterpreting the experience of stress.
- Although much of consulting involves "head work," consultants should be aware of the mind-body interaction. For example, taking better physical care of oneself (e.g., attending to nutrition, sleep, exercise) can often reduce stress and increase capacity for coping.
- Stress can also be reduced by increasing other resources, including sufficient preparation and the minimization of uncertainty, pacing, altering one's perception or interpretation of resources, and increasing one's support system.
- Mental skills are important to the performer not only for optimal performance but for management of stress as well. Among the most important for stress management may be relaxation techniques (e.g., diaphragmatic breathing), imagery, thought management, and attention management.
- Numerous types of reframing allow the performer to put the performance situation into perspective. Stress is subsequently reduced by decreasing the importance of the outcome of performance.
- The use of humor is a particularly effective "reframing" that is common particularly among performers who work in high-stress situations.
- Work–life balance is a crucial factor in coping with stress over extended periods of time. As such, time with family and loved ones can ultimately be a performance enhancer.

You're On! (Performance) 11

The night of the performance, there is no more studying, you just need to be there. That work (studying) is what should have been done over the last two years. The experience is like emptying yourself out of everything that is not essential so that you're hyper-focused on communicating that which cannot be communicated in any other way. It is an act of emptying and eliminating everything and then you just add in the music once everything is gone.

—Harold (conductor)

n the previous chapters, we have reviewed the common elements necessary for peak performance. We noted the importance of achieving an optimal pre-performance state and of having a performance plan, as well as an understanding of the ways in which adjustments can be made to maintain focus and the optimal performance state. This chapter addresses the point at which planning stops and performance begins. We look at the actuality of excellent performance in terms of both the performer's process and experience.

Flow and Peak Performance

When Ravizza (1977) asked athletes to describe their "greatest moment" in sport, their responses contained the following elements: no fear of failure; no thinking of performance; total immersion in the activity; narrow focus of attention; a sense of effortlessness in producing action; a sense of being in complete control; disorientation of time and/or space; and experiencing a sense of "oneness" with the universe. Furthermore, the athletes described these greatest moments as being temporary and somehow beyond their voluntary control.

These elements are similar to those often described when one is "in the zone," or in a state of flow (Csikszentmihalyi, 1990). In the world of athletics,

> To feel completely at one with what you are doing, to know you are strong and able to control your destiny at least for the moment, and to gain a sense of pleasure independent of the results is to experience flow. (Jackson & Csikszentmihalyi, 1999, p. vi)

Nine factors comprise the experience of flow: (a) balance between the challenge of a situation and the athlete's skills; (b) mind–body "oneness"; (c) clear goals; (d) unambiguous feedback; (e) total focus on the task at hand; (f) a sense of control; (g) a loss of self-consciousness; (h) experience of a transformation of time; and (i) an "autotelic" experience, one which is intrinsically rewarding, exhilarating, and an emotional "high."

Flow is a psychological state (Jackson, Thomas, Marsh, & Smethurst, 2001), alternatively described as an ideal "recipe of emotions" (Hardy et al., 1996, p. 245), or individual zone of optimal functioning (IZOF; Hanin, 2000). Flow (or one of the comparable terms) facilitates peak performance, but the two are conceptually different. Flow is an experience, whereas peak performance is optimal functioning (Privette & Bundrick, 1991). This distinction was confirmed by our performers: Their descriptions of memorable and optimal performances included emphasis on what they did as well as how they felt while doing it. We use those two broad categories—the process of performance, or what the performer does, and the experience of performance, or how the performer feels—as the general framework for our discussion.

The Process of Performance: What the Performer Does

FACTORS ESTABLISHED PRIOR TO PERFORMANCE

Several of the factors that influence flow, as indicated above, are established prior to performance. In performances that follow a predetermined pattern, such as a script or musical score, one typically knows or is able to anticipate the balance required between skills and challenge and has a general expectation of what will be encountered while performing. Ideally, clear goals will have been established as part of thorough preparation. The variability of the performance context often determines the cognitive and attentional processes required for success (Hardy et al., 1996). The more predictable the circumstances, the more a performer can rely on automated processes that require little conscious attention or focus. The more variable the situation, the more a performer must direct

When I started in this orchestra, my [music] stand partner was a totally jaded older guy. Although he could play very well if he wanted to, he was lazy. He couldn't stand the job, played like crap, and didn't care.

One night, after I had been in the orchestra for a couple of months, we played a Mozart symphony and this guy just shit all over it. It was terrible, I was upset, and I stayed behind in my dressing room, crying. I left the hall at the same time as [the conductor], and he looked at me and said, "I know why you're upset. I can see what's going on. I know it's frustrating for you because you want it to sound good. Well, you know he's been here a long time and unfortunately he hasn't figured out how to stay happy with what he's doing. He's unhappy and he just takes it out, and the worse he plays, the more unhappy he is because it doesn't sound good. There's no reason that he has to let that happen, but you also don't have to be affected by it. It's a terrible influence on you, and I'm going to speak to him." And he did.

—Diane (musician)

attention to assessing the situation prior to choosing a response strategy (which may then be an automated process).

The dynamics of the performance group are typically known and established prior to performance. These dynamics influence both flow and peak performance. Research with athletes indicates that team dynamics such as cohesiveness, trust, commitment, and positive focus are associated with athletic success (Gould et al., 1999).

Our performers noted the importance of interactions with (a) other performers within the performing group, (b) the immediate supporting group, or (c) the administrative group. Brenda (actor) offered metaphors of both music and sports when she emphasized the centrality of group dynamics within theatre:

The one thing you learn in the theatre is that if you don't work together you've got nothing at all. Interaction is what it's all about. You've got to be willing to do that; otherwise you've got to plan to be a soloist all your life. You have to have an instinct for working with other people and be interested in what they are about, because then you can play ball. Of course, it's only playing when you know what you're doing. Then it can just be so much fun, it's just marvelous. If you don't know what you're doing . . . I'd rather open a vein.

Tension in relationships can affect performance. Straightforwardly, Diane (musician) commented: "Your relationships with people you're performing with can drastically alter how your performance is. It would be nice to be able to avoid people or performance situations that made you uncomfortable, but this is what we do."

Not surprisingly, the performers whose work involves directing others on stage (conductors) were keenly aware of group dynamics. From the vantage point of her role as a conductor, Ellen reviewed both the relationship between performers and the concert sequence:

> What goes into a good performance? I think the way people are getting along and the work they've done to put it all together is very important. If there's been a lot of tension in the rehearsals, that will be reflected in your performance. You have to keep very focused, and yet you have to give everybody a sense that they are participating. If they sense that their input doesn't matter in rehearsals, then in the concerts they're going to have that same sense. Why should their input suddenly matter then? You want them playing their [best], so a lot of that work has been done ahead of time about how people feel about their participation, their role.

The dynamics and subsequent quality of performance change with repetition. Ellen continued:

> We do each concert four or five times. There's a certain cycle that seems to repeat itself. At the first concert, the energy for me and probably everybody else in the group is usually pretty uptight. The first night is very careful and precise and often not as flowing as you might want it to be. The second night is sometimes a little bit careless, parts are a little bit unfocused. And then it starts really coming together. The third and fourth you do really great—they're usually the best concerts. And then you have to be careful if there's a fifth one that it's not just too relaxed.

The group dynamics in broadcasting were described by Grace:

> Part of working on a team involves recognizing that we are not all friends having fun here. It is more like, "We have a job to do and if we don't do it, this team disbands." For a while, we cycled through employees whom we did not manage properly. They did not do the job and ultimately there had to be firings. That is always hard, because they are people you like. A friendship develops. If the person does not do what he or she is supposed to do, you begin to feel taken advantage of and resentment kicks in. You can hear on the air that something is not quite right. You do not want them to lose their job; it's devastating. This is a fun job and when they get fired, you don't celebrate.

It is so important that you have total trust. When you are doing improv, you need to know that the other person is going to be in there swinging. As soon as layers of resentment and anger build up, trust disappears. I have learned the hard way that it is so much better to be very clear about your expectations and to correct people midstream, rather than at the end when it is hopelessly screwed up and you can't work together any more.

In the world of medicine, interaction with one's immediate supporting group takes on a vital role. Frederick, the emergency room physician, said:

I function best when I operate in a collaborative way. I rarely order nurses to do things. I say, "We are going to need to do a pelvic on this person." I don't say, "Do this or do that." The result is the same, but it's all a matter of style.

The key is to be careful about what jobs you layer on to your nurses or any other providers. Because you are the person giving most of the orders, you delineate who is going to do what under what circumstances. You have to know the operating capabilities and not pour a lot of stuff onto people. If somebody is out there doing something, you say to them, "No hurry; any time within the next 15 minutes if you get a free time, I need you to be a chaperone for a pelvic examination." And don't say, "I want to do that NOW." In the emergency department if you take on that type of air, you become colossally inefficient. I say, "Here's a window—find me," because a lot of times I can be more flexible than others on the team. I can bounce around; I can leave the room, go do something and then come right back in.

It is all team, much more so than being an internist where you have "your" nurse. There are a couple of things that the nurses do that I can't do, like get into the drug machine and get out narcotics. I am absolutely not allowed to do that. But I can change a stretcher or make a bed. There are all sorts of jobs that everybody can do and everybody should do them, so it truly is a teamwork proposition.

FACTORS DURING PERFORMANCE

During the actual performance, our performers emphasized an ongoing, interactive process that included assessment, presentation of self, willingness to risk, and maintenance of an optimal performance state. Maintaining an optimal performance state is a process that entails a number of elements: total focus on the present, adjustments in response to external feedback (from the audience), and adjustments in response to internal feedback (self-corrections in relation to mistakes or errors).

Assessment

As noted earlier, performances can be broadly categorized into two groups: those in which the action follows a scripted pattern with minor variations, such as in dance, theatre, and notated music; and those in which the performer must react to changing situational factors that may proceed along any of a number of paths. With this latter group, performance excellence is contingent on correct assessment of a situation and effective subsequent choices and actions. Many performers in the high-risk and business categories must be prepared to make critical decisions at the onset of performance. Improvisational performing artists, such as jazz musicians and improvisational comedians, rely on "reading a situation" (the resources available) in directing their performance efforts.

Accurate initial observation and ongoing appraisal are obviously essential to high-risk performers. George, the medic, described the need for both narrow and broad focusing skills (Nideffer, 1976). Initial assessment typically involves a broad scan of the situation. George illustrated this method of broad attentional focus: "I would have an awareness [of what is] around me. The situation may dictate that I'm being shot at or things are happening around me. I can't get so focused on one patient that I become a casualty."

Frederick, the emergency room physician, referred to the initial assessment of a situation as *gestalting*, that is, rapid evaluation of the overall situation. He noted the critical nature of this initial snapshot on the triage that is part of an emergency situation. It must be done as accurately as possible:

> Gestalting is dangerous. If you come to see a patient, your gestalt on a patient may not always be right, but it always has an impact on your process.
>
> Gestalting the patient is very important, not so much as to their disease but as to intensity: Just how sick are they? It's sort of an instant image of the circumstances in the room that becomes very important. It's a quick read: How sick is the patient? Not what type of sick, not surgical sick, medical sick, disease sick—just sick sick. Is this somebody who is about ready to die, or is this somebody where I can waste time? Can I be more efficient with somebody else and put this person on hold?

Frederick's second quick read involves assessing the dynamics of the human beings in the room. Recognizing the key family members and attending to what they believe to be the problem is "absolutely critical."

These are the people who have the most information about the patient and the most influence on the patient's life after discharge from the hospital. Their support and cooperation is crucial to a "relationship-centered" approach (described in chap. 4, this volume).

Business performance can often entail a challenging blend of pre-performance strategy and adjustment to variations. A person may have an initial predetermined agenda, but ongoing assessment and feedback may necessitate dramatic modification of one's original plan. The ability to assess a situation both rapidly and accurately is the foundation of achieving excellence in these settings. Arthur (lawyer) commented:

> The key in what I do is *pace*. It's like using a clutch and an accelerator. Knowing enough to be quiet and listen and to try to really read what needs to happen. And then to take a stab at it. And still to listen, to figure out whether it worked or not, so that you don't over-commit too much to one way of doing it but are open to changing very quickly without appearing flighty. In that context, it's more like being focused on what's going on, trying to be wide open so that you can understand what everybody needs and decide whether you can accomplish what everybody needs.

Presentation of Self

Another factor of peak performance involves the way in which the performer presents himself or herself. Even when one doesn't feel the basic attribute of confidence, conveying a sense of self-assurance is the most important element of self-presentation. Like the character in the musical *The King and I*, sometimes it's a matter of whistling a happy tune: "For when I fool the people I meet, I fool myself as well." Ellen (musician) commented that

> a certain amount of being a performer is the sense that when you don't feel the confidence, you can fool yourself and fool everybody else into believing that you have the confidence, so that you get into whatever the role is that you have to do to perform the music. If you're not really confident, that's going to be an effort. But that's part of the job; you can't seem as insecure as you sometimes feel.

Norman (musician) asked the key questions:

> How are you going to be able to get up there and just act like you're having a good time, the way kids do? And even if you're not, can you psyche it up to the point where you can convince the audience that you haven't got a care in the world, or that if

you've got a care it's only about what's inside the music and not about your own fear in approaching your instrument—or approaching the audience for that matter.

Successful performance includes presentation of self that may be at odds with one's actual feelings at the moment. Grace (broadcaster) described the dilemma of authentic connection with one's intimates, yet maintaining full engagement in one's performance self:

> One of the things I hate to hear [from my husband] is, "What do you mean, you're tired? You didn't sound tired on the radio." The only thing that works is to be direct. You just have to be really honest and you have to repeatedly remind the other person that it's a job. This is what it entails—accept it. It is hard. I deal with it. My co-anchor deals with it. Everybody who does this deals with it. And the only way around it is constant negotiation. I have had to tell my husband: "Listen, when I go to work I am at work, I am going to do my job. The day I sound tired on the radio, I am eating cat food and living under a bridge."

Music is an aural medium, yet in performance it contains a visual element as well. As a violinist and conductor, Ellen commented on one of the disjuncts between musician and audience:

> People are very visual in our society, and music is not very visual. Music is a very abstract art form. People come to look as well as to enjoy the sound. And we (musicians) tend to be totally focused on the sound, on the music. You have to have a bit of at least a sense of what you look like.

(One of the great pleasures that I (KH) experienced while observing "Ellen" perform was a particular way in which her face suffused with delight at certain moments. Ironically, especially in light of her comment above, when I described this vivid audience experience of mine, she was not at all clear which moments I was describing.)

The regulation of emotion while in performance is necessary in all domains. As noted, surgeon Eric spoke of his "calm assuredness" in the operating room. Anna described an overarching sense of confidence that lawyers project. How this gets conveyed may vary, in part, by gender:

> There's a certain male style of litigation. I think it is sort of a waning style, but nonetheless it's very much there: this sort of cowboy style. It's all performance. There's not much behind it, and yet it can be very successful. It's a very aggressive gladiator approach to things. In my experience the really, really good lawyers have that ability to read their audience and synthesize

things in a way that takes whatever that sensibility is into account.

About ten years ago, I went to England to do a Gilbert and Sullivan operetta. On opening night, there was a sea of "penguins" (men wearing tuxedos) out there. It was a very stiff audience and we knew we had our hands full. We had a difficult show. I had a wonderful role and it seemed to go quite well [in rehearsal], but I was worried. I was quite out on a limb with the characterization of my part.

I did it, and the audience didn't laugh at one thing I did, because I was so desperate. They (the audience) did home in on the other three performers. They (the other three) had the confidence. They connected. I realized later that I didn't have the confidence for the British audience.

It doesn't matter if you're wrong; you have to believe totally in what you're doing. If you don't, you have to manufacture those qualities. So I started doing that. I wasn't changing anything externally. Timing wasn't changing. It was an internal journey.

—Larry (actor)

In addition to presenting oneself as confident, the performer must be clear about the role of emotion during performance. Here, we are distinguishing between the emotions one actually experiences and the emotions that are conveyed during performance. As we noted earlier, the ideal role of emotion during performance varies according to performance domain. An actor's ideal performance state might include a combination of nervousness and uncertainty, whereas the role may call for the display of outrage and anger. The performance plan for a businessperson may include presenting a proposal in a fashion that emphasizes logic and reason and minimizes the display of emotion. That same individual may have an ideal performance state that includes feelings of anger, competitiveness, and even a little fear. It is critical for the individual to achieve his or her Individual Zone of Optimal Functioning (IZOF) and then to display emotions according to the performance plan.

Two performers with markedly different personalities both commented on the value of being deliberate with one's emotions during performance. George, who performed as both medic and sniper, recognized that he was an emotional person. At the same time he admitted that his performance was best when emotions were minimized and not displayed.

For a professional sniper, a lot of different mental tasks need to be carried out continuously, until the situation is resolved. It's important to keep your mind occupied and pull yourself away a little bit, kind of stand outside of the emotional sphere. Keep those emotional things covered. In both cases, as a medic and a sniper, I'm trying to keep them bottled up until afterward.

One time five of us went to meet this group of decision-makers. The first set of questions that were thrown at us were ones that other people in the room were trying to hit and they were just whiffing. I finally stood up and said, "You know, this is really a disaster. You may decide not to hire us for what I am going to do now, but I am just going to say we are going to start over again. You are asking questions and we're not listening, or you are asking questions that are impossible to answer. Let's take it from the top. Let's try to refocus the time that we have together, or let's end the time we have together, because this is not working. I know it's not working. You know it's not working. We are not going to do this anymore."

What I was doing was listening and watching the body language. I was making an on-the-spot diagnosis of what was going on. In some ways, it was pretty easy. It was like Janis Joplin—there was freedom, a sense that "there is not much to lose here; we are dead in the water here. Maybe we can salvage our pride. Maybe we can surprise everybody and they'll decide they like us, because I am going to do something that is really, in this social context, relatively risky. I am going to tell the truth."

—Arthur (lawyer)

David (banker) described himself as being an unemotional person. He also preferred to keep the display of emotions out of business performance.

Some people just have terrible tempers and throw temper tantrums. They're passionate about everything, whether positive or negative. In my eyes, it hurts them. My style is kind of "Well, let's look at the facts, let's think about it, let's talk about it, what do you think?" For these people, it's "GOD, WE'VE GOT TO DO THIS! I MEAN, I CAN'T BELIEVE YOU GUYS ARE STILL DOING THAT!"

Frederick (emergency room physician) elaborated on the importance of changing his presentation of himself to fit the demands of a situation.

You walk into a room and the first person you see is a person who is dying—I'll use the most extreme thing—and then dies. You go see the family. The way I do it, I extract myself from it and I really think of myself as an actor. And I go in playing a certain role when I talk to the family of a loved one who has died. That is, there is a certain way you should be. There is a certain process you should go through. There is a certain set of theory and dogma related to how you start the grieving process, how you process that, how close you should be to

> High-level performers have a kind of stubborn persistence and belief in self. It's like: I can do this. I can succeed. This is a good idea. They are willing to take a risk to get the goal.
>
> One guy I worked with had been a friend of my father's. He made quite a bit of money. He went broke a couple of times in his life. He risked it all. He lost it all. He built it back up again. He sold and did a bunch of things and became just a money maker after a while. He just really believed in himself. He believed and knew it was the right idea. He had a lot of experience to the contrary for a period of several decades before he finally succeeded.
>
> —Dr. Brian Bell (consultant, family business)

somebody, whether you should be touching them or not touching them. I assume that identity, I do the job, and I walk out of the room and quite literally walk down the hall into the room of a person who has got a minor problem and I'm jovial and laughing, because that person requires an entirely different set of behaviors from the caregiver.

Willingness to Risk

Loss of self-consciousness is regularly reported by athletes as an element of flow (Jackson & Csikszentmihalyi, 1999). We characterized a similar phenomenon as a *willingness to risk*. Radio host Ian commented:

> One key skill in doing a talk show is trusting yourself. It may be opening yourself up to your own life experience. Trusting yourself comes from experience and opening your own life experiences up comes from not being afraid to be open and honest—being who you are. I say that I play this person on the radio, but there are lots of real elements of me that I am not afraid to let out. I admitted the other day on the radio that it was very painful for me as a teenager to be in phys ed class, because I was lousy at it. I was always the last person chosen to be on a team, and I couldn't dribble a basketball and nobody wanted me on their team. It was horrible. No guy admits that he is no good at sports. It was a painful time in my life, but we were talking about a topic where it seemed appropriate to admit that.

As a businessman, Barry described the "risk inherent in doing what has never been done" as very inspirational. Jerry, a dancer, characterized "having the courage to go out and do something unknown" as "emotional courage," for which "you need to have a very strong sense of knowing what you're doing and believing in what you're doing."

For an actor, willingness to risk relates to being emotionally present, open, and vulnerable to what one is experiencing in the role and then sharing that vulnerability with the audience. Larry (actor) commented:

> Sometimes I like the challenge of a piece. There's something about it that is a psychological, mental, or physical hurdle to get through. Part of my own being has always believed that if you have a fear, you've got to walk up to it, you've got to look at it, and hopefully to walk through it to the other side.

Elaborating further, Keith shared his own sense of vulnerability, particularly around auditioning:

> As an actor, I use what I have. I'm very much of the belief that whatever I use is within me. Any characteristic that you play, any element of the human spirit, is somewhere inside you. It's a question of what's foreground and what's background, and what choice you make. How open can I be? How open will I be? That's the biggest challenge for me, not so much in performance but more in auditioning. You feel incredibly vulnerable because what you're working with is you. These are your materials. And especially if you're of the view that you're not putting on something, that it's all coming out of you, you feel tremendously vulnerable. And the sense of rejection then is at its greatest when you feel you're most open.

> Physical tension is something you want to have as a dancer. You don't want to have *gripping* tension, but you do want to have—maybe attention is a better word than tension. Even in your stillness you need to have vibration, and a present energy. You don't want it to be a locked tension but a kind of vibrating tension. You actually need that all the way through the performance. Even still moments have to be very intense.
>
> —Helena (dancer)

MAINTAINING AN OPTIMAL PERFORMANCE STATE

In chapter 8, we discussed the importance of achieving an ideal performance state, or IZOF (Hanin, 2000). Performance excellence is based, in part, on sustaining that ideal state, using the mental skills developed during preparation for performance. Our performers described two critical tasks: maintaining focus within the present moment, while at the same time being able to make minor adjustments in response to external or internal cues. We refer to these, below, as focus, interactive feedback with "audience," and self-correction.

Focus

Total focus on the present is one of the key methods of maintaining an optimal performance state. Performers in all domains mentioned this point. All the skills of attention management (see chap. 8, this volume) come into play to maintain focus on the moment.

As a conductor, Michael commented that it is particularly critical for conductors to develop the skill of focusing totally on the music itself. With the music as foreground, interpersonal or systemic issues can become background.

> You're dealing with such numbers of people who make music, and they have their own problems, whether it's their personalities or circumstances. I don't get involved with that; I just say that I just work on the information; I just keep focused on the music itself. I've discovered that that approach is most productive, and it also makes it easy for me to deal with lots of hard situations that come up in all my travels working with different orchestras in different parts of the world.

Maintaining focus on the task at hand is useful in many domains. David (banker) commented: "I think of myself as being very disciplined, which I think is a positive. I don't get caught up in the deal or the hype of the moment. I stay focused and disciplined."

Making an analogy to physicians' challenges, radio personality Grace emphasized the need to be totally focused on the present situation:

> I really have no patience with people who: (a) can't get it together and (b) do not understand that this is a job. If I'm your doctor and I had a fight with my husband and I come in and screw up your operation, is that fair? It is totally unacceptable. I'm expected to put it aside. If you're married to a doctor, you don't call your spouse and say, "I hope Mrs. Jackson dies because you screwed up her spleen. You're too tired to help me with these kids, so I hope that woman dies." You would never do that. . . . You have not lived until you've had a knock-down, drag-out marital argument at 4 a.m., right before you have to get in your car for a ten-mile commute [prior to going on the air]. When I get in the car, I take a deep breath and say to myself, "He will be there; and so will [the problem]." At that point I have to move on.

This skill is also one that radio host Ian found invaluable:

> I can compartmentalize things really well. Even if I have had a horribly bad day or I had a car accident on the way in, I just

At a recent concert of Baroque music, one of us (KH) met one of the performers, Francis Colpron. He wore a lapel pin in the shape of a table knife. When asked about it, he commented that he wears it to remind him to stay "sharp," that is, alert or focused.

have to focus. You focus. The car accident was in the past. Yes, I'll have to deal with the insurance company when I get off the air, but that can't be in the picture now. I have to talk to [the guest] now.

Performers know where to put their thoughts at which time. Ilene (musician) contrasted the experience of practice with the total focus of performing. She also spoke to the importance of being able to "hold the line." One needs not only to attend or focus, but also to stay focused, concentrating throughout an entire piece of music.

When you practice, you're always editing and you're always thinking backward, you're always evaluating. If you play a phrase, you stop and think back: "What can I fix, what would be better there?" But if you do that while you're performing, then at the moment that you're thinking backward you're not thinking about the music that you're playing at the moment. What became very helpful to me was to try, instead of saying, "Okay, do this here"—which is what you get into when you're practicing—to just sing it through. When you're singing inside your head, you usually can't think thoughts. You usually can't think verbally. Your whole head is used up with thinking of the music. What you don't want is an interruption, because music goes on linearly. If you're thinking all those little corrections, your concentration can break down. But if you're thinking the line, it shouldn't break down. The musical term for it is *audiating*, hearing music inside your head and thinking the music.

The deliberate use of sound or silence marks certain surgical operations, stages of surgery, or level of complexity at any one time (Katz, 1999). Neurosurgeon Eric's description of the ideal performance state reflects this factor as the performance plan becomes a reality:

Everybody in the operating room is aware of those difficult cases. There is just a general decline in the background noise. Things tend to be a lot more efficient and there's just a more businesslike, "get the work done" approach to those types of cases where there are pretty serious consequences. Without any prompting, without the surgeon saying, "We've really got to pay attention to this," there is just kind of a general pattern that everybody picks up and follows. It's a lot more intense. It also involves sticking to the same [known] procedure. If you have too much anxiety or too much fear, it's counterproductive. You almost have to go into it with kind of a calm assuredness that you can deal with it. The other thing is that everything around has to fit into that same pattern. The smoother things go and the more streamlined the process seems, the less anxious you can be as a surgeon.

For Harold, conductor and keyboard player, focusing—and at times, refocusing—is clearly the key to performance.

That is a crucial thing. When I'm playing a keyboard in performance, one of the bad things that can happen is that stupid things will just come into my mind. And then you obsess about the fact that you're not thinking about the music. And then you start to have this war within yourself and that becomes the disintegrator of the performance. If you are focused, those things don't happen—or at least they're less likely.

Rather than being concerned throughout a piece of music, Diane (musician) uses focus deliberately to isolate difficult passages.

If I know that I have something hard coming up, I really try not to think about it during the rest of the performance, because if you allow those six or eight bars to control your entire performance, you're going to tie yourself up in knots; you're not going to be where you are. It's okay to think about something else during the thing but not about another part of the piece. That just upsets you. If you've done your work, if you've ever even sung it right or played it right once, then you know you can do it.

Intentional direction of one's attention is a central aspect of being "on." At times, the performance relates to one's task. At other times, it involves attention to one's audience. Norman (musician) elaborated on this process:

When you walk out on the stage and look at the audience, that's the time when you belong totally to the audience. That's your time to be humble in front of them—that's what the bowing indicates. You're humbling yourself in front of the audience and saying, "I'm your servant and I'm going to play for you." Then as soon as [the bowing is] over, it's "Screw you, buddy, now I'm going to show you what I've got," and you can't ever look back until the piece is over.

Norman's style fit his description, albeit not quite so blatantly: One of us (KH) attended a concert in which he performed. He was utterly engaged with the audience before and after the piece of music. During his playing, however, he and his musician colleagues were entirely fixed on their musical creation and interaction. Depending on the domain, some performers can seem or be nearly oblivious of their audience. For others, feedback from the audience during the performance is crucial to maintaining optimal performance.

Interactive Feedback From Audience

For many performers, interaction with the "audience" is a vital source of feedback and is integral to the quality of the performance experience. Here we are referring to audience in the broadest sense. For different domains, audience has different meanings. It may refer to an abstract audience, a virtual audience, an actual audience, or an interactive recipient of a procedure or idea.

A musical conductor focuses on the relationship with a hypothetical audience through programming choices. Michael described this aspect:

> My basic viewpoint as an artist is that you are there to actually serve others in addition to yourself. Depending on your application of that principle, the sky is the limit. You would like to affect as many people as you can, because that's the purpose of it. That then affects your relationship with those you work with. It affects your relationship with the public; it affects your attitude toward the programming policies you have, what pieces you choose to give to your public.
>
> Many conductors don't care what anybody thinks about what they program. It's almost as if they're out there for themselves only, and the public be dammed. They sort of hide behind the apparent exaltedness of, say, new or contemporary music. I try to make choices that are targeted for people who can get the message. Relative to something new, unheard of before, my program is to gradually build up the audience's knowledge and appreciation so that they can be with me the whole way along. I care about what my audience is experiencing.

In acting, subtle distinctions can be made regarding the audience, depending on the specific medium. Keith discussed the differences between doing comedy, live theatre, and film:

> Playing comedy is—it's the power of laughs. It really is intoxicating, no matter what my mood, to get that immediate charge. And there's a huge sense of power from that.

In contrast, working in straight dramatic theatre is often difficult. As with comedy, there's a live organism—the audience that's out there—but they just don't actively feed a piece in such a tangible way as they do when you're playing comedy.

Film is entirely different, because you're playing to one "person": the camera. That's a whole other very interesting medium, because you have the rapt attention of that one person. It's trained on you. On stage, in contrast, you're always aware of the battle to harness people's focus and energy.

Larry noted the dynamic between actor and audience in live theatre:

The point is to try and find some communication, some kind of acceptance with the audience. If things aren't going well, one tendency is to overact, to try to grab the audience. The other tendency is to be dismissive, to say: "Well, fine, if you don't like it, I'll move along." But you've always got to care for people. In my life as a performer, if I'm not sharing with an audience, and trying to reach them in some way, then I'm not doing my job.

Norman observed that musicians vary in regard to the sense of connection with their audience. As with athletes, the breadth of attentional focus may be a function of individual differences (Nideffer, 1976), type of music, or type of performance:

How do you relate to the audience? How much attention do you pay to what's going on out there? Some are going to say, "Oh, did you hear that incredible thing that happened in the third movement when somebody dropped their teeth?" Others will respond: "I don't know, I didn't hear a thing." Some people will be open to an outside stimulus or a variety of outside stimuli. And some people just aren't open to outside stimuli. They go out and perform and have no idea whether it's hot, cold, bright, or dark.

The dynamics between performer and audience are a factor even when the audience is unseen. In radio, talk show host Ian said:

I think people like to know who you are. They like honesty. I think people like vulnerability. Vulnerability makes you attractive to some people to a certain degree. They don't want you to be a whimpering pile of crap in the corner, but if you're willing to show that you're not perfect, that you have cracks in the veneer, it makes you human.

In the world of business, the client becomes the audience. For Charles, the insurance business revolved around his interaction with his clients:

What I do best is create relationships with people. I don't think I'm the world's greatest salesman. But I do have a very good technical knowledge of my product, and I think that I'm very good at creating relationships with people.

We're not selling a copier where we come in and convince you that we have the best copier and we're gone. Or office supplies. Or a stock. We're selling a relationship. I want to sell you insurance, I want to help you do your financial plan, and this is a long-term relationship. You have to have confidence in me.

Frederick adopted a holistic perspective in relation to emergency medicine, emphasizing the primacy of interpersonal skills even over medical knowledge. His task involved the entire dynamic range of everyone in the examination room.

When you walk into the room, if there are four people in the room including you, at minimum there are three diseased patients. You might be, too. Whether you are or not depends on your mood or whether you are a pathologic dork. But there are at least three dis-eased people. What you have to do is find out what it is that you think is wrong with them and treat that. But that is secondary to finding out what *they* think is wrong with them and treating that. You have to treat both. If things are really going poorly and you are one of the diseased people, you have to figure out what it is that is bothering you, causing your disease, and you've got to treat that.

Never kick anybody out of the room unless the patient wants them out of the room—never. The odds are that the other people in the room are going to be involved in the caregiving, so if they are engaged from the very beginning it is more efficient.

The key is to engage the patient and engage the caregivers so that they will know the plan and will carry out the plan, because 90% of the therapy that you are prescribing, you won't do right there in the emergency room. And they think you are God and you strut around like a God. They are not that much better when they leave, but they just have to be enabled and have to have a plan to be optimistic about.

Self-Correction

During performance, the performer's focus and relationship with the audience does not necessarily continue at a steady state. Performers get off-

> I think good salespeople connect with people deeply and quickly. I think we (consultants) are different from salespeople, but really good salespeople connect on the basis of really trying to help a person. They think they've got a product that is good and they think it will help. I think we are somewhat like that.
>
> —Dr. Brian Bell (consultant, family business)

track, and thus, one key skill is the ability to make minor corrections to one's actions during performance. For instance, a coach of our acquaintance described trampolinists' activity (with a certain dour anticipation of catastrophe) as continuous "disaster control." An element of danger in performance exists. Depending on performance domain, this danger of derailment may be psychological or physical. For example, in order to think clearly and maintain his fine motor skills, whether for a medical procedure or a steady rifle hand, George deliberately slowed down his actions:

> When I feel that I am too aroused, I just start moving in slow motion. When I'm on the range training with the sniper rifle, when I get down in position and I just start making my hand movements very slowly, my whole body calms down.

In addition to his emergency medicine practice, Frederick has responsibilities as a hospital administrator. At times, his shift in the emergency room is disrupted by an administrative matter that immediately interrupts his sense of flow:

> What drops me off the peak is getting a sense of frustration because there has been a break in my continuity. If I do get frustrated, I won't get mad, but I will get inefficient. I operate much less efficiently when I don't get over it. So I sort of start over. If I was in some place where I can just get back in, I go there. If not, I go to the board—a computer that has the names of all the patients and where they are—and I basically run the board and go through every patient. Then I prioritize what I am going to do. I reorder. It may not be in the same order that I had been going, but you have to start over.

Larry commented on the actor–audience connection in theatre, an ever-changing opportunity for self-correction and course adjustment. "Theatre is a living entity . . . a changing thing. If your character is in the right area of your mind and you are physically with the character, you can adjust to the variations that the audience will take you to."

Although Arthur was an attorney rather than an actor, he too was sensitive to the interaction between himself and his clients, as noted in his earlier comments about pacing. In addition to reading the process of

When I was a sophomore in high school, I sang "Over the Rainbow" in the Amateur Hour. I never had stage fright and it never occurred to me that I would ever be nervous on stage. Until I walked out there the night of the performance, I'd never had stage lights in my face. I walked out there, the lights were in my face, and I couldn't see any audience. I couldn't remember a word of that song. I was wearing this blue gingham dress, with a big basket of lilacs, so I knew I looked really pretty. I thought, "Well, I'm not going to crash out here," so I la-la'd the whole beginning and when I got to "Somewhere over the rainbow," I just made up something, and it all rhymed.

I was sort of mad at myself when I got off stage—I should have gotten first prize, and now some other singer was going to get first prize. I got second prize. I was mad at myself, but it didn't make me depressed, or think that I shouldn't be a performer. I thought it was funny. It just made me think, "Well, at least I rhymed." I turned it around to be humorous, some kind of learning thing. And I've still never come off stage depressed or thinking "Well, I'm obviously in the wrong field."

—Faith (singer)

interaction, he attended in particular to language. He noted which words elicit specific responses and adjusted his performance accordingly: "I've learned something about the power of the straight word. I don't measure what I'm going to say—I think it pretty much flows—but I am really careful about hot words."

How does the performer handle mistakes and move beyond them? For Michael (conductor), the issue is intention:

If your aim is to be perfect, then the moment you make any mistake, you've already failed. But for me, the main purpose of, let's say, my doing a Beethoven symphony is to deliver the intent of the music. The technique of the piece itself is there to serve the dramatic ends of it. Your focus as an artist should be to master the techniques sufficiently to live with that dramatic intent. There can still be mistakes in the performance, there can still be lack of perfection in performance, and yet you can still fulfill the purpose.

Charlotte (dancer) illustrated the distraction and interference that can occur through a focus on perfection:

The performances that went badly were the performances where I was distracted from what I wasdoing. I was worrying about pressure, and letting every little mistake I made take my mind off what I was doing at that moment. If I made a mistake during the beginning of the performance or did something a little roughly or did some little step at a level less than that I thought I should be doing

If you look beyond the garage band, self-taught kind of musician, criticism has been an integral part of the music world since whenever. You have to do it right. If you listen to musicians talk to the conductor or their teacher or even their peers, the initial focus is always on "What did I do wrong?" or "How could I do better?" Typically, there's very little emphasis placed on "This was really good, this was really fine, this was really nice, now here are some changes you could make." That kind of aura is not out there. So kids come in, since childhood, with this perfectionistic kind of belief, and I work real hard at changing that. There's more to making music than just following the notes on the page.

If you recognize that you're the one making music, you're the one saying this, then it's harder to fall victim to the perfectionism that's intertwined with performance anxiety. Because performance anxiety people are tied up in "Oh my god, other people are judging me and I have to be perfect." They're tied up in what others are thinking as opposed to what they're thinking, what they're saying, through the music that they're making. I think probably the best mental kind of attitude is, "Hey, this is my music, I'm saying it."

—Dr. Nick Norris (consultant, music)

it—and these are things that nobody would notice but me—I would just dwell on how angry I was with myself, instead of letting it go and getting on with the show. And all that would do was make me blow the rest of the show. I really got caught up in that. I had to teach myself, to discipline myself to let go of mistakes and forgive myself for not being perfect every time.

Similarly, musician Norman recognized that musicians need to know both that they'll make mistakes and that they can't undo them. "I don't need to be in control of the mistake, but I need to not let it stop me from doing what I'm doing and try not to feel guilty about making a mistake."

Ian (broadcaster) indicated that maintenance of the optimal performance state consists of a delicate interplay of focus, audience, and self-correction. He described the importance of maintaining focus throughout an interview, using techniques of self-talk and thought management:

You have to remind yourself that you know you can do it. You can do it, you have done it before. I am not one of these Pollyanna people who think you should never have negative thoughts. That is bull. But when you are in the moment of doing it, inevitably if you think you can't, then you can't. You have to think, "I can recover from this. It is not going well and I can get out of this." Or "Oops, that was a mistake but I can recover from this."

DEALING WITH OUTCOME

Both positive and negative performances lead to their own distinct and unique set of challenges. Positive outcome and the accompanying celebrity status can wreak havoc within one's personal life, as Grace (broadcaster) noted earlier. At the same time, negative outcome often leads to a crisis of confidence.

Radio host Ian described the poignant challenge to the successful performer—that of being a public figure. Anything that one does is going to be noticed by others:

> You have to develop a realistic picture of who you are and you have to be open to recognizing your faults. And that is hard to do. It takes a certain amount of confidence to get up on the stage or to get on the radio every day. Sometimes you are not willing to look at the things that you are not good at or the things that you failed at or the things that you could use improvement in. If you tell me on a Wednesday that I am not good at something and I have to use that skill tomorrow, how can I use it? I am going in there knowing one of my weak points—I am naked out there. It is not like a desk job. If I am having a bad day everybody knows it. If the guy at BellSouth is having a bad day, not everybody knows it.

Bandura's (1986) self-efficacy theory posits that a person's confidence is most influenced by prior efforts and accomplishments. After the performance is completed, there is a feedback loop of assessment of the outcome and this in turn influences further performance. Dealing with negative outcomes becomes a crucial aspect of this process.

Speaking of auditioning, actor Keith described under-achievement in action:

> Sometimes I feel like I've sabotaged myself, especially in auditioning. It's much easier for me to walk out of an audition and feel that I somehow inhibited the communication, that I inhibited the performance, through fear, so that if there's a rejection, then it's like "Well, of course there was a rejection because they never saw what I have to offer." To lay yourself bare, and *still* have somebody say, "It's not what we want or what we need," is really profound. It really is profoundly saddening and hurtful, no matter how many times it happens.

Taking a more philosophical position, Larry (actor) commented: "I have to learn from failing. It's a process of making mistakes. Babe Ruth, who was the home run king and has never been equaled, was also the strikeout king. You have to get things in perspective."

Using a baseball analogy, also, advertising executive Barry said:

I think there is a resiliency that you need. Things can fall apart in the first minute. You lose your belief in yourself if you throw a couple of balls right out of the gate. You've got to be resilient enough to bounce back from that. You have to have failed a lot and be used to failure and have the ability to overcome it and not let it destroy you.

Because of the long-term implications of decisions made in his business, David focused on the importance of being able to live with his decisions and avoid dwelling on them after the fact:

They're partial victories or partial performances, indications of performance, as opposed to somebody who's in the business of selling cars and one Saturday they sell more cars than they've ever sold before. Boom, they've done it. They can measure it and it's done. Here, sometimes it's winning a deal. That's a partial victory but at the same time you worry, "Did I really want that? Is it good that I won it?"

We have discussed the process of optimal performance chronologically: relevant factors prior to, during, and after the performance event. What of the performers' *experiences* during optimal performance? Here, we come back to the transformative experience.

The Performance Experience: What the Performer Feels

A final theme that emerged in our interviews with a number of the performers is the way in which performing may contain transformative qualities, whether those relate to a sense of "oneness," alteration in the experience of time, spiritual issues, or a sense of "flow" (Csikszentmihalyi, 1990).

While in the flow state, athletes routinely experience a transformation of the sense of time (Jackson & Csikszentmihalyi, 1999). Several performers we interviewed described similar perceptions. Norman (musician) deliberately attended to this through what he called "the creation of time." He commented on two pieces of contemporary music that were performed on the same program, one exceedingly slow and spacious and the other with many rapid notes:

To play the first, I simply had to tell myself that I'm going to create a certain kind of time between the notes; that I'm not going to allow myself—*ever*—to force a note to be where it doesn't want to be. Because there the microscopic nightmares of infinity are not even microscopic, they're huge. The gap between the notes is very large. And then to go to play the second one right afterward—it's only because I've drilled myself to do it, to be able suddenly to divide time into very small chunks. But even when I play the first, I'm also dividing time into small chunks for myself, because a note for me will have a beginning, a middle, and an end.

During surgery, time disappears. Eric elaborated:

It may take two or two and half hours to complete the procedure, but mentally it's five seconds. There is absolutely no pause in time. It just collapses when you are in the midst of it. If you look back over everything that occurred you realize that it has been a pretty prolonged period of time, but it just all runs together and collapses. For a lot of these operations, you just start and then finish and the concept of time is just stopped.

A number of transformative experiences were described as a sense of "oneness." Ellen (musician) spoke of music performance as a 300% experience, containing the physical, spiritual, and emotional or mental.

It's completely physical: You have to be completely physically coordinated. It's spiritual in terms of the way you're connecting with the audience and with the other performers. And then it's emotional or mental, because if you're really nervous or upset, that's going to create a block. If something isn't working, you have to focus on that and somehow get that going. A lot of the time I'm just sort of trying to get those three things in balance. I may feel like I'm simply tight somewhere, I need just to focus on relaxing muscles—it can be that physical and that basic. Or it could be that the energy is not focused in the group, which is mostly the spiritual thing. Or that we're not communicating with the audience and we need to somehow get something more focused happening and more together. It's very seldom that all three things come together at once in a perfect way. But that's the goal. You get there, you touch it, and you come away. I think that's the nature of performance.

Early in her career, Charlotte danced with a passionate, frenetic style that created a transformed, but unaware state. Although the audience loved the energy of her performances, she had no recollection of the process after the curtain fell. She shifted to a systematic and deliberate calming of herself in order to relish the full awareness of her dancing.

Although I hated galas, I went to [X] because of the money. They were doing the full length version of Apollo, with the unwrapping from birth. The role is physically very taxing and I thought, "Oh my god, how am I going to do this, plus it's a gala, and the stress."

At the time, I was very busy with becoming a parent, and the cycle of life. While I loved my current ballet company, I felt that sometimes they were so focused on the newest, youngest, most exciting, most remarkable things that they ignored or forgot that as dancers became 30 or 35, they add a depth of experience that actually informs abstract ballet. To be doing a role that I had done many times, with the story put back in, and in my own life to be going through that sense of growing up, to be dancing as an adult with people who were from my childhood as an artist—all of those were part of why I looked forward to it.

They got me all wrapped. One of the first things is the Handmaidens come on and lean you backward, and you open your mouth and cry. I opened my mouth and made as if I were a squalling baby. I had this sudden vision of my own son lying there squalling, and that's the last thing I remember. But I know that it was a very good performance.

—Jerry (dancer)

Helena, also a dancer, spoke of the ways in which, for a number of performers, verbal language loses its meaning during performance:

I've never really been able to describe very well what's going on in my mind when I'm performing. I don't actually *think* when I'm performing. A little part of my mind is thinking about the technical aspects of holding on to this muscle to get this limb where it needs to be, or how to do this turn without falling over. But that's just one layer of what's going on. I think it is quite possible for people to be acting in a way, to be trying to inhabit a role as they perform, but I often don't find myself doing that. I find myself being the music, or being the movement.

Norman (musician) spoke of "shine," referring to the quality of the note and rhythm:

I draw every drop of inspiration from the notes and rhythms that I play. You want to find the flow, the groove, the spiritual feeling, the inner self, your own paradise that you created. I try to say: "This note has got shine on it." I feel the shine. I don't see the word, but I look for the quality of the note and the rhythm, and I feel those two things are locked together. And that the rhythm and its place—those things are locked together. If there's any way to create it, I would create it by a sense that those two things, the note and the rhythm, are totally locked hand in hand, like Siamese twins.

Ellen (musician) was aware of the evanescence of extraordinary moments during a concert:

> My experience in performing is that in most concerts, if you're lucky, there's a moment—the moment may last for 30 seconds or on a good day for even two minutes—a moment when you feel completely at one. Everything is growing and it's all happening just the way you mean it to be. Most of the time there's something in the way. You're either nervous or something's not functioning in the group quite right or there's a loud noise or somebody is chewing loudly or coughing. Or there's something distracting you—your mind is wandering or you're tired. But there are certain moments in a good performance when everything is just working and all that stuff doesn't matter or it's not happening, it's just totally focused performing.

Describing her deep level of concentration, radio personality Grace illustrated her experience of focus and corresponding effortless action.

> There are times when you are firing on all cylinders, and when that happens, everything darkens around the edges and you're super-focused. When I am listening very intently to someone, I do not hear anything else. It all starts shutting down around me. And when I am listening, my brain is just firing like a computer. Everything the person is saying is tripping a hyper link—an association, an idea, a concept. As you're telling me something, I am cross-referencing in my head. I am not trying to do it; it just is happening. It just seems so beautifully obvious that it seems almost embarrassing to say it out loud. Like, "This is what we're ALL thinking!"

Some of the performers—none of whom defined themselves as especially religious people—specifically described the transformative experience as containing spiritual aspects.

Diane spoke of the interaction between performer and music:

> For those of us who really love it, music is like a religion to us. I say "us" to include people who really feel a great affinity for what they're doing. I'm sure there are a lot of bored musicians who would just as soon be doing something else, but music to me is a very spiritual thing. We have this connection with these composers. Bach's been dead how many hundreds of years and how many people have experienced his music? I always feel like every time we play something, I think of the connection with all those long gone people, and that we're almost reliving what the composer and the people that have heard it and

played it have experienced. To me it makes some sort of sense of the universe a little bit. There's a sense of connectedness there.

Somewhat mystically, Norman (musician) alluded to stripping away the veil of illusions in which we all swath ourselves. Extraordinary playing

is often described as a religious experience. Is it the veil of illusions that all writers and poets talk about? We don't have one word that says what that veil of illusions is. There are no real words in it. Whatever that feeling, you have the illusion that the prison that you create for yourself, or the paradise that you make for yourself, that it's all not true. Really the only thing is about tapping into the source of your own imagination, and your own source, the place where you find your inner temple, and inner space. It includes the ability to create time rather than be a victim of time.

For Larry, the relationship between actor and audience can take on a spiritual dimension:

It's visceral communication; it's almost a spiritual communication. You just know. There's a sense of awareness, you actually feel your audience breathing. Although the concentration is on you and turns on that, it's a sharing process, it doesn't feel selfish. I perceive it with a stillness; there's a tranquility and stillness from the audience and from the performers. There's no effort involved in it. That sense of sharing comes through, there's a generousness to your whole being.

Recommendations to Consultants

- Several of the factors influencing flow are determined prior to the commencement of performance: clear goals, a performance plan, refocusing strategies, and group dynamics.
- In contexts where performance is more open-ended and involves problem-solving activities (such as medicine, business, and many of the high-risk activities), accurate assessment of the performing context is essential. Critical cues or elements in the situation must be recognized, and a course of action selected, based on that assessment.

■ The manner in which a performer presents himself or herself may differ significantly from his or her ideal performance state. A sense of confidence, or creating the appearance of confidence, is considered important in all domains. Consultants should help performers learn concrete skills to appear confident, even if they are not.

■ The willingness to risk and push the limits of one's abilities is an important part of peak performance.

■ Sustaining a performer's ideal performance state requires focus in the immediate moment and ongoing minor adjustments in accordance with feedback. Feedback may be external (from an audience or action) or internal (awareness).

■ Peak performance does not require flawless performance; it does require accepting mistakes, making any necessary adjustments, and continuing to maintain focus on the moment. The best performers are not the ones who are perfect, but the ones who are best at handling their mistakes.

■ Transformative experiences often involve a sense of time distortion, effortless activity, and (at times) a sense of spirituality or oneness with the universe.

■ Although one can set some of the conditions for transformative experiences to occur, in all domains these experiences appear to be outside of the performer's conscious control.

IV

What Do Performers Want?

The Help They Need: 12
Assistance Performers Want

I tend to over-analyze and over-complicate things. You need somebody
who can just calm you down and get you to focus on what's important
and boil things down to the essence.

—Barry (advertising executive)

We turn in part IV to the interaction between performer and consultant.
Performance consultants use a number of methods to offer assistance,
depending on their training, interests, and styles. Each consultant may
have a niche, a specialty, or a method that shapes his or her perception of
performers' needs. A consultant's specialty, however, may also be a liability. We are mindful of the aphorism attributed to Abraham Maslow:
"When the only tool you own is a hammer, every problem begins to
resemble a nail."

We asked both consultants and performers what areas or concerns
might require assistance. In analyzing the responses, we began with the
performers' perspective by asking the following question: "When you
think of the ideal consultant, what kind of skills or assistance would they
provide?" We have supplemented their responses with those of our consultant interviewees. We have also highlighted some of the contrasts
among consultants, differences that are a result of their training, background, or objectives. Consultants may find these comparisons a reminder
to consider a range of intervention options, rather than just "to look for
a nail."

We explored the issue of performance assistance in two ways. First,
we simply asked each performer what assistance he or she would like a
consultant to provide. For a number of our interviewees, the area of
performance consultation was a new concept; many were unaware of
the range of services and assistance available. Therefore, at the conclusion of our open-ended interviews we inquired about assistance a sec-

ond time, in a slightly different fashion. We offered a checklist of skills and services that have historically been provided by performance consultants who work with athletes (Appendix B). We asked whether the performer thought the skill or service would be helpful within his or her own milieu. Overall, this checklist of options often elicited enthusiastic support for services previously not considered. This response suggests that in many performance domains, considerable education is required to raise performers' awareness of the range of options available within performance consulting.

The responses can be clustered into four overall categories: assessment, education, support, and career development. Accurate assessment may involve appraising the individual or the system. The educational function includes the vast majority of interventions. Among these are technical information, interpersonal skills, mental skills, and intrapersonal skills. Support may include the emotional assistance, affirmation, and encouragement that are traditionally associated with counseling; it also can mean debriefing after critical incidents. Career development potentially focuses on issues in advancing within one's performance domain or exploring vocations in other areas.

Assessment

From the perspective of our consultants, a thorough and accurate assessment of the consultative situation is a critically important first step. The foundation of any consultation typically includes a determination of strengths, identification of problem areas, and the establishment of goals. Not surprisingly, assessment is consistent with the training, skills, and beliefs of psychologists who consult with performers. Traditional psychological training grounds one in the medical model of diagnosis necessary to inform treatment decisions as well as the use and interpretation of formal assessment instruments.

From the performer's perspective, however, the centrality of assessment was much less evident. To the extent that performers spoke of assessment, they acknowledged the value of assessment in its broader sense rather than formal testing or evaluation. Performers want a consultant to identify strengths and capabilities to help address problem areas—a perspective consistent with solution-focused or positive psychology. For example, as an insurance agent, Charles observed that a personal assessment of strengths would be helpful. Ian, in broadcasting, suggested that knowing the performer's weaknesses and insecurities allows the consultant to provide feedback without undermining the performer's confidence.

Performers in various domains underscored the value of observational skills, one of the elements of assessment. They emphasized both observation and interaction. The consultant should not only observe, but more importantly, give direct feedback on the observation. For example, in medicine, Eric suggested that it could be useful to work with a consultant

> with good behavioral observation powers, someone who could watch somebody work, especially in the operating room, and be able to turn that around and say, "These are some of your characteristics and traits, and with this type of characteristic and trait, we have found that you could probably benefit from this change."

Diane, a musician, also noted the value of observational skills:

> It would be helpful if they have good powers of observation. They could point out things that I may not be noticing about what I'm doing. They might notice tension at particular times. Or maybe they come and watch me perform as part of the consultation and try and see what they can figure out from there.

Various performers mentioned balancing evaluation with rapidity of feedback. Ilene (musician) said that it would be useful for someone to work with the performer long enough to be able to observe and provide feedback on patterns. At the same time, an important skill would be the consultant's "ability to read you quickly."

This speed of engagement, assessment, and development of potential suggestions was a defining characteristic cited by a number of different performers in various domains. Arthur (lawyer) suggested that it would be helpful if the consultant were able to develop "hypotheses" fairly rapidly. Characterizing lawyers as impatient, he commented that

> it would be important for someone to make at least a reasonable hypothesis rather quickly and start going down a path based on that hypothesis. Assuming it's half right, the person would be able to take small steps, to make adjustments, to see what works and what does not work.

Similarly, Barry (advertising executive) thought that it was important for the consultant to be blunt at times. "Don't be too sympathetic an ear and don't wait too long to allow me to come to the right answer. Sometimes, my performance really needs to be maximized quickly, so just tell me what to do."

What is it that should be observed or understood? Larry, an actor, presented a traditionalist perspective on assessment. He saw it as important "to have a good psychological understanding of the person, to know the roots of the person, to know what his or her family background was like."

For others, consultation assessment should be broader than the mental or psychological. Norman (musician) suggested a comprehensive role for the consultant:

> Depending on what level the psychologist is involved with the subject, if it's not a class but maybe it's a personal consultation, you have to look at every aspect of the person, the kind of work they do, the schedule of work they maintain, the whole range of what goes on.

In some areas of performance, assessment may involve teasing out the interaction between physical and mental concerns. Diane (musician) thought it important that the consultant be able to review and distinguish physical (as compared with mental) problems; that is, the consultant should make certain that the performer is doing everything possible for physical preparation.

This differentiation between physical and mental is critically important in ballet, which demands particular physical skills that are in part a function of individuals' anatomy. Jerry suggested that it would be useful to have an objective assessment of dancers' abilities and limitations and the extent to which they are physical or mental. He offered a potent example where accurate assessment would be critical in selecting the appropriate intervention. A dancer could experience anxiety about anatomical or skill limitations: "I don't turn well and I'm frightened." Alternatively, anxiety might determine the response: "I don't turn well because I'm frightened."

As reflected in these examples, most performers thought of assessment only as it related to their individual skills and abilities; almost none mentioned assessing relationships and interactions with others in the performance setting. One exception was Barry (advertising executive), who thought that it would be helpful to have assistance in understanding (i.e., an assessment) the needs and motivation of his most important audience. He meant his boss, the CEO to whom he reports. He said that he would want someone who could identify the CEO's emotional triggers as well as the appropriate responses that he (Barry) might make.

Education

Performers want a consultant to have more than basic counseling skills. They want someone with expertise to address specific concerns in their area of performance. In this section we discuss the background and special skills that they would like an ideal consultant to possess.

TECHNICAL INFORMATION

Technical information can encompass a number of elements, including the mechanical, physical, and physiological aspects of the domain. Many of the performers wished for a consultant who was knowledgeable about both the technical issues of their specific field and the more general skills of performance consultation. In advertising, Barry suggested that it would be useful to address mechanical or technical skills. He would want a consultant to be able to review and prescribe. The consultant should be able to say: "This is the area you should probably be looking to cover mechanically, technically, intellectually. These are the triggers that you should be looking for, and this is what you should be prepared to do."

Similarly, in banking, David would want technical skills from someone highly knowledgeable and experienced; someone who has been in the field for a while:

> I think in our business, what people would respect is the
> technical side of it, somebody very experienced. I don't see
> how anybody can help us if they don't really know our
> business. You have to really understand it. Having spent 15 or
> 20 years in the business field would be almost a prerequisite to
> being able to really help us in performance.

For those who perform with their bodies, technical expertise can involve knowledge of the physiological as well as mental aspects of performance. As a musician, Diane was aware that many musicians play their instruments while in pain. She thought a music consultant should be knowledgeable about the physical and mechanical factors involved in creating and sustaining pain. Beyond that, the consultant should be skilled in helping the performer cope with both the physical tension and the fear that often accompanies pain.

The two ballet dancers, however, differed in their assumptions about technical knowledge. Charlotte said: "I wouldn't be able to talk to [the consultant] on a technical level, because ballet is such a complicated technique, unless you've spent years and years at it."

Yet Jerry thought that it would be critically important for the consultant to be knowledgeable about the technical aspects of dance in order to assess a situation accurately:

> The consultant would have to know a hell of a lot about dance.
> I think it would be very important for the psychologist to have
> an objective judgment, to be able to know whether the

concerns that the patient has are real or not. Is the problem that the person has concerns that aren't valid?

In sports and athletics, performance consultants often serve as educators, providing reliable and accurate information on areas of concern. Ellen, a violinist, was the only performer to speak directly to this straightforward educative function. She thought it especially valuable for a consultant to educate performers regarding the interaction of physiology and fear:

There are some physical things that happen when you get nervous that get in the way. For example, there's a vestigial instinct that we all have as ex-apes. When we're scared, we grab. The apes do it, the monkeys do it so as not to fall off the branch—it's a fear response, and we all do it. It doesn't do us any good as human beings, but it's still there. If we get that fear response and we start grabbing, we can't play the violin. It happens to everybody, and people complain about it all the time. Or wind players who hold their breath and aren't able to breathe deeply. That's a very normal physical response to fear.

Whichever instrument you play, there's going to be a physical response to fear which is getting in your way. It's one that is absolutely instinctive, that every human being shares. Beginners—children, for example—play the violin and don't have any experience with performing, and the bow shakes on the string.

So what do you do when you have the fear? Somehow you have to deal with that physical aspect which is coming from an emotional place, fear. You have to learn to control it. I have learned that no matter how scared I am, this bow is going to go straight. It's not exploring the fear, it's just figuring out how to deal with it when it's there, and letting it flow, and not resisting and saying, "I'm afraid, I can't be afraid because then my bow is going to shake," [because then] it's going to shake worse. You have to somehow not be afraid of the fear.

INTERPERSONAL AND RELATIONSHIP SKILLS

Among the businesspeople, the attorneys were the ones who focused on intragroup and relationship skills. Anna commented about her colleagues:

There are some very successful lawyers who have no people skills. They may be good with clients but they're horrible with their partners or associates. The best lawyers I know have an ability to read other people, an ability to empathize with other people.

Our other attorney, Arthur, was focused on the value of teamwork: "I just keep coming back to 'teams, teams, teams.' Making people aware of how roles work together and how they sometimes don't work together; how people can find ways to communicate and listen a little bit better."

The importance and challenges of intragroup relations was recognized by a number of performing artists as well. As we noted in chapter 5, Charlotte pointed to the complexities of hierarchy, systems, and team dynamics within the world of ballet and other performing arts institutions. Chamber music groups and other small music ensembles are notoriously complex systems (e.g., Brandt, 1993; Steinhardt, 1998). In our own practices, one of our most challenging consultations involved a professional quartet attempting to deal with rivalries, interpersonal violence, and substance abuse. Norman (musician) commented on the value of guidance in working with others. He mentioned an organization, Chamber Music America, which holds an annual conference:

> Chamber Music America sometimes will have sessions at their conferences, almost like a counseling session. A trio may be having problems and decide to consult somebody. Maybe the violinist and cellist aren't getting along well. They're sick of each other. "Do you want to try and resolve the situation, or does one person want to leave?" Maybe neither one wants to leave, but each one wants the other dead. The psychology of it can get to the point where the group is not playing well because of the friction among the players. Usually it comes down to the relationship between two players.

From the consultant's perspective, Dr. Owen Osborne (consultant, theatre) described some intragroup situations in which a consultant might be of assistance: "Sometimes it's necessary to resign from an impossible situation. If an actor is being emotionally abused by a director or being asked to endure impossible work conditions, then that actor really has to look at resigning as an option." This example also illustrates the ways in which a consultant ought to understand the theatrical world and the interplay between actors and other personnel, as well as the individual with whom one might be consulting. What is endemic and contextually relevant, and what goes beyond the bounds of appropriate consultation? We explore this balance more fully in chapter 15.

MENTAL SKILLS

Mental or psychological skills training is a hallmark of consultation with athletes. A number of performers wanted assistance with the development or use of these skills. The spontaneous mention of these skills seemed to be strongly related to whether there had been prior exposure to mental skills concepts. George, the medic and police sniper, had pursued a formal study of mental skills training to address performance issues. He suggested activation management skills, positive self-talk, and confidence building as specific issues that a consultant might address. Although the physicians did not mention any specific mental skills during the open-ended questioning, they endorsed a number of the mental skills on the checklist as areas where assistance would be helpful. These included imagery, refocusing, pre-performance mental readying, confidence, dealing with fears, and dealing with loss.

The mental skills specifically requested by businesspeople included goal clarification, imagery, and attention management. With regard to goal clarification, Arthur (attorney) suggested that it would be important to "try to articulate goals and set standards." On seeing the options on the checklist, each businessperson noted the importance of dealing with loss. For Barry (advertising executive), it would be helpful to "be able to define success and failure, and know how to respond appropriately." Another attorney, Anna, reflected on the issue of losing cases. Despite the intellectual knowledge that it was to be expected and that she had endured the process numerous times, each loss was difficult.

Among the skills described in more detail were imagery, performance plan, and attention management. Performers gave examples of the ways in which a performance consultant might assist the performer in developing these skills.

Imagery

Charles described the value of a consultant teaching him how to visualize specific upcoming situations in insurance. For him, this type of mentally scripted imagery is central to the success of a call.

Ellen, a musician, was well aware of the power of imagery and would want a consultant who could facilitate those skills. Although she used the more restricted term, visualization, she was describing imagery in its richest sense, as she spoke of the sensory, emotional, and contextual details of the mental experience of peak performance:

> People aren't clear about what it would feel like to be a successful performer. In a quiet, relaxed moment when you're not performing, think about—in other words, visualize—what that would be. To you, what would feel like a really great, satisfying performance? What would it *be* like, what would it *feel* like, what would it *sound* like, what would it *look* like, what would be the audience's experience? What would you experience? What would your colleagues experience? How

would the music be different from a humdrum performance, a "just another day, another dollar" kind of thing? What would really be a peak experience for you as a performer? If you know where you're going, then you can spend some time visualizing it, trying to get there from here.

Performance Plan

As someone who struggles with the discomforts of auditioning, actor Keith would welcome assistance developing a performance plan. He had tried various methods with intermittent success; he recognized that a predictable plan could allow him to trust his knowledge and skills:

> Particularly in auditions, keeping myself *open* would be the biggest gift I could get or give to myself. I like to go to an audition space maybe a day before [to become accustomed to it], but I'm always disappointed that at the audition, the smallest things seem to really throw me off. There might be a person there who I didn't expect to be there. Suddenly I just spiral so quickly, and I find that it builds on itself. The next time I go, I feel like, "Oh, I'm feeling really good today," but then I replay the previous experiences and I feel so frazzled, I'm like, "Oh all it's going to take is someone coming in through that door with a cup of coffee and I'll be thrown off." I really distrust myself.

Attention Management

Concentration and focus are a primary concern for the majority of performers. Among all the performers we surveyed, only one did not endorse assistance in refocusing as beneficial. This sole exception was David, a pragmatic businessman, who dismissed the subject: "I think people are very focused, usually focused the way they need to be." This was in marked contrast to other performers in the business domain. In addition to imagery, for example, Charles suggested that learning how to focus was an important aspect of working in the insurance industry.

In dance, Helena commented: "For people who get almost totally freaked out by stage fright, I think a technique of finding a way to center, finding a way to almost get into a meditative grounding state, would be very valuable." Similarly, Charlotte noted the central function of concentration. Elaborating on her perspective that a performance consultant need not know ballet technique per se, she said: "The ability to concentrate is the most important thing. If they (performers) can concentrate, they can improve everything about their performance, technique included."

INTRAPERSONAL SKILLS

Self-Confidence

The desire for assistance in developing confidence was clearly noted in both the open-ended questions as well as the checklists, with 100% endorsement of the latter by all the performing artists and those in high-risk professions. In dance, Charlotte commented on the complex balance between retaining a sense of humility while maintaining confidence.

An expectation of perfection is the normative stated message in some performance areas. As we have noted, the importance of adaptive, as compared with maladaptive, perfectionism is one that is currently under investigation among sport psychologists (e.g., Gould et al., 2002). Its application to other performance areas, such as dance, is being explored as well (Gould & Pennisi, 2002; Hamilton, 2002; Hays, 2003; Krasnow et al., 1999). Reworking perfection strivings can have a salutary effect on performance and self-confidence.

Lawyers may experience a conflict between the demands and roles placed on them and their own needs. With clients who are dependent on them, lawyers may wish for someone who can bolster their own sense of self. Anna suggested:

> Some lawyers need someone to sort of pump them up. They need to have a relationship with someone else that is similar to the one that the client has to them—someone who is more an authority figure for them and is going to give them a sense of self-confidence.

Problem Solving

Some performers want assistance in dealing with specific identifiable problems rather than enhancing an already satisfactory performance. In certain instances, problem solving may relate to group or systemic issues. In others, the concerns may be endemic to the profession or specific to the individual.

Banker David illustrated the ways in which a performance consultant might assist with problem solving.

> We had an administrative assistant working with us who was 29 years old and died of breast cancer. That was really tough on a lot of us. We never dealt with that firsthand—not her death, but the time while she was very sick. Nobody knew how to go about it.

In dance, Charlotte recognized that pressure is not restricted to the principals and soloists; it exists through the entire dance hierarchy: "No matter who they are, whether they're in the corps de ballet and they're being thrown into a new place in the corps de ballet or whatever, they have to cope with pressure."

Diane (musician) suggested that learning how to get beyond prior negative experiences would be an important skill. Larry noted the challenge actors experience because of performing in public. Actors may need assistance in learning how to handle the experience of public failure.

Frederick (emergency room physician) suggested that it would be useful for a consultant to deal with a flaw that needed correction, such as temper or anxiety management.

Balance and Perspective

A consultant might assist the performer in developing and maintaining a sense of balance and perspective. While articulating her own resolution of this issue, Grace (broadcaster) suggested that a consultant could be of help in this regard. She found that the way to maintain a sense of balance was to locate herself in the present moment and to maintain focus in the here and now:

> It would be helpful to have the big picture. For me, I have the big picture: We're all dying here, and a minute only takes 60 seconds. That's the big picture. Once you look at that, you can narrow it down a little bit. The next shutter down is: I have this four hours in front of me. That's what I need to do right now. That's where I am. It's very Zen; I'm in the moment.

Support

The types of support our performers wanted were described in a number of ways. Barry, an advertiser, would look for reassurance: "Let me know that other people have overcome this and it is not as difficult as I might have thought. Or if it is difficult, prepare me for what I need to do." Additionally, he would value "a motivational kick as well, the old 'you can do it.'"

Similarly, Larry (actor) suggested that it was important to convey

> a strong sense of belief in the performer, "Yes, you can do it."
> And it's also important to allow [performers] to understand
> that when they're out there, they're not alone. Or that if they
> are, to be comfortable with that aloneness.

George underscored the experience of aloneness of the performer and the resultant need for support. With the stress of potential incidents in his roles as medic and as sniper, he commented on the importance of having someone available for support and debriefing after an incident.

Having encountered a negative consulting experience in which the consultant had not maintained confidentiality, Ian (broadcaster) was explicit in his insistence on a consultant's personal support and commitment. Ian had disclosed what he had thought was confidential information; the consultant had not kept that information confidential, and as a result Ian lost his job. He expressed the importance of feeling as though the consultant were working for *his* benefit rather than for management.

The value of support in assisting performers to appreciate the importance of their striving was also recognized. Using a more psychotherapeutic perspective, Jerry (dancer) suggested that support is useful because

> once a person doesn't feel so bad, so guilty, so ashamed about what it is they're doing that they see as shameful, then they'll stop wanting also to see their expression of themselves on stage as something that they need to be criticized for.

Career Development

Career development was not typically mentioned during the open-ended questioning, but it was gladly welcomed when proposed on the checklist. Every performing artist who completed the checklist saw career development as a desirable skill. Charlotte (dancer) noted the importance of a developmental focus in consultation, "to help people cope with wherever they are, at whatever stage they are, and do the best they can at that stage. If they do well enough, they'll move onto the next stage." It is also noteworthy that international programs have been developed for issues of career transition among dancers (Hamilton, 1997, 1998).

The attorneys were particularly vocal about the importance of this area. Anna exclaimed, "Oh boy, there's a huge market for that! Lawyers are desperately unhappy." As noted in chapter 3, as she was leaving the law firm in which she had practiced, Anna heard directly from her colleagues of their distress with their professional lives.

In contrast to the other performers in various domains, the physicians interviewed did not see discussion of career development as relevant to the possible functions of a performance consultant, even when proposed as a potential area of focus. This lack of interest may have been an artifact of the small number of interviewees in each category, or it may reflect career satisfaction in a profession in which the performer can anticipate considerable longevity.

Recommendations to Consultants

- Many performers are unaware of the range of assistance that a performance consultant might offer. Consultants should be prepared to engage in extensive education regarding the options, resources, and potential benefits of performance consulting.
- Consultants who have a unique niche, specialty, or method should be cautious in "selling their product" to performers. Because of their lack of familiarity with consultation, performers may not have the knowledge to make informed choices regarding consultation. A conscientious consultant will educate the performer of the range of options available and be guided by what best meets the performer's needs.
- It is critical that a consultant be capable of providing rapid (a) assessment of a performer's abilities and needs and (b) subsequent feedback and suggestions for intervention. Performers appreciate information that is shared in a direct and collaborative manner.
- Most performers think of assessment as involving observation and interaction rather than psychological measurement. Direct observation of performance may be required for performers to consider feedback to be valid.
- It is crucial that an assessment distinguish between concerns that are based on physical skills and technical abilities and those that are mental or emotional in nature. Depending on the referral request and the consultant's proficiencies, the consultant may provide these disparate roles or enlist the services of someone with the appropriate expertise. As we discuss in chapter 15, a consultant should be conscious of the pitfalls of engaging in more than one role relationship with a client.
- Performers' expectations of consultation range from specific problem solving to providing feedback on virtually all aspects of performance. Consultants should clarify the scope and focus of efforts at the onset of consultation. If the consultant does not have expertise in the areas the performer wishes to address (e.g., specific technical knowledge, or expertise in relationships or group dynamics), the consultant should acknowledge those limitations and recommend other appropriate resources.
- A performance consultant should have a model and expertise in addressing issues of self-confidence and dealing with mistakes. These are fairly universal concerns among performers.

- The specific techniques of goal clarification, imagery, attention management, and performance planning are mental skills that performers comprehend and welcome.
- A successful consultant balances encouragement with open feedback within a supportive relationship.
- Providing support is important for all performers and is often intrinsic to the consultation role. It is especially important for those in isolated, isolating, or dangerous occupations.
- Many performers have significant concerns about career planning and development, but they may not know that consultants address these issues. Consultants may want to consider developing expertise in this area, whether to facilitate a performer's advancement within her or his performance domain or to assist in career transition planning. The demand for these services is likely to be greater in domains in which career duration is restricted by physical limitations (e.g., ballet) and in which there are high levels of discontent (e.g., law).

The Ideal Consultant 13

In our business, a lot of consultants have preset ideas about what works. They think that if it works in one place, it will work everywhere. To a degree that is true, but very often it does not work exactly the same. People resent that attitude. They want to be consulted on their own unique gifts, challenges, and shortcomings, not on what has generally worked in a broad way. We all feel special. We are all unique. Consultants sometimes forget that people still want to be snowflakes.

—Grace (broadcaster)

n addition to the question of optimal assistance or services that a consultant might provide, we looked at the question of optimal consultant characteristics. We asked: What kind of personal characteristics would you look for in an ideal consultant? We then asked specifically whether age, gender, or ethnicity would be a factor in working with a consultant.

We noticed that many of our performer interviewees were unfamiliar with the concept of a performance consultant or performance psychologist, let alone having known of one or worked with one directly. Lack of familiarity may result in the creation of a person of mythic proportions, someone truly superhuman. However, our performers were reasonable in their expectations. We have included numerous samples of their comments to provide a collage of what performers are seeking. Performers' responses were clustered to reflect issues of credibility, the consultant's style and manner of consultation, and aspects of interpersonal functioning. We augmented these responses with comments from our consultants.

Credibility

Credibility can be established and recognized in a variety of ways. As professionals, we often think of formal credentials as being a cornerstone of credibility. In truth, the performers never mentioned formal credentials when discussing the ways in which a consultant might be knowledgeable and skilled. For them, credibility derived from a combination of experience, knowledge, and valuing of the domain. The consultants underscored the importance of experience and knowledge.

EXPERIENCE AND KNOWLEDGE

Across a number of areas, performers described direct experience in the domain as one of the most important criteria. Pianist Ilene said that a performance consultant for musicians should be "someone who has been or who is a musician, so that there is an understanding of what it's like."

Describing the world of theatre, Larry suggested that having direct experience with acting would be useful, although it needn't be at a professional level. A consultant who had taken an acting class or could claim "I did the backstage thing, I did community theatre, I've been out there alone" would understand and appreciate the complexities and challenges of the profession.

Speaking more broadly about performance, violinist–conductor Ellen recognized that there can be similarities among those who have stage experience: "It's helpful if somebody has been a performer of some kind at some point, having had the experience of getting up on stage and knowing what stage fright is, so that there would be some common ground, some shared experience."

Jerry (dancer) also recognized the value of generic performance experience: "My ideal consultant is someone who was a performer and moves into [consulting] out of interest. Being able to identify some area of your life as performance would be quite important if you want to help performers."

General rather than specific experience in the field may have particular advantages. Barry expressed concern about personality characteristics of people in advertising. Thus, he would want to work with someone with experience, but perhaps in a related area of expertise:

> I would probably trust someone who has experience in the
> field. But I have been finding that people in advertising tend to
> be very arrogant and to me that is kind of a turn off, so I
> probably would be looking for somebody who has a personality
> similar to mine and who has faced similar issues, but one who
> is in a business other than advertising.

Breadth of knowledge was emphasized by some performers. Considering a number of different performance domains, violinist–conductor Ellen thought that consultant knowledge of physical movement would be useful:

Movement is an important part [of music] and the more I think about the other performing arts, it's even more important for them. A lot of the problems are just not letting your body do [what's needed]. Working it out, working it out physically, because that's how we're doing it. We're all expressing ourselves through our bodies, whether one is a singer or a violinist or a dancer—and certainly in theatre, it's your body that is your vehicle. I can't think of an exception. Maybe one part of your body more than other parts, but somehow, you've got to get that going. So I think what would be important is somebody who has some experience performing, and somebody who's experienced working with movement, rather than just the talking part.

Knowledge, an important component of expertise, was emphasized by a number of the businesspeople. For example, David (banker) felt that the primary requirement would be extensive knowledge, experience, and understanding of the business, and he pointed out that this kind of knowledge takes time to accumulate. Charles (insurance broker), similarly, would look for someone with prior experience of successful consultation in the field.

Ian, in broadcasting, would want some demonstration or indication of practical credibility:

I'd look for credibility in a consultant: that you have some knowledge of what you are talking about and that you can actually help me be better. How can you help me? What is your track record? What are the skills or philosophies that you bring to the table that I can buy into?

VALUING THE DOMAIN

Along with having some knowledge and experience in the domain, having enthusiasm for and interest in the domain is valued by performers. This aspect was emphasized by a number of musicians and a dancer. It also reflects a perspective underscored by expert sport psychologists. In interviews with 11 well-known sport psychology consultants, Simons and Andersen (1995) found that despite various paths to entry into consulting, all "shared a love of sport, exercise, and human performance" (p. 452).

Recognizing the important mix of experience and appreciation, Norman (musician) suggested that the consultant should have skill in or passion for music. Faith, a singer, elaborated further. She said that it was important that the consultant have an interest in and appreciation for music and energy and enthusiasm for the kind of work the performer does: "Especially if they want to specialize in working with musicians, it would be helpful that they have some interest in music, some appreciation."

This interest may have to be broader than the specific field in which one consults. For example, music, as well as movement, are central to the dance experience. Thus, Helena (dancer) suggested that an important characteristic of a dance consultant would be being "open to music."

Michael (conductor) described a number of ways the consultant could demonstrate knowledge or valuing of the domain:

> There has to be some kind of affinity there. Consultants who deal with musicians would maybe actually love music and know a bit about it or be avid concert-goers. Or they would have seen or been around situations that musicians were in. They might have an easier time being trusted than those who have never seen a symphony play and are trying to work with a conductor. In that case, it might be a little bit harder to get enough connection going, enough trust.

Presentation of the Consultant

The way in which the consultant presents himself or herself can be an important determinant of successful consulting. We looked at a number of elements that enter into self-presentation, including physical characteristics as well as affective, verbal, linguistic, and attitudinal aspects. Some of these descriptors could be neatly separated out, although for a number of performers, it was the cluster or gestalt that would be significant.

Some professions value certain specific physical characteristics. In broadcasting, for example, Grace reflected: "My business is a little more open to diversity of appearance than others. Bleach your hair, pierce your nose, whatever. In fact, to be honest, we tend to think those people may be a little more creative."

Some individuals have specific preferences. Faith (singer), for example, would want to work with a consultant who is neat in appearance and whose workspace is tidy.

Numerous people mentioned the importance of empathy to effective consulting. Without empathy, a consultant's knowledge and expertise are useless. World-renowned business consultant Dr. Adams proposed that empathy is the very cornerstone of effective consultation.

You need to be a cultural anthropologist. You need to be able to study that world to see how to present yourself in ways that speak their language and that make them comfortable. I don't think most psychologists feel that comfortable with some of the worlds that we're in right now. They don't present themselves in ways that would be acceptable to a businessperson. They would be quickly discounted, their skills would be quickly discounted or discarded because they're not presenting it in the business culture, which means having the right kind of language, the right kind of clothes, the right kind of presentation.

—Dr. Claire Crown (consultant, business)

Prior experience can affect one's current consulting preferences. Barry (advertising executive) drew on his athletic experience, using the model of an athletic coach as a prime example of the general style he would want in a consultant:

In the past, I responded best to coaches who were brutally honest and straightforward and sometimes even a little hurtful, but very motivating. Sometimes, you need somebody to help you step out of your own body and figure things out. I would probably respond well to somebody who is more like a classic [athletic] coach.

My son went to some hockey camps last summer and he hated half of them and loved the other half. He most recently said, "Boy, Dad, it seems like the camps I hated the most were the ones that did me the most good."

The type of affective intervention he would want also derives from Barry's athletic experience: "Sometimes things were said in a nice way and sometimes things were said in a humorous way, but it was always in an emotional way. I have always responded well to kind-hearted but emotional coaches who talked straight."

Throughout the interviews there was consistent reference to the importance of a consultant's verbal skills and language. The quality of voice, the lack of didactic or repetitious language, and the use of the performer's language were all mentioned by various performers. This latter element—speaking the person's language in a pragmatic, easy-to-understand fashion—was critical across performance domains. This point has long been recognized within sport psychol-

I used to always dress up and wear a coat and tie and so on and then after a while, I got to saying "Hell, one of us ought to be comfortable."

—Dr. Brian Bell (consultant, family business)

In working with people in marketing and some other areas of business that are more sales oriented and where there's actually more women in the group, I've actually found situations where some of the sports analogies that I've used have just drawn a complete blank, like "That story about the New York Yankees was great, but what are they? Are they a soccer team? I don't know what you're talking about."

—Dr. John Jarrett (consultant, high-risk)

ogy consulting (e.g., Gould & Damarjian, 1998; Orlick & Partington, 1987; Simons & Andersen, 1995; Van Raalte, 1998). Dr. Gates, for example, commented on the importance of being "one of the guys" when working in high-performance sports: "It gets you in the door; but even more than that, it allows you to communicate with them because you are not 'too good' for them. There is the entry stuff, but also, you speak their language."

Combining physical, affective, linguistic, and general attributes, Arthur suggested that a consultant working with lawyers "would need to be at least half spry . . . [and] to be able to work the room physically. Even if the room was only eight people, or even if one were sitting, the consultant must not be very sedentary." It would be important that the person look experienced and present with confidence. From an affective perspective, "One would have to be relatively demonstrative, but also relatively controlled." The person would need to have a strong voice, one that is neither grating nor a whisper. For lawyers, Arthur thought, it would be important that the person not seem to be a consultant. "They would have to be very careful about using psychological jargon. Avoiding jargon is really critical. Lawyers will pick apart words. They'll kill you with words. Working with lawyers would be hard, because we live and die by words." As for the content of the language, Arthur suggested that "lawyers are now all sizes and shapes. Sports analogies sometimes don't work anymore, and I always thought they did."

ATTITUDE

Attitude refers to the general or global impression the consultant makes regarding his or her interest in the domain or consultee. Some of the preferred characteristics might be specific to the profession; others may merely reflect personal preference. A few characteristics cut across professions. For example, Jerry (dancer) suggested that what would be best would be someone who was low-key, unflappable, and detached from the outcome of the performance. Acknowledging that a performer is often already struggling with expectations and attempting to please other people, he would want "somebody who doesn't look like they have a hell of a lot invested in what you do." Similarly, Norman (musician) described the value of "a sense of warmth without a lot of personal involvement." Diane (musician) suggested that she would appreciate working with someone who was "very honest and forthright."

More generally, Norman emphasized the importance of the consultant having a "healing" rather than "Svengali" mentality. This ability to connect and support in a profound way was one that he compared to playing with other musicians:

> Some musicians can draw the other musicians into playing better than they are. But some people are brilliant and exclusive when they get on stage, and actually make other musicians sound worse by their own performance.

This interactive quality was mentioned by Grace (broadcaster):

> Good listener. Self-deprecating. A person who is able to laugh freely and openly. There is nothing worse than a didactic consultant and there is nothing worse than a consultant who cannot conceal their boredom with you and the task at hand because they have dealt with it a dozen times.

Larry (actor) suggested that what was important was a strong sense of support for and belief in the performer:

> It's that gut level of awareness and empathy that actors crave, that they search for. I think a trainer should honor the performer—not the performer in himself, but honor the task they have at hand. It just centers everybody, because we all look for that respect and honor. It's a noble profession.

As an actor, Keith commented that what mattered was "someone who was caring, nonjudgmental, experienced, and also willing to learn." It would also be important that the person be collaborative and not "just say, 'Hey this is the way to do it.'"

The businesspeople emphasized various attitudinal characteristics. Both lawyers underscored the importance of presenting with confidence. Barry (advertising executive) cautioned that the person not appear arrogant, however.

This may be something of a contrast with characteristics preferred by performers in medicine and high-risk professions. A low-key approach appeared to be of more interest to them. Eric (neurosurgeon) noted that surgeons typically do not like to be told what to do. Consequently, it would be helpful to present with "Not a real forceful approach, more of a 'we could try this and this, and work with it awhile and see if it makes a difference and if so . . . '—less of a director and more of a facilitator."

George (medic–sniper) thought that an ability to relate and be casual, "shooting the breeze and hanging out with the boys and drinking beer," would be useful.

Frederick (emergency room physician) suggested minimizing paternalistic, trite framing:

> Make sure that you minimize in every way possible being the great white father. Don't use old hackneyed phrases like "I learn as much when I come to a different place . . . " [or] "I think of myself as being an insect, because all I am doing is cross-pollinating. I am taking things I learned from one consulting job and passing them on to the next consulting job."

INDIVIDUALIZED INTERVENTION

Orlick and Partington's (1987) analysis of critical components in consulting with Olympic athletes suggested that individualized intervention was one of the key elements in effective performance consultation. In our research, several performers specifically mentioned the importance of individualizing the intervention. Frederick (emergency room physician) suggested that the consultant should be "a non-black-and-white thinker. You have to operate at least to some extent in the gray zone and feel like there are multiple answers to any question, or you are dead meat."

Highly skeptical of performance consultants, actor Brenda was specifically clear that a formulaic approach would not work. Larry pointed out the importance of being able to communicate in the sensory mode that works best for the particular actor (physical, auditory, visual, taste, sound, touch).

Cellist Norman emphasized the importance of observation of the performer in action as a necessary condition for credible, individually tailored intervention:

> A performance therapist would have to really get to know a person and see them perform often. They would have to actually come to their performances and see them before, after, and maybe during to really be able to help them with performance strategies.

Barry (advertising executive) emphasized the need to balance experience with not giving pat solutions. He would look for someone who has considerable experience and can therefore put things in context: "Make me feel like you have had experience with 10 or 20 other people who have faced the same thing." Although he wouldn't want "a solution that comes out of a can," he would look for support. That might take the form of additional tools to prepare him for a difficult situation, or reassurance that the issue is not as problematic as he'd thought.

Interpersonal Relationships

A number of interpersonal factors contribute to the effective functioning of a consultant. We looked at the consultant's role function, the nature of the relationship, and the nature of feedback that is given.

ROLE FUNCTION OF THE CONSULTANT

Prior experience often determines future attitude. Having been "burned" in his earlier dealings with a consultant, Ian (broadcaster) would want to make sure that a consultant's role was to serve the client rather than to promote management's agenda:

> Most traditional consultants in radio are all working for management. I want to know your agenda. "Why are you there and who hired you? Are you there because the boss thinks I suck or are you there because the boss wants it to work here?" I would want to have confidence that you really are there to make me better.

There may be some domain-specific differences. Powerful physicians, such as Eric (neurosurgeon), suggested that physicians would look for a facilitator rather than a director, whereas the attorneys stated that strong leadership might be preferable. Arthur commented that "lawyers aren't going to want to lead, but at the same time, they are going to demand to be led."

NATURE OF THE RELATIONSHIP

One of our consultants, Dr. Benton (business), suggested that it was important for a consultant to be "someone who has two ears and one mouth and [who] uses them in that proportion." Knowing how to listen in an engaged way is critical: Dr. Bell commented that with businesspeople who are used to running the show and listening just to themselves, "if you are too tentative or too wishy-washy, too laid back, too much of a listener, you don't ever get to play."

In broadcasting (Grace) and music (Diane), mention was made of the importance of having the consultant be a good listener. Perhaps somewhat more cynical, Frederick (emergency room physician) spoke of the importance of good social skills. "The single best social skill is simply to constantly give the impression not only that you are listening but also that you are actually paying attention and analyzing what they are saying. That is the key."

For a full understanding of the performer's patterns, Ilene (musician) considered it important that a relationship exists in an ongoing manner over time. This is consistent with feedback from Olympic athletes, who in different studies have noted the value of working with the same sport psychologist over time (Greenleaf et al., 2001; Orlick & Partington, 1987).

Similarly, Charlotte (dancer) described the value of general availability:

> We have a physical therapist who works on [dancers'] knees and their ankles and stuff like that, and she ends up being a psychologist most of the time. The dancers go there and unload while she's working on their joints. She feels that some of them go to PT (physical therapy) all the time because they actually need to talk about things. They don't even need so much PT; they just need to talk about how they're feeling about what's going on in their career.

NATURE OF FEEDBACK

Performers want consultants to provide direct feedback on relevant issues in a timely fashion. They want results, and they want them fairly rapidly. Ian (broadcaster) commented: "Early on, I would need to have from you some little victory, some piece of wisdom that you impart or something about me that I am able to incorporate that makes me better."

> Consultants need to be able to connect with other people deeply and quickly and communicate that. They need to be able to cut to the chase to get to the core issue pretty quickly.
>
> —Dr. Brian Bell (consultant, family business)

Ellen (musician) suggested that visual feedback through videotape would be useful. She also spoke of the value of concrete and specific focus on the present situation:

> I wouldn't spend a whole lot of time exploring the depths of fear. Fear is the most normal thing in the world. I think what you have to do is learn to cope with it: identify it and own it and then get past it. Dwelling on its source may be a worthwhile activity at some other point, but I don't think that's going to help the performance now. You're better off just saying: It's the most horrible thing in the world to be afraid, standing up there in front of thousands of people, when the stakes are high and you can't mess up. You're going to have normal fear reflexes, so let's talk about what you're afraid of and how you're going to deal with the fear when you feel it

coming up. What are you going to do? Are you going to resist it, push it away, or are you going to just incorporate it? How are you going to get it out? How are you going to let it go? I would deal with it rather than analyze it.

Performers in a number of domains expressed a strong preference for informative, collaborative consultation rather than directive consultation. Diane (musician) commented that the consultant can bring issues to a performer's awareness that they can then address. Eric (neurosurgeon) suggested a kind of smorgasbord approach:

I would like it if a consultant could provide me with a list of patterns or activities that people utilize to prepare for surgery. Personalities are so varied that you are not going to find that the whole list is beneficial to everybody, but I think you would be able to look through a list and say, "This may be something that could really be helpful" or "That is not anything that I could utilize." You'd need to do this knowing that we are fairly ignorant about all that. We do not have any history of saying, "Joe Blow does this and that is kind of neat. I want to try that technique," or "I'm not interested in that." Trying to steer somebody down a path is probably going to be less successful for neurosurgeons than to kind of give options and make them feel like they are directing it themselves. You're building the ego, so to speak, but you're allowing a self-discovery process that probably would be adopted and utilized faster.

Michael (conductor) suggested an alternate form of information sharing through diffidence:

A person has to have his own realizations and needs to decide for himself what is true. Anybody can help a person who is doing a good job. And the person can look at the factors that are in his life, what is going on there, and take a look at them, and put two and two together and make a better go of it because of that.

If I was consulting with someone, helping somebody, I would certainly ask, "Have you thought about this, have you thought about that?" I like to put things in this way: "This is what I have found for myself to be very helpful." And it resonates with the individual, and he or she can say, "Oh yeah, I can see that, I see that in my own situation, yesterday blah blah blah, and that's what happens with me." And it helps to improve a person's life. I'm very careful in that I don't want to enforce my views on somebody else. I like to simply put it in terms of letting someone know what has helped me.

Biases

Having asked about various personality and style characteristics of the ideal consultant, we were also curious about bias in the different domains. We wondered whether performers had certain biases with regard to the obvious visible characteristics of age, gender, and ethnicity. Recognizing that there could well be a tendency to present a "politically correct" image of utter neutrality, we asked not only about the specific performer's own preferences but also about their expectation of others in their profession. In regard to age, for example, Diane (musician) commented that the age of the consultant was not an issue for her personally and that, more broadly, it would not be relevant for others in music.

At a general level, Keith (actor) commented: "I don't really feel like it would make an enormous difference. I've found some valuable insights in some of the least likely places." As a realist, Dr. Bell (consultant, business) recognized that whereas demographic characteristics might not be significant after the initial contact, they might well affect the likelihood of "getting in the door."

AGE

We had anticipated neutrality for the most part but were surprised (and, given that we've been around for a while, personally somewhat relieved!) to find that to the extent that performers saw age as relevant, they expressed interest in working with someone older rather than younger. For some people, it was a matter of working with someone within their age range—and our interview participants, by virtue of our expertise criteria, were themselves not beginners. For others, this preference was directly tied to an assumption that age most likely related to number of years of experience and competence.

A number of people in the business domain responded to this issue. Charles (insurance broker executive) suggested someone older than 35. Barry (advertising, age 43) would want a peer or someone a bit older. Arthur (lawyer, age 51), was quite specific: "Probably being 40 is better than being 30. Looking 40 is better than being 45 and looking 35. Maybe someone who is a little older and has taken a few turns around the track." Making the age aspect relational, Anna (lawyer, age 51) commented:

> To me, gender or ethnicity are irrelevant. I think age *is* probably a factor for me. I doubt that I could have the type of relationship that I would envision wanting from such a person, with somebody who was very young. I would probably want somebody who was within my age group. I probably wouldn't

Initially, I think age is kind of important. There are some impressions that you might have to get over. We've got a lot of high-tech companies around here and mostly the people that do those are young. In a lot of family businesses, members of the founding generation are my age or near it. They don't do e-mail, they don't do computers, but their kids sure as hell do. So, they kind of take to me at first figuring that I don't know one end of the computer from another. Sometimes I use that. I *do* know one end of the computer from the other, but I may disparage that and say "Well, you can't high-tech everything. You've got to know what the hell you are doing, too." All that does is just help you get in the door, get some rapport.

The younger ones are more likely to assume that because of my age [64], I don't know diddly about what they are trying to accomplish: getting a management information system and people who are computer literate, and getting the old man to understand that there is more to running a business these days than just yakking on the telephone. We all start with these kinds of vices and assumptions. We have to work with those or against them or overcome them.

—Dr. Brian Bell (consultant, family business)

want somebody a lot older or a lot younger. You might have a problem really believing that a younger person could have insight that you wouldn't have.

Pragmatically, Eric (neurosurgeon) suggested that age would be irrelevant to neurosurgeons unless there were a large age discrepancy: "If there is a huge age difference, it probably wouldn't be as beneficial to them. It's kind of that 30–55 stretch where time stands still." Similarly, Dr. Dean (consultant, business) commented that age can become a factor if the mismatch is too great.

A few people noted the likely relationship between age and experience. Ian (broadcaster) said that he would discount information from a person who was both young and inexperienced. David (banker) articulated this interaction:

Age would matter only to the extent that it translated into relevant experience—and that indirectly would correlate with age. If somebody walked in 18 months out of graduate school, that would be a lot different from somebody who has been doing it for 20 years. There would be a lot more chance of respecting that person's opinions. They wouldn't have to prove themselves as much. The new graduate might still win everybody over, but it would be a harder sell.

GENDER

A number of the (male) businesspeople suggested that businesspeople would prefer working with a man, as Charles (insurance broker) com-

> I sometimes have difficulty with somebody who's significantly younger than me trying to tell me, "You should be doing this, that, and the other." I went to a sports clinic a couple of days ago, and part of the time I was feeling like an old curmudgeon and saying to myself: "Come on, Helena, now just relax. These people probably know lots, and they can be really helpful to you." But I just found it very difficult to get over thinking that I was practically old enough to be the doctor's and the physiotherapist's mother. And I just found myself resenting the fact that they hadn't gone through half of my life experience, and so they just don't have the frame of reference that I'm coming from. Maybe they'll luck into exactly the information that I need, but I somehow trust somebody who's got at least the mileage behind them that I have.
>
> —Helena (dancer)

mented, "because it's a predominantly male business." This observation was acknowledged by some of the male business consultants. Among Dr. Colin Cross's staff are women business consultants. Confounding gender and professional background a bit, he nonetheless commented with considerable frustration,

> Whether we like to accept the fact or not, we still have people in decision-making positions in the industry who are male. And if given a choice between a male with a sports background or a female without one, invariably they'll choose the male. About 80% of them will choose the male with the sports background.

However, the only female performer we interviewed in the business domain, Anna (lawyer), commented on the variable nature of preference for one gender or the other. She reflected that "depending on the interaction—the dynamic—sometimes it can be a real plus to be the opposite sex, and sometimes it can be a real plus to be the same." Dr. Adams also thought that being female or an ethnic minority could be advantageous at the present time. He believed that affirmative action had created an atmosphere of opportunity for women and ethnically diverse individuals.

The performers in high-risk medicine were clear about preferring to work with a man. George (medic–sniper) said that a man would be easier to open up to. Eric said:

> Gender in the field of neurosurgery probably would be an issue at some point, because there are very few women in the field of neurosurgery. I don't think anyone has a strong preference, good or bad with it, but it's just that the field hasn't been heavily penetrated and I think you would find that some people would not be as comfortable with a female.

Similarly, in emergency medicine, Frederick saw gender trumping ethnicity—though less because of gender per se and more because of heterosexual energies:

> I think that by and large the white male emergency room physician would relate much better to a white or black male. When you are spilling your guts, you don't want any issues of sexuality to play a part. I think it would be much easier for a woman to go to a man because women don't look at every man and think whether they want to go to bed with them or not.

Helena (dancer) would also opt for a same-sex consultant. For her, issues of sexism and heterosexuality could then be eliminated from the initial interchange:

> I usually feel more comfortable talking to a woman. Generally, if I'm talking to a man who is in a sort of counseling or therapeutic position, there's a bunch of defenses that I have to get over before I can deal with whatever the issues actually are. It's easier for me to start without those defenses so that I'm closer to dealing with whatever the actual issue is at hand.

Interestingly, some of the consultants working with high-risk performers saw potential advantages to women as consultants in these fields. Dr. Gates suggested that women working with race car drivers might have some advantages, as long as they minimized sexual cues in their dress and demeanor and were able to tolerate a traditional and blatantly sexist environment. Some of Dr. Lindsay's female students were unexpectedly more effective in working with Navy SEALs in training than were the male consultants. He hypothesized that the naval trainees felt the need to maintain a "macho" façade with male consultants, whereas with female consultants, they "didn't have to act any part."

> Because I'm in a helping profession, sometimes I don't realize how Machiavellian business often is, or how sociopathic people will behave, or how much the sole motivator is often money. I've often projected some of my own needs or experiences onto the situation, whereas in fact it's a different culture and I've misread it.
>
> Women in particular have been misreading the men's world and men's motivation, thinking that relationships count more than they do. People have done things that totally shocked us. We never expected them to do such dirty or manipulative things. And they do. And then our coaching hasn't been as effective.
>
> —Dr. Claire Crown (consultant, business)

These very mixed perspectives on gender suggest that there may be increasing fluidity even within some traditionally closed systems. It may also be important to distinguish between issues of entry and issues of acceptance. Ultimately, a female consultant entering a traditionally masculine environment must be deliberative about how she establishes legitimate credibility and professional relationships.

ETHNICITY

All of the performers interviewed were White. Few had any comments about ethnicity. Frederick (emergency room physician) raised the possibility that a Black male physician might think that a White male wouldn't understand his perspective. As mentioned, Grace suggested that in broadcasting, diversity is accepted and valued. "In radio we are much more open and loose. I actually have a slight bias against the Caucasian gray suit–wearing man, because we have had some bad experiences with them."

Recommendations to Consultants

- Although professionals may place a great deal of stock in formal credentials as a means of establishing credibility, performers do not. Performers assess credibility by looking at a consultant's experience, knowledge, and his or her valuing of the performer's craft.
- A consultant will typically be viewed more positively if he or she has some form of performance experience. It does not have to be at the same level or necessarily in the same domain. The mere fact of having experienced the demands and expectations of performance enhances the belief that the consultant can empathize with the performer.
- It is crucial that the performer experiences the consultant as empathic. This is the cornerstone of an effective relationship and consequently the foundation of successful consulting.
- Each performance domain is a unique culture. A consultant is advised to become a "cultural anthropologist" and learn the culture's language, customs, and attire. The consultant can "mirror" that knowledge by selecting the "appropriate" language, attire, and actions.
- Performers value a consultant who shows empathy and support and can work with them in a collaborative fashion that recognizes their own strengths and expertise.

- Preference for the manner in which feedback is presented may vary from performer to performer. Consultants are encouraged to explore with the performer how he or she best receives feedback and then respond accordingly. Consultants accustomed to a traditional, nondirective approach most likely must learn how to be more engaged and direct.

- It is important that the consultant be able to rapidly establish a trusting relationship with the performer, assess the situation, and provide feedback in a timely fashion. Providing feedback and suggestions that prove beneficial to the performer is perhaps the most potent means of establishing credibility.

- More youthful consultants may be at a disadvantage in performance consulting, as numerous (experienced) performers preferred older, more experienced individuals. Younger consultants are advised to be respectful of these concerns, to acknowledge the limitations of experience, and to emphasize their usefulness as a collaborative resource rather than an "expert with the answers."

- It is not clear whether gender or ethnicity biases play a role in the selection of a performance consultant. There has been some indication that being male might be a slight advantage in gaining initial access to consulting in high-risk domains, but there is also compelling evidence that women may be equally (if not more) effective in dealing with stress-related issues in that same domain. This topic requires further research and clarification.

- There are several indications that the ideal consulting relationship is forged over a significant period of time. Consultants must be prepared to be available to the performer "for the long haul," albeit at varying levels of involvement.

Consultant Efforts That Hinder Performance 14

It would be troublesome if I got the message that indeed I am wrong, that there is something wrong with me. That would just perpetuate my cycles of crumbling.

—Keith (actor)

lthough one hopes that consultant efforts would have positive (or at least neutral) effects, consultant contact potentially can be negative or harmful. We asked: Are there things a consultant might do that might actually hinder performance? We asked because we wanted to know what consultants should avoid doing and because we thought responses might shed light on the antithesis: defining best practices. It was also an intriguing question because it offered performers an opportunity for spontaneous comment rather than routine responses to predictable questions. In addressing this topic, we also turned to our consultants, whose humility and insights from their own failures guided our understanding of the risks and liabilities in working with elite performers.

The athletes in Orlick and Partington's (1987) study of preferred consultant attributes described the worst consultants as having the following characteristics: poor interpersonal skills, poor application of psychology to sport, lack of sensitivity or flexibility to individual needs, limited one-on-one contact, inappropriate behavior on site, bad timing, and inadequate feedback. These issues were described by our interviewees as well.

We clustered potentially harmful consultant activities into three general categories: those that are off the mark, those involving poor skills, and those that involve problems with the consultant's personality. Performers also expressed various attitudes toward and biases about consultants and consultation that might have additional negative effects.

Off the Mark

Consultants can hinder a performer if they offer suggestions that are of little use or are unrealistic. The lack of domain-specific knowledge, resulting in advice or interventions that are unrealistic or inaccurate, was a potential concern mentioned by several performers. Arthur (lawyer), for example, commented: "A lot of law consultants come in and don't have a lot to say [of substance]. There is no listening going on and no diagnosis, but it's entertaining."

Our consultants observed that problems of unrealistic or inaccurate advice were typically related to problems with assessment. Although performers didn't use the same terminology, they shared the same concerns. Within the highly traditionalist, structured framework of ballet, Charlotte (dancer) noted that a performer's capacities could in some ways be impaired:

> If someone (a dancer) whose ego was already a little out of control was convinced that they were even better than they thought they were. Part of being mature in dance is that you have to understand your place in the organization. Not everyone can be a principal dancer.

In dance, anatomy is destiny. No matter how hard you work, you may not be able to be a professional. If you don't have the turn-out or the feet or the extension, it's not going to happen. [Dancers can be adversely affected if the consultant] assumes that because they want this so much, all that is necessary is to focus on helping them get it without recognizing their personal limitations. The role of the consultant as a psychologist may not be helping them to perfect their techniques or even deal with performance anxiety— it may be helping them to find another career.

—Dr. Donna Desmond
(consultant, dance)

Similarly, Norman (musician) suggested that it would be harmful if the consultant were to pump up performers beyond their abilities and not acknowledge the discrepancy between their expectations and abilities.

Harold commented specifically about the ways in which imagery training could be problematic to a musician. Because music is abstract communication, a particular mental image could restrict the broader expression of the music.

Experience may inure the performer to a consultant who gives poor advice. Ilene said that she had thought so much about performance issues for the past 30 years that "I doubt I would take any suggestions that I thought were bogus. I'm just really judgmental. If I thought they weren't telling me anything that was useful, I wouldn't listen to them any more."

One issue is not being adequately sensitive to the actual physical demands of a performance. I'm going to describe a sports situation, though it's equally applicable to the military. It's less so in business because there you are talking about cognitive skills more often than the physical requirements of performance.

A discus thrower was having a hard time staying focused. She just had too many distracting thoughts. I suggested: "As you get in the ring, why don't you just pay attention to the feeling of the weight of the discus in your hand." The idea was that you can't simultaneously really feel that, pay attention to it, and be distracted by thoughts going on inside your head.

I wasn't aware that for a discus thrower to focus on the weight in their hand means they lose awareness of their lower body. That is where the strength comes from for their throw.

This person just used her arm for throwing. She didn't lower her body to get the drive through the power of her legs. My suggestion actually interfered with her performance. A lack of sensitivity to the biomechanics and the actual physical demands of the performance situation meant that an intervention that made sense from a concentration standpoint, when put together with what the body has got to do, was not the right thing to suggest.

—Dr. Kenneth King (consultant, military)

David (banker) conveyed a similar attitude:

As strong willed as everybody is here, if somebody didn't think something was right and didn't want to do it, they just wouldn't do it. They might listen, they might try some things, experiment, but not for long if it's not working. They'd be quick to speak up and say, "Bullshit!"

From David's perspective, rather than hindering the performer, "the only harm would be the time and materials—the cost in dollars and time away from doing other things."

Dr. Bell's summary of "off the mark" consulting captures the flavor of this type of work. As a consultant specializing in work with family businesses, he recognized that inaccurate assessment, knowledge, or presentation can be problematic:

I think the biggest mistakes in working with family businesses are failures to really understand the family. If you haven't paid a lot of attention and you don't understand that family and what is going on there, you just do things that are dumb, naïve, and misdirected. It may be a great idea, but it is not going to work because you didn't deliver the message in a way that it could be heard.

Poor Skills

Sometimes a consultant may lack or be weak in certain skills, which hinders his or her ability to serve performers. Some weaknesses may lead to problems with presentation, not being able to match interventions with individuals, creating overdependence or undermining confidence, and providing inadequate support. We discuss these shortcomings in this section.

PROBLEMS WITH PRESENTATION

Difficulty with presentation may include problematic language, poor timing, or unskilled pacing. A number of these are basic clinical or consultation skills. However, as reflected by both the performers' concerns and the consultants' experience, in the pressure of a new contact or different use of one's skills, some seemingly ingrained skills can at least temporarily get derailed.

Trying to impress the performer can backfire. Barry (advertising executive) said, "Don't tell me all the great people you know right up front. Focus on me."

Sometimes, it's a matter of poor basic communication skills. Barry continued: "You have to be there in the room with me. It would be a problem if there were signs that you were distracted." Actors, commented acting consultant Dr. Owen Osborne, sometimes describe this kind of distracted inattention to the present as "phoning in" one's performance.

Problematic timing or pacing could involve giving the person too many things to focus on, suggested George (medic–sniper). Experienced consultants echoed the importance of pacing and incremental change as central to success. Dr. Cross, for example, used a term first developed by inventor Buckminster Fuller, trim tab adjustment, and elaborated:

> You don't try and change everything. If the Titanic had turned a half a degree south as it left England, there'd have been no movie. And the same thing is true with us. Yesterday I was doing a coaching workshop. One of the things the participants had to do was take a single goal and break it down and then come up with a performance goal. Then they got coached in it. We were trying to build self-awareness and self-responsibility in other human beings. One of these goals was building rapport with people. Someone picked an item and said, "Well this is not very big." And I said to them, "Think about it: if you start to work with building rapport with your people through more two-way communication and more two-way dialogue, in three months you're going to have a whole different relationship with them. You don't have to change the world, just this one small thing. You start to give people your undivided attention when they come in to speak to you in your office; four months later you will be in a whole different place with those people and understanding them.

Arthur (lawyer) suggested that the consultant is ineffective if he or she is merely entertaining rather than acting as an agent of change:

> A lot of law firm consultants specialize in what I would characterize as gossip. Sometimes information is involved, but mostly it ends up being gossip about other law firms and how other law firms practice, but the person who comes in with the gossip does not know how similar you are to what they are talking about. If there *is* a knowledge base to it—pay, where people went to law school, and that sort of stuff—hearing about another's corporate culture or deciding whether that corporate culture fits your own practice requires more than gossip; [but] you can't do that on an entertainment budget.

POOR MATCH BETWEEN THE INTERVENTION AND THE INDIVIDUAL

Pro forma solutions do not take the individual, the situation, and the consultative focus into account. The lack of an individualized approach can signal problems with consultant skill (Simons & Andersen, 1995). Charles (insurance broker) gave an example:

> If somebody in my business were not detail-oriented and the psychologist said, "This is an exercise that's very detailed. For the next two or three days, record what you do during the day, every fifteen minutes," I think a lot of people would bail out.

OVERDEPENDENCE

A consultant fostering over-investment by the performer can create difficulties. Simons and Andersen (1995) interviewed 11 well-known sport psychology consultants regarding their consulting practices. Dr. Ronald Smith, at the University of Washington, commented to Simons and Andersen about the problems of fostering athlete dependency: "I've . . . seen lots of instances where athletes have formed tremendous dependency relationships with sport consultants, and they can't make a move without that person. That's one thing I think is a negative rather than a positive" (p. 465). Among our own interviewees, Norman (musician) suggested that an over-reliance on the consultant could be problematic:

> If [the consultant] were to lead you to believe that your performance was somehow based on his or her helping you and you felt that you couldn't do it without the other person's help, that would be a detriment. "I've got to see my teacher

before I play this concert, I've got to get to the guru, I've got to see my spiritual counselor," that kind of thing.

TENDENCY TO UNDERMINE CONFIDENCE AND DISCOUNT EXPERIENCE

Support, including a sustaining sense of confidence in the client's capacities, would seem to be a basic element of counseling or consulting skill. Yet a number of performers recognized the delicacy of performers' beliefs in their own knowledge, skill, competence, and confidence. This category was one of the most frequently mentioned by performers in various domains. Whether in broadcasting, insurance, music, or medicine, the potential negative interaction between a consultant's power and a performer's ego loomed as a real threat.

Ian (broadcaster) remarked:

If a consultant criticizes in the wrong way or points out shortcomings in a way that undercuts your level of confidence, then that could hinder performance. You are out there on your own every day. There is no script and you bring to it what you bring to it. You have to bring a certain mental confidence. If [the consultant] undermines that, you can't perform.

Charles (insurance broker) indicated that performance would suffer if the consultant discounted the performer's experience and hitherto successful methods. Faith (musician) said: "The only thing that would be a detriment is if this practitioner made you have doubts about yourself."

Both physicians reflected on this issue as well. Eric (neurosurgeon) described the possibly serious, genuine life and death implications of such an interaction.

If someone is a successful practicing surgeon, I think you could undermine competence by trying to aggressively change this or that—to demean what people have been doing. I can picture someone coming in and saying, "Oh no, you've done this all wrong. You've got to do this and this differently." If someone really took it to heart, it could seriously shake his or her confidence. In surgery, you have to be confident in what you are doing. If you can't walk into a case and feel confident that you're going to get through that case regardless of what is thrown at you along the way, that's going to affect your ability to perform the surgery and the patient will suffer.

Frederick (emergency room physician) recognized the ways in which self-confidence can be undermined and the implications of that:

Let's take a person who has a poor self-image. You can obviously do things to further screw their self-image. You can do that to anybody. It doesn't matter whether they are in emergency medicine or anything else. If you've got somebody that is frail in that regard, a person who has grave self-doubts, if you want to, obviously you can take them out.

INADEQUATE SUPPORT OR FOLLOW-THROUGH

Consultants, but not performers, specifically mentioned the problem of inadequate support or follow-through. Dr. Barbara Benton (consultant, business) said, "Lack of follow-up or follow-through can be a problem. Even consistent top performers occasionally hit a wall. They need to see you ASAP and it would be a drawback if you're not accessible."

The importance of access was echoed by performers when discussing characteristics of the ideal consultant and was one of the key points made by athletes in the Orlick and Partington study (1987). Dancer Charlotte was explicit on the importance of availability, and Ilene (musician) underscored the value of an ongoing relationship over time.

The Personality of the Consultant

In today's practice climate, competing methods are used to attract potential customers. Though consultants may reason that the best way to obtain or retain business is to present a specific package to clients, a number of performers were leery of this method. Our expert consultants also saw packaging as an ineffective business method.

CLAIMS OF HAVING "THE ANSWER"

Performers were especially cautious about consultants who have The Answer. Arthur (lawyer) commented: "You can have somebody who is ineffective because he or she's come to sell one thing. He's got The Answer and he's going to share it with you and you're going to be happy." Barry (insurance broker) described this approach as "thinking you know it all. Having the answer right away."

The Answer can at times indicate a variant on the lack of individualization. Keith (actor) said:

> I would just find it very difficult if someone felt that they had it figured out, like: "This is what works for the sprinter I work

[To assess consultants' competency], I would want to see that they were the embodiment of what we were talking about here [training, professional credentials, etc.]. And even though they may be the embodiment of it, they shouldn't be evangelical about it. Some people go away and take a course and then they come back and they turn people off because they [claim to] have The Answer.

—Dr. Colin Cross (consultant, business)

with, so this will work for you. I know there are different circumstances, but this will work for you."

Maybe that *is* true, I don't know. But I'm a curious, inquisitive kind of person, and I don't take really well to people laying it out for me. So I suppose if that was true, I would like somebody to lead me to that conclusion and at least pay me the lip service of taking in all of the cruel and unusual demands of *my* industry, and *my* life. And then at the end, they could say, "Oh, this is exactly the same thing that we did for the sprinter."

In their interviews with expert sport psychology consultants, Simons and Andersen (1995) commented: "None of our consultants endorsed a 'cookbook' approach to mental skills training, and none of them claimed to hold the 'one true method'" (p. 458). Although this strategy for presentation may appear appealing to some, clearly neither performers nor expert consultants see it as valuable.

Grace (broadcaster) said that performance was actually hindered when the staff at her radio station were provided with

the molded stuff, the carbon stuff, the preconceived stuff. We were required: "Here is this promotion/concept/bit. It has worked really well in [another state] and so this is exactly how you should do it here." We did that here with an on-air contest that bombed miserably. It had been a huge success in [another city]. We "Xeroxed" the concept here and it bombed, because our city is not that city and this is not that radio station. Things are different here.

From painful personal experience (as he related in chap. 9, this volume), Michael (conductor) was vividly aware of the detrimental effects of the consultant-as-authority:

The consultant shouldn't set himself or herself up as an authority, because whoever needs help has to discover what's true. That's the only thing that has to happen. The person has to discover what's true for himself or herself. If the consultant can help the performer do that, that's great.

> You may have the competence to give technical advice, but it would be inappropriate because it isn't your place to do that, especially if the advice clashes with the advice of those who are responsible for the performance. That's a dangerous position to be in. Moreover, that leads to a kind of triangulation which happens all too frequently in the theatre world: People end up carrying the opinions of other people on their shoulders and that messes them up.
>
> —Dr. Owen Osborne
> (consultant, theatre)

OUTSIDE THE BOUNDARIES OF THE CONSULTING "CONTRACT"

What is the consultant's level of knowledge in the field? What are the services to which the consultant and performer have agreed? Although Jerry (dancer) thought that an ideal consultant would be someone who has been a practicing performer, he also said that for mental skills training, "I would think most consultants would have a hard time maintaining their credibility if they actually gave technical advice."

Performance can be adversely affected if the practitioner blurs the distinctions between consultation and psychotherapy. We discuss this issue more thoroughly in chapter 15. Differentiating between the roles of performance consultation and insight-oriented psychotherapy, Ellen (musician) suggested that in performance consulting, performance fear should be addressed in terms of normalizing and developing coping mechanisms rather than addressing historical roots. Historical understanding and reconstruction can occur at some other point and is essentially a different "contract."

UNETHICAL PRACTICE

Few performers described conduct that they would actually consider unethical. Ian (broadcaster), however, had personal experience of consultation with unclear boundaries and ultimately, a violation of confidentiality:

> The one radio consultant I worked with was a guy who focused on psychological aspects. He wanted "to get into your head and see where you were at and see what kind of person you were and help to mold you into being a better personality," when in fact he was collecting information for the general manager— who repeated it all back to me as I was being fired. So don't come in here and tell me it's all between us. There *has* to be a doctor–patient relationship. It has to stay confidential and I have to trust that; otherwise you are not going to help me, because I am never going to open up to you.

Two potential liabilities related to the consultant's personality or ego were mentioned only by consultants: loss of perspective and lack of congruence. Consultants' awareness and concern about these factors may reflect their own experience and observations of colleagues' behavior.

LOSS OF PERSPECTIVE

The consultants recognized that being "in awe" of the performer would likely render them inefficient at best and possibly hinder the performer's efforts. This observation has also been made in the sport psychology context (Gould & Damarjian, 1998; Simons & Andersen, 1995). An awe-struck consultant is more likely to indulge the tendency of some performers to act with immaturity. Dr. Owen Osborne commented:

> Some performers say, "I'm the artist. I get to be the baby. I get to be outrageous. In fact, it may even enhance my image as somebody who is truly artistic." Sometimes they've had people in their life who did that—their mother treated them like they were the Second Coming and indulged the hell out of them or made excuses or protected them from life. Sometimes an artist attempts to operate out of being imbalanced in their life and thinks that their talent or their commitment to the field is going to somehow compensate for that or protect them. If the consultant accepts that, if they indulge that, watch out. Bad news.

It can be a fine line, suggested Dr. King, maintaining a balance between showing respect yet not putting some performers on a pedestal. Effective consulting may well be compromised when the consultant becomes swept into the performer's orbit. Dr. Gordon Gates provided an example (see chap. 15, this volume) of a situation in which a "sports groupie's" awe about the status of his client (a race car driver) limited his effectiveness.

CONSULTANT BEHAVIOR NOT ISOMORPHIC TO MODEL

Consultants whose work focused on team dynamics and leadership issues were particularly sensitive to the potential hazard of "practicing differently than one preaches." Dr. Colin Cross described his own approach:

> If you don't match up with what you're trying to teach, I think that's inappropriate. If you're trying to get managers to be more open-minded, to involve their people more, to ask more questions, to use the wisdom of the group, then you better

meet all of those behaviors to the nth degree. You've got to model it big time. And that's certainly true in working with corporate people. You need to model what you want them to do. And it's so easy sometimes to want to violate that and say, "Well we don't have a lot of time, so let me just tell you this."

Biases and Attitudes About Consultation

Many of the performers were unfamiliar with the concept of using consultants to work on mental skills. Some had had unpleasant or difficult prior experiences with consultants; others were skeptical. It is useful for consultants to be aware of the preconceptions that may color performers' receptivity to working with consultants.

In certain domains, specific attitudes toward consultants were noted. In broadcasting, Grace commented: "As a rule, we hate consultants in our business." Dave (banker) has found large leadership conferences, his primary contact with consultants, stultifying and obvious:

> To me and to most people in my group, these leadership conferences have not been all that helpful. You're told you need a vision and need to share the vision for the company, and you need to express it to people, and you need to be a team player and you need to be a good listener . . . all that sort of thing. Frankly, most of us know those things, even if we don't necessarily do them.
>
> So much of it (leadership conferences) is, to me, common sense. Or things that never even occur to me, like "never pick up a piece of paper but once." There are a lot of things I handle once, but there are a lot of things I like to have just sit on my desk. I like to put them aside and then handle them again. To me, that is productive. Or: making a list, prioritizing—no shit, of course, you know. My problem is I so much love making lists and checking things off, when I make a list I tend to do the quick and easy things first and then I can check seven out of nine things off. And I'm left with the two really big and important ones and I've done the unimportant.

Concerning consultation for lawyers, Arthur said:

> A bad consultant will ruin it for the next three good ones. Lawyers bring a certain level of skepticism about a consultant

being able to help them, no matter where they are. If you end up with someone who comes in with only one approach or someone who is just an entertainer type, then the next time when something is seriously wrong, [the lawyer won't be willing to make use of a consultant]. Let's say you're half-dysfunctional and you bring in somebody who is bad. By the time you're fully dysfunctional, you're probably sunk, because the next guy is never going to have a chance.

As a businessman, David initially thought that a consultant would be called in only if something were really going wrong and needed to be fixed. Regarding his own tension headaches, for example, he said:

I was just having a headache. I wasn't on the verge of anything serious. A certain amount of stress is good. People get stressed out, people blow up occasionally, things happen—but it's just short term. It's natural in a very competitive but difficult environment with high stakes. I think I would need to see some serious problems before I would call a performance consultant.

On the other hand, he could see the relevance of performance consulting in the world of athletics and sport psychology: "Obviously, in the athletic world it has done an awful lot." However, he questioned evaluating effectiveness in a situation with a sample size of one: "The problem is you never know whether it had any impact because you never know what would have happened if you hadn't done it or if you had done something else."

Ultimately, he acknowledged that there might be ways in which learning could be more effective and efficient by using a competent consultant:

We're continually doing nonremedial thinking around here. We're trying to figure out how to improve what we do. We actually do that consciously and are always talking about it. We ask our newest young people a couple of times a year, "Hey, you guys just came from the outside, tell us: Do you think we can do better? We may laugh at you, we may not; but we want to know. You're coming in blind; you don't know the history of a lot of stuff." Or when a new associate comes in: "See if you can come up with three things that don't make any sense. Let us either explain them to you or stop doing them." And we try to do that sort of thing in our periodic meetings: "How can we improve the process, what can we do differently?" Not that we're doing anything *wrong*, but what can we do [better]? So I think we make a very conscious effort to continually improve stuff that's not broken. And I just want to make that point, because I think that is very inconsistent with my preconceived notion about the consultant. I think if I could have learned a lot of things that I've learned over a long period of time, if that could have been helped a long time ago, to learn those sooner and faster and better—maybe learn some other things, too—that would be great.

Recommendations to Consultants

- The greatest concern expressed by performers is that a consultant might undermine their self-confidence. Consultants are advised always to be respectful of the performer's abilities and to build on existing strengths and resources.
- Even more than domain-specific knowledge, the consultant should consider what is appropriate for this specific individual in this unique setting within this specific domain. We refer to this capacity as *contextual intelligence* and discuss it further in chapter 16.
- As indicated in earlier chapters, assessment is crucial to ensure that challenging but realistic goals are set.
- A consultant can be well meaning but nonetheless hurt an individual's performance by not demonstrating appropriate pacing, or not matching interventions to the particular style and strengths of the individual.
- A consultant who is entertaining rather than informative will ultimately be viewed as a waste of effort and may hinder efforts of subsequent consultants in that setting.
- For many performers, crises may not fit a predetermined consulting schedule. From the onset of services, consultants should plan for adequate support and follow-through.
- At the same time, consultants can hinder a performer by creating overdependence on the consultant. The ultimate goal of consulting should be the performer's autonomous success.
- Failure to recognize the idiosyncratic nature of each individual is likely to lead to ineffective consultation at best and may even have adverse effects. A "one size fits all" model may seem to ease the demands on the consultant; however, it is likely to be a disaster.
- Being "a fan" or in awe of the performer renders consultation ineffective. Consultants need to maintain perspective on their role: assisting a person in the process of change.

▪ While having performance experience in the particular domain may be an asset for developing credibility and empathy with the performer, it may also be a liability if the consultant strays from performance consulting to giving technical advice.

▪ It is crucial that a consultant have a clear understanding of issues falling under the domain of performance consultation and that of psychotherapy. This is discussed in greater detail in the next chapter.

▪ It is important that consultants "practice what they preach." This is particularly true with consultants who focus on the organizational climate and the decision-making process in a performance setting.

V

What Consultants Need: Training, Ethics, and Practice

A Good Fit: Training, Competence, and Ethical Practice

15

Whether a person considers performance consulting a distinct profession or a subset of professional knowledge and expertise, there is no doubt that the field is in a process of evolution. The consultants we interviewed, like the performers, came from varying backgrounds and differing levels of involvement with assorted types of performers. In beginning to map out appropriate expectations for training, competence, and ethics, we wished to tap this very diversity, reflective of the field.

We were curious about the practicalities of performance consulting. How does one become and stay competent? What best prepared them for what they are now doing? How would they assess a colleague's competence?

Training and Turf Concerns

A number of consultants expressed concern about other consultants. In some instances, the concern was expressed in terms of professional categories of training; in others, consultants shared specific concerns about other consultants they knew or knew of. Within the community of consultants, some of these red flags are well recognized, and some are red flags for "bulls" with different types of training. It is instructive, therefore, to understand what some of these concerns are.

Various consultants expressed concern about the current variety of paths to coaching and the lack of regulation in the field. Dr. Brian Bell (family business) noted that the field of performance coaching is presently wide open to people with, at best, minimal training. His sardonic summary: "Some of these people remind me of reporters who have reported on a lot of wars and after a while they decide they would make pretty good generals."

Lest those of us with advanced degrees scoff at these reservations, the concerns of others merit some reflection. For example, Dr. Cross (business), whose background is in sports sciences, commented on the ways in which psychologists who lack experience in sports may superimpose inappropriate values on their clients:

> I can remember a psychologist who went in to work with a group of athletes and he said to me, "It's an abusive environment! It's this; it's that." He didn't understand sports. I don't know a lot of Olympic athletes who love their coach. They like their coach, they respect their coach, but they always feel like they're being overworked. It's not that I'm siding with the coach *or* the athlete. I don't. I often represent the athlete to the coach. But you have to understand what that world is all about. You don't have to know the intricacy or the strategy of the game, but you have to understand what training is all about and how hard it is, and how someone is trying to move someone out of their comfort zone and getting them to stretch. So, too, it is with the business world.

Dr. Daniel Dean (business) shared his concerns about the arrogance demonstrated at times by practitioners who do not obtain additional specialized training. He sees supplementary education as especially important when one attempts to consult with businesses. He compared the learning process in business consultation to that of sport psychology. Practitioners learning how to become sport psychologists often do so, in part, through volunteer activities. The business setting, however, does not provide "amateur" opportunities:

> I don't know too many who have the luxury of having a formal training program like I had at ___ . Frankly, I think a lot of times [lack of specialized training] comes from confidence— and a lot of times I think it's false confidence. My sense is that a lot of people are going into [business consulting] as solo folks without a lot of experience and just sort of winging it. They should not be confident, because they are walking into a disaster! It is easy in the sport area to say, "I'll do this for free to get some training. It is only junior high soccer, so I am not going to do much harm." It is very hard to do that in a

corporate setting. To call up the local office of the Xerox organization and say, "Hey, do you guys need some team building? I am looking to get some training in that area. I'll give you a talk!" You have to go in with both feet and "b.s." some people to be able to pull it off, unless you have some formal consulting group where you've got folks who can mentor you.

Essential Ethical Concerns

Issues of training, competence, and ethics are highly interwoven. Ultimately, the "big picture" of ethical practice means doing "work that is good." There are two basic ways of measuring that: (a) obtaining appropriate preparation and (b) practicing in a competent manner. This concept is linguistically supported: The derivation of the word *competent* comes from the Latin *competens*, "being fit." It is appropriate that fitness implies both health—perhaps the health of this new field—and capacity.

The development of competency in performance consulting must include more than the obvious acquisition of techniques and skills. The knowledge and skills required to treat pathologies are not necessarily the same as those needed to facilitate excellence (Seligman & Csikszentmihalyi, 2000; Sheldon & King, 2001). It may be equally important to attain perspectives and attitudes that emphasize strengths and excellence rather than deficiencies. These sentiments are consistent with recent observations from the positive psychology movement.

A discussion of ethics is often left to the end of a book. At times, we're sure this is because practitioners may approach ethics discussions with a paralyzing combination of boredom and fear. Instead, we subscribe to the idea that ethics frame and shape our best practice. Accordingly, we consider a discussion of ethics as an opportunity to reflect on the central issues and values of performance consulting.

It is in the context of ethical beliefs, values, and practices that the practitioner can move with some sense of confidence into a new area of practice. This framework is well articulated by Pope and Vasquez (1998):

> [Learning] ethics is a process through which we awaken, enhance, inform, expand, and improve our ability to respond effectively to those who come to us for help. . . .
>
> [Ethics codes] cannot do our questioning, thinking, feeling, and responding for us. Such codes can never be a substitute for the active process by which the individual therapist or counselor struggles with the sometimes bewildering, always unique constellation of questions, responsibilities, contexts, and competing demands of helping another person. . . .

Ethics must be practical. Clinicians confront an almost unimaginable diversity of situations, each with its own shifting questions, demands, and responsibilities. Every clinician is unique in important ways. Every client is unique in important ways. Ethics that are out of touch with the practical realities of clinical work, with the diversity and constantly changing nature of the therapeutic venture, are useless. (pp. xiii–xiv)

The ethical concerns of performance psychology are similar to the concerns of sport psychology, which have been expressed in that literature for the past 20 years (see, e.g., Andersen, Van Raalte, & Brewer, 2001; Brown, 2001; Nideffer, 1981; Sachs, 1993; Whelan, Meyers, & Elkins, 2002). The Association for the Advancement of Applied Sport Psychology has developed its own Code of Ethics (Meyers, 1995). Although based fairly extensively on that of the American Psychological Association (APA; 1992, 2002), the Code of Ethics recognizes the particular circumstances and situations that apply to those consulting within the athletic setting. These various resources highlight essential concerns regarding competence, confidentiality, multiple relationships, self-representation to the public, marketing, and advertising. Many of the sport examples described in the literature could apply equally well to other performance domains.

All of our consultants emphasized the importance of having an ethical framework and of recognizing the limits of their competence. For example, Dr. Gates (high-risk) suggested that he would make a referral to consultants "who know enough to recognize their own limits and know not to take a referral if they're not going to be able to do it well." More generally, Dr. King (high-risk) suggested:

I look at performance along a continuum. And along that continuum, I think it is fair to say that everybody has some situations they can be successful in and everybody has some that they are going to fail in. The key for me has more to do with individuals' recognition of their own limitations and their areas of competency.

Dr. Bell (business) raised important reflective questions in considering consultants' competence: "Do they have formal training in a relevant discipline? Do they have some professional association that would help hold them to some ethical guidelines of some kind? Do they have appropriate experience in what they are trying to do?"

Within APA, the area of sport psychology has recently been recognized as a proficiency, and initial descriptions of that field and its practitioners have been developed (APA, n.d.). The Education and Training Committee of APA's Division 13, Society of Consulting Psychology, has

> Anybody can occasionally make an error and may occasionally do things that might appear to be incompetent. In many cases, the training you have had and your ability to document it become important in order to make the point that "I am in fact competent in this."
>
> —Dr. Stanley Jones (former director of the APA Ethics Office)

established Principles for Education and Training at the Doctoral and Post-Doctoral Level in Consulting Psychology/ Organizational Consulting Psychology (APA, 2000). The document "outlines the expected competencies to be obtained by persons receiving training at the doctoral or post-doctoral level in Consulting Psychology (CP)."

Ethical issues in performance consulting appear to be similar to those recognized within sport psychology and consulting psychology organizations. Because the field of performance consultation is in the process of development, its ethical standards may be even more ambiguous than those of more established areas. To address concerns of ethics in this new field, we were guided in large measure by an interview we conducted with Stanley Jones, the former director of the APA Ethics Office (1990–1999), and a consultant to that office since then. Dr. Jones was willing to extrapolate his understanding of professional ethics in developing areas to address concerns about performance psychology. In contrast to our broader interviews with the performance consultants, our interview with Dr. Jones focused entirely on issues of the ethics of professionals moving into a field that is still in the process of being defined. Our discussion drew from the *Ethical Principles of Psychologists and Code of Conduct* (APA, 1992); however, in the present discussion we have extrapolated his comments to the recently published revision (2002; we refer to both as the *APA Ethics Code*).

Although we focus on a document that has specific application to psychologists, we recognize that nonpsychologist practitioners may be more familiar with and have greater legal and ethical responsibility to uphold the ethics framework of their particular profession. We commend them to the documents pertinent to their licensed professional identity.

In a litigious society, issues of risk management are also embedded within ethical concerns. In particular, being able to document one's development of competence in a particular area takes on potential legal as well as ethical significance. A practitioner with substantiated training may be in a position to place a one-time mistake in the perspective of a history of ethical practice. In contrast, if a practitioner committed the identical act, but lacked a track record indicating the development of competence, the error might be perceived differently. In regard to these issues, we appreciated the opportunity to review some of the relevant risk management factors with Eric Harris (personal communication, January 28, 2003), a psychologist and legal consultant to the APA Insurance Trust.

The sections that follow are designed to review training, competence, and ethics from a variety of angles. We begin with a straightforward application of the current professional standards regarding boundaries and maintenance of competence to the area of performance consulting. Then we incorporate the perspectives of our consultant interviewees on the elements of training and experience necessary to their own development and maintenance of competence. A slightly different perspective is offered as we consider the task of assessing another's competence. Ethical concerns that move beyond issues of competence are then reviewed. Finally, because practitioners approach this field from various backgrounds, we describe in detail the training and practice of three of our performance consultant interviewees.

THE BOUNDARIES OF COMPETENCE

Standard 2.01 of the APA Code of Conduct, describing the Boundaries of Competence, speaks directly to the issues of training and competence.

2.01(a) Psychologists provide services, teach, and conduct research with populations and in areas only within the boundaries of their competence, based on their education, training, supervised experience, consultation, study, or professional experience.

Standard 2.01 recognizes a broad array of ways in which one may develop competence in a particular area. The linguistic changes in the updated APA Ethics Code suggest that in a number of practice areas, psychologists are expanding their knowledge by a variety of means. This standard describes the attainment of competence fairly broadly by virtue of the word *or*. In situations where formal education is available, prudence would suggest that such education be obtained. What that training includes, however, is not defined within the standard.

Standard 2.01(c) is especially relevant for practitioners who have already obtained training in, say, clinical or counseling psychology. This section addresses situations in which graduate training occurred in one field and the practitioner wishes to add a different area of practice:

2.01(c) Psychologists planning to provide services, teach, or conduct research involving populations, areas, techniques, or technologies new to them undertake relevant education, training, supervised experience, consultation, or study.

This standard notes that the intention to engage in another area of practice should include deliberative relevant learning. Again, the method by which the practitioner learns and the necessary amount of learning needed may vary.

A further complication results from the interaction of individuals with varied backgrounds working within a field (i.e., performance consulting) in a state of development. On the one hand, a practitioner psychologist already trained in the use of relaxation or imagery skills might benefit from a weekend workshop that elaborates on the use of these skills in performance settings. On the other hand, if a person's background and training is in comparative psychology with minimal understanding of methods of working with people, this same workshop would at most only touch on the necessary knowledge for this psychologist.

Standard 2.01 (e) refers to truly emergent areas of practice. It reads:

> 2.01(e) In those emerging areas in which generally recognized standards for preparatory training do not yet exist, psychologists nevertheless take reasonable steps to ensure the competence of their work and to protect clients/patients, students, supervisees, research participants, organizational clients, and others from harm.

The challenge of defining "reasonable steps" or "relevant education" for performance psychology is that the field is neither totally new nor fully defined. Furthermore, it makes use of techniques and populations that have been and are within the purview of others. It exists in a middle or gray zone, with elements of both emerging and truly established areas of practice. Because the field of performance consulting includes elements and techniques with which many psychologists may already be familiar, some psychologists will legitimately argue that this area is a "subspecialty" of their general practice. As an emerging area, it is still not clear whether the exact emphasis of training should be at the graduate or postgraduate level. In particular, the lack of a developed graduate curriculum and other similar indices suggest that it is not yet a fully established field.

Until such guidelines are formally developed, the APA Ethics Code (2002) indicates that "*reasonable* means the prevailing professional judgment of psychologists engaged in similar activities in similar circumstances" (p. 1061). This suggests that if a clinical or counseling psychologist is seeking to expand his or her practice to include performance consulting, information from colleagues engaged in general practice is not likely to be sufficiently "informed" to meet the definition of "reasonable" efforts. One must look to those who are established and active in performance consulting for guidance regarding appropriate standards. In the sections that follow, we have incorporated the opinions of our consultants in order to provide a meaningful reference for persons seeking ethical expansion in this area.

MAINTAINING COMPETENCE

Psychologists who have developed expertise in an area are also ethically obligated to maintain that level of skill. The new standard that addresses the issue of competence maintenance is brief but to the point. Standard 2.03 reads:

> 2.03 Psychologists undertake ongoing efforts to develop and maintain their competence.

Although the methods used to develop and maintain competence are not explained, we suggest that for minimal compliance, one must have an awareness of the current journal literature and engage in relevant continuing education. As noted earlier, for the benefit of both risk management and maintenance of ethical practice, practitioners are advised to secure credible evidence of these efforts. This may be in the form of certificates verifying workshops or specific consultative or supervised experience in the new field. Nonetheless, the conundrum remains: What constitutes relevant education and training?

As the field evolves, formal ways will undoubtedly develop to help practitioners become knowledgeable and specialized. At present, the consultants we interviewed described a combination of factors relevant to the acquisition of their knowledge and skill.

As recognized experts in the field of performance consulting, our interviewees offered insights concerning the nature of appropriate education. Because this general field does not have formally developed criteria or career paths, each consultant had come to his or her present consulting practice through a somewhat idiosyncratic combination of formal and informal education and experience, as well as formative life experiences.

Aspects of Appropriate Training

In reviewing the training experiences of performance consultants, we conclude that a solid foundation in either psychology or exercise science is essential, along with relevant supplemental training. This additional preparation may involve formal training through coursework or free-standing educational programs, in domains where this is available. A combination of performance experience (generic), informal learning, and useful life experiences currently provide the additional relevant knowledge.

FORMAL ACADEMIC TRAINING

The majority of the consultants (the psychologists in particular) mentioned their formal academic education as the foundational structure for developing consultation skills. Dr. Frank Fiske (business), for example, suggested that the generalist knowledge base of psychology allows for transfer of knowledge from one setting to another.

Dr. King (high-risk, military) emphasized the importance of having a theoretical frame to guide interventions. He was also quick to differentiate between knowledge and its manifestation in practice behavior. Theoretical understanding should be translated into usable ideas that are then expressed in the form of pragmatic techniques when working with the performer: "They don't want theories; they want to know it works."

The generic knowledge base developed through psychological training was highlighted by those with and without a specific psychology degree. Dr. Andrew Adams, a nonpsychologist and former professor of organizational development, is now a highly successful business consultant. He observed that psychologists, in contrast to management consultants without a psychology background, understand the interpersonal dynamics that are an important aspect of the "sea change" of the current business climate. Dr. Dean pointed to the extensive knowledge that psychologists gain in graduate school: expertise regarding individual human needs, as well as training in group dynamics. He asserted that the full range of graduate education—from social psychology to developmental psychology to abnormal psychology to nonverbal communication—forms an unparalleled foundation on which further specialized knowledge can be built.

Several consultants specifically mentioned cognitive–behavioral treatment as a useful grounding for performance consulting. Dr. Alice Austin (business) commented that the cognitive–behavioral treatment framework of both questioning and firm but caring confrontation was an important element of her present consulting practice. Whereas he recognized that psychodynamic, existential, or gestalt training might be of use for certain performance consultations, Dr. Jarrett (high-risk) noted that he found an excellent "fit" between cognitive–behavioral treatment and sport psychology and performance consulting.

In addition to having a theoretical framework for assessing situations and making decisions, those trained in psychology programs typically learn particular counseling and therapy skills. Specific subareas of knowledge may be vital as well. Dr. Brian Bell, who does extensive consulting to family businesses, said that his training in family therapy, in addition to general clinical experience, has been essential to his consulting success.

If you come from a purely [industrial/organizational] background without the family systems orientation, you may not recognize that in a family business, there are the problems of regular business plus a few that families "manufacture." And they are always mixed up together. Sometimes there is some defensiveness [in the consultant]: "Well, how are we going to work around this? I am not here to take care of that for them."

If you have worked a while as a therapist, you know that, as in therapy, family members don't always want to solve the problem. They don't always give you the straight scoop, and sometimes they do try to sabotage you, or they set it up in a way that makes it very difficult. By the time you find out about some other key family members, you've already spent enough time with them that it is really difficult to switch [focus to include the new information] and be believed. Families are families. They sometimes do a lot of hurtful things to each other.

—Dr. Brian Bell
(consultant, family business)

Dr. Edward Evans (business) mentioned a number of relevant skills and perspectives that he obtained during his training as a behavioral clinical psychologist: training in functional behavioral analysis, individual interviewing and listening, and an internship experience involving knowledge of group functioning and intervention.

Those consultants whose primary degree was in the sport sciences offered a slightly different perspective than those trained primarily in psychology. Consultants such as Dr. Lindsay (high-risk) and Dr. Benton (business) recognized the importance of training in psychology but also saw the distinct knowledge base of exercise and sport science as essential to becoming a competent consultant. They suggested that the ideal consultant is one who has an integrated, systematic foundation of knowledge in exercise science, psychology, and sport psychology.

This first element that consultants rely on, their formal graduate training, points to a common core of underlying skills necessary for specialized consulting. These are the foundational building blocks of successful consulting. As Whiston and Sexton (1993) noted, the relationship skills that form the backbone of clinical and counseling psychology programs are the necessary but not sufficient conditions for performance consulting. Because consultants' work moves beyond this generalist level, other types of learning serve to augment that base.

An individual considering practice expansion who recognizes particular deficits in knowledge or experience has an ethical obligation to rectify these deficiencies. Structured postdegree training is especially important for those without a background in psychology. It is also useful in domains where formal training exists, such as in the fields of business consulting and coaching. For other performance domains, it may be necessary to extrapolate from existing training. More informal methods—

[Cognitive–behavioral training provided a worldview that connects cognition, emotion, and behavior], and that has greatly colored who I am, the way I operate, and the types of interventions and ways that I work with performers.

You just cannot be effective unless you're a good people person with terrific working skills. Graduate school and internship training improved me a thousandfold as a listener and a counselor. There must be other factors in there as well, but getting good training as a counselor is going to increase the odds of your being an effective counselor in the real world. I think it's enormously important in terms of performance consulting.

I have had training in a lot of the other areas of knowledge or expertise as a postdoctoral professional. I've learned to understand people's performance patterns in relationship to their nutritional habits, their fitness, their sleep patterns, and so on either from the ___ Center or through some of the sport psychology and sports medicine training experiences that I've had. Similarly, a lot of the training I've had in leadership studies and teamwork has been postdoctoral and has been tremendously helpful in my consulting. I know that I will continue to seek out new learning experiences, because that's the only way to keep improving.

—Dr. John Jarrett (consultant, high-risk)

including performance experience, independent study and reading, and life experience—may prove valuable to some, as attested to by a number of the consultants interviewed. By definition, these are tailored to the individual's knowledge, background, and training needs as well as the performance domain. We offer several examples of postdegree training below.

STRUCTURED, POSTDEGREE TRAINING

For some, formal postdegree training has served to supplement and expand consultants' prior knowledge base. For example, Dr. Marc Martin (music) was originally trained as a musician, performing, conducting, and composing. For him, taking coursework in neuro-linguistic programming (NLP), and training with Virginia Satir and Milton Erickson were the paths to providing consultation to others. The effectiveness of combined imaginative and pragmatic interventions, such as those of Satir and Erickson, was also noted by Dr. King, working in an entirely different domain with high-risk performers. Practitioners interested in practice expansion may want to give special attention to these resources, which appear to have appeal and direct application to performers' concerns.

Dr. Jarrett (high-risk) described postdoctoral study in leadership and teamwork as especially useful. Dr. Benton (business) and Dr. Dean (business) have both obtained extensive training and experience in a formal, postdegree free-standing business consulting organization. Dr. Dean commented that this organization-based training felt comparable to graduate school. "There is classroom training, formal mentoring, observation, session taping and then feedback—the whole nine yards."

PERFORMANCE EXPERIENCE

Several consultants commented that their own performance experience was significant in preparing them for their eventual consulting role. For some, earlier experience in a performance domain evolved into practice focus. For others, the experience of working with elite performers in high-pressure situations has provided the foundation for applying skills in new domains.

The most straightforward transfer of performance experience occurs when one becomes a consultant in a domain in which one has performed. The many years Dr. Donna Desmond spent as a professional ballet dancer informs all her work with performers. The experience has provided insights into both the individual issues that dancers face and the systemic issues of working in the world of professional dance. Dr. Marc Martin (music) commented on the rapid rapport that can develop from such history: "It helps if you understand performing, understand the battle-field conditions, so that in a few moments, the performer can say, 'Oh they know what I'm talking about.'"

Dr. Owen Osborne (theatre) cited a number of different intersections with theatre performance that assisted in his preparation for consulting with actors. He performed improvisational team comedy for a number of years. Through his wife (an actor), he has been involved in the theatrical milieu, whether sitting in on rehearsals, being involved in theatre projects, or in social interaction. These experiences were instrumental in the development of his own consulting model, one that integrates elements of performance and psychotherapy.

On the road to becoming a business consultant, Dr. Bell cited the importance of his business experience as a university dean. His understanding of both business and business consulting was then expanded when he was asked to consult with the university's board of trustees. Within an informal context in which he felt respected and not under pressure to perform, it was possible to gain considerable knowledge that now serves as one of the foundations for his consulting practice.

Dr. Cross (business) elaborated on the importance of knowing the world in which one is consulting. He described his work with athletic coaches:

At one time, I used to coach and that's been invaluable.
Coaching has been much more valuable to me in making my

connections initially than my sport psychology credentials; because [the coaches] know I know their reality. You don't have to know the intricacy or the strategy of the game, but you have to understand what training is all about and how hard it is, and how someone is trying to move someone out of their comfort zone, getting them to stretch.

Performance experience can also include the learning that is acquired as a performance consultant. Generalization provides its own unique education, occurring in two ways: applying what one has learned in relatively easy situations to more complex ones; and transferring knowledge from one domain to another. For example, a sport psychologist typically refines his or her consulting talents and techniques by working with amateur athletes. Consultants have to prove their abilities with "low-risk" situations before they are invited to work with "the crown jewels" of performance. As Dr. Gates (high-risk) aptly explained, "I wouldn't want to run into a major NASCAR team and kind of figure it out as I went."

Several consultants whose original training and work was in sport consultation told of businesspeople who sought their performance expertise, even before the consultant recognized the possible link. Commenting on his own transition, for example, Graham Jones (2002) recently wrote:

> A number of years ago, when I was still a full-time university academic engrossed in research into the area of competitive anxiety and consulting with elite athletes, I was approached by a senior executive in a large global company. [He] was seeking a sport psychologist who would give him an insight into the psychology of coaching and implement a coaching intervention that would help his already successful senior management team to achieve even higher levels of performance. (p. 268)

In his current work within the business world, Dr. Cross emphasized the similarities of role and function between his athletic experience and the business situations in which he consults. He gains credibility by having been a university athletic director. Businesspeople know that he understands what it's like to be an administrator and that he, too, has had to manage staff, do performance appraisals, and fire employees.

Dr. Franklin Fiske, a former elite athlete, has enhanced credibility in the business world because of his experience as a high-level performer:

> You don't have to have been a world class athlete to be a successful sport psychologist; you don't have to have been a vice-president of a company to be a successful consulting psychologist; but I think it helps. Actually, I've been hired

several times because I was a world-class ski racer. That background seems to carry a lot of weight because they know that I know what it's like to perform in high-pressure situations.

INFORMAL TRAINING

Informal training experiences—such as learning through reading; experiencing the domain; or being coached, mentored, or supervised—provide important opportunities for gaining proficiency. The expansion, breadth, and depth of this informal training allow the practitioner to understand commonalities across domains and gain specific knowledge within particular domains. A number of our consultants commented on the value of these experiences in which they participated.

"For some, it's been a matter of reading." Dr. Cross (business) commented. He said that he applies less than 1% of what he learned in graduate school to his current work, but has found it very helpful to read broadly across a number of disciplines. Similarly, Dr. Daniel Dean(business) has found reading to be instructive: "Just like in any other field, the more you work with people, the more you understand and recognize common themes. Like 'Oh, that's a common theme; that's not unique to this person.'"

For some of his more recent work in high-risk sports, Dr. Gates has learned informally through using computer games to gain general information and learn some of the jargon specific to the sport. Simply being curious and asking questions can be a remarkable source of informal learning. Dr. Ingram (public safety) said that "hanging out with these people" is one of his primary modes of education. Dr. Lindsay (high-risk) learned informally through observing all phases of the training program with which he then consulted.

Informal learning may also include developing a network of colleagues who can serve as a sounding board, resource, or means of "peer consultation" when the consultant encounters challenging situations. For example, although he obtained his doctorate 16 years ago, Dr. Fiske (business) turns to two other well-respected practitioners "when I'm stuck or when I'm scared or when I don't know what to do or when something is a little over my head."

FORMATIVE LIFE EXPERIENCES

Successful consultation is more than the application of knowledge and techniques; it includes the use of oneself—personality, values, and perspectives—all the things that are essential when one human develops an authentic relationship with another. One cannot schedule, predict, or structure some of the significant life events that mold our being and that appear to be elements essential to the process of becoming an effective consultant.

Varying circumstances of family and development helped shape individuals to their current practice. These formative life experiences comprised perhaps the most interesting category of training reported by our consultants. The specifics are varied; it is the commonality of having been informed by these experiences that is thematically constant. Consultants have made use of these experiences in guiding their interests and developing a communicated empathy with their clients.

For Dr. Bell (family business), consulting to family businesses has been influenced by having grown up in a family business as well as his own in-depth psychotherapy and psychoanalysis. Dr. Adams (business) observed that his own family and emotional stability have been an anchor in his work with others.

Dr. Kenneth King (military) mentioned a number of developmental influences that shaped his subsequent comfort in working with the military:

> I was raised in southern California on a farm. I grew up with guns. I've been shooting all my life. I hunted when I was younger. I was born in 1942, so when I was going to school, there was still all of this patriotism. I got a lot of patriotism instilled in me. I was in the Civil Air Patrol. I was in the military. I studied the martial arts. So, there is a lot of empathy for the kinds of things that [the military] do.

He also spoke of the ways in which he uses his own experience to empathize and affirm others' experience:

> I've had my own failure experiences, so I can certainly empathize with the situations that people find themselves in. It's the ability to draw on those experiences and then generalize them to what the other person is going through, but to do it in a way which doesn't sound like "Oh, I know what you do because I've done bigger things." Instead, it's doing it in a way that affirms them and yet shows some sensitivity to what they have to deal with.

In a similar manner, Dr. Colin Cross (business) deliberately has used many aspects of his life history as a way to connect with people and increase credibility:

> The biggest thing that has helped me is I have had a very broad spectrum of experiences in my life. Each of those has provided me with the background that I need for different groups and at different levels.

You connect with what you have going for you and you share that. Sometimes I'm in rural areas, and I make it very clear that I come from a rural area. And when I'm in ___, I talk about how I used to live there. My background is working class. My father worked 42 years underground in mines. I spent my summers working underground in mines. So when I have to deliver the mental fitness material to laborers—and I've done this many, many times, in lunchrooms and other places—I'm able to do it in a way that they can accept. I speak their language.

Dr. Ingram (high-risk) also grew up in a working-class environment and uses his experience to understand and connect with public service employees in high-risk jobs:

I grew up in a blue-collar family. I grew up using my hands. I grew up with a great deal of respect for entry-level personnel of one kind or another. My dad was a plumber. I've always respected the skill that people have, whether it's an electrician or a carpenter or a plumber, a firefighter or a police officer. I'm just fascinated by how people do their work. I can't even count the hours I've spent in patrol cars and firehouses. I don't pretend that I can do their job, but I do know enough about the nature of their jobs by having actually performed those kinds of things with their help or watching them do it.

Some consultants find that shared character traits can form an entrée for "joining" and being accepted by performers. In contrast to Dr. Cross and Dr. Ingram, whose early life experiences served as a foundation for empathizing with the performers with whom they work, Dr. Norris (music) described his connection with musicians as related to similar aspects of personality. Although he has not had any formal instruction in music, he has a strong sense of creativity. Another characteristic is a term he takes from drama: "the ability to be a 'quick study.' In working with any musician, no matter what the genre, I pick up the nuances of the craft, of the art, and then can integrate that not only into how I talk with them but how I hear them."

Serendipity sometimes plays a major role in shaping the informal training that later proves essential to performance consulting. Up until the age of 35, Dr. Marc Martin (music) was a professional musician. "[I] got bored with playing, and the way my life was going. I decided that I wanted to study the other arts. So I studied acting, dance, mime, ballet, fencing, theatre directing—all the theatre arts." These broadened skills and abilities are central to his current consulting work.

The best preparation for me has been working in a lot of different fields—the television that I've done, working as a psychology expert for a national network for many years. That required learning how to translate and do things in different ways. The elected and appointed positions that I've held in APA have also involved watching what works and doesn't in terms of teams and effectiveness. Really listening and learning from my clients' experience in the business world. Modeling successful behavior that I'm comfortable with in terms of my own values.

I need to do something more than just clinical work. I've done it for so long, I want to do some other kinds of things. I found that [business consulting] was a really good application. Although I was trained analytically, I'm very action oriented, so it's a better fit for my temperament to be able to have action and identifiable results. It is a great antidote to burn-out, and very financially lucrative. It's allowed me to work in partnerships with a lot of other psychologists who I really like, so I don't feel alone or isolated. We do certain projects together but we don't have to be encumbered by a business partnership—we are all working together as independent contractors.

I can't teach anybody else if I haven't mastered the coaching skills myself. So it's challenged me personally, and I like that as well.

—Dr. Claire Crown (consultant, business)

Assessing Competence

One of the ways of determining the "relevant education" and "appropriate steps" to becoming competent as a performance consultant is to look at the ways in which expert consultants have developed their own expertise. Another potential angle on the same question is to ask a somewhat projective question: "How would you assess whether a colleague was competent to provide such service?"

As the field and practice of performance consultation becomes more clearly defined, standards and guidelines for assessing competence will undoubtedly be specified. For the present, our consultants suggested a number of methods of review. These may serve as a starting point for evaluating whether one has established competence. They include formal training, direct observation, outcome, experience, personal characteristics, and the presence of some form of ethical consciousness.

FORMAL TRAINING– KNOWLEDGE BASE

Formal training was the most frequently mentioned measure that consultants would use to evaluate a colleague's competence. Because consultants noted their own formal education as the foundation of their consultation preparation (mentioned earlier in this chapter), it is not surprising that they would start there in assessing others' competence. The minimal criterion most commonly cited was education that involved psychology, counseling, or psychotherapy.

The combination of athletic and formal course experience works for me in the sports world. I was a runner-up for the Olympic basketball team. Athletes realize that you have been an athlete and can relate. The best sport psychologists for athletes have played competitive sports at a pretty intense level.

I also had formal education in sport psychology. I did not train myself [just] by reading books. I took course work [on] concentration, relaxation, anxiety, and stress.

In the business world, I have spent over ten years now at ___ and that experience, combined with my education is pretty powerful.

When people come to our leadership training program and I introduce myself, I tell folks that I am a sport psychologist who works in the area of consistent top performance. Peoples' eyes light up and they think, "Boy, I can't wait to learn from her." I tell them, "This week while you are here I hope to share some techniques with you that will help you develop yourself at work and teach you how to develop other people. And if I can, also help you with your kid's soccer game."

So many workers ask me how to be a better parent to their kid who is playing tee-ball. It's incredible how people call upon my sport psych in the athletic arena while they are here for business development.

—Dr. Barbara Benton
(consultant, business)

The pragmatic stance of the leadership organization where Dr. Daniel Dean (business) received his postdoctoral training illustrates the importance of formal training. This organization has mostly drawn its trainees from those already licensed in psychology. Although the organization has turned to psychology to obtain competent practitioners, Dr. Dean suggested that the "implicit prestige factor" might actually be the determinant: "If you are going to present yourself to corporations and executives, having those paper credentials can help sell the product."

It is significant that this formal academic degree, although necessary, was not considered sufficient. The specifics of the additional training varied, in terms of both practitioner and domain. The most directly relevant additional training was that of an MBA or its equivalent, as suggested by some of the business consultants. Even if a person does not have formal postdoctoral training, Dr. Dean suggested a consultant may demonstrate competence by developing some formal system of mentoring, such as working with and being supervised by someone with business knowledge. As noted earlier, consultants whose original training was in the exercise and sport sciences strongly recommended that persons with clinical or counseling backgrounds, interested in becoming sport psychology consultants, need to demonstrate mastery of the distinct knowledge base of sport psychology.

Rather than a specific kind of additional training, a number of consultants spoke to a type of training or experience. For example, with a background in kinesiology and current work with high-risk performers, Dr. Leo Lindsay emphasized the importance of the joint knowledge produced by a background in psychology *and* some area of applied performance. He cited music performance as an example, indicating that it was the focus on performance application that was key.

For Dr. Fiske (business), the isomorphism, or consistency, between training and experience would be one means of measurement. Dr. Gates (high-risk) suggested that the knowledge base should include either specific knowledge or knowledge about knowledge: "Consultants should have a thorough knowledge of the field and also know enough either to understand the specific context or learn about it."

In addition to formal training credentials, a number of other factors were suggested for assessing a consultant's competency. These include some combination of direct observation, the consultant's reputation with regard to outcome and experience, and personal characteristics of the consultant.

DIRECT OBSERVATION

A number of consultants indicated that direct observation of the person's work, perhaps through working together, would be the preferred mode of assessing competence. Dr. Marc Martin (music) observed:

> The best way of course would be just to watch them work. But I think if I had a conversation with somebody about working with performers, I would be able to get an idea in a short time of how they approach it, and how successful they would be, just by their general attitude.

OUTCOME

Probably the most pragmatic assessment of competence involves looking at outcome: Does a consultant's effort produce the desired results? Dr. Adams (business) stated that the long-term outcome would be the most significant indicator: "I think ultimately the test is the pragmatic test over time in the marketplace."

Several interviewees suggested that outcome alone is not sufficient, however. Dr. Jarrett (high-risk) recommended the combination of effectiveness plus positive feedback over time as critical factors. Dr. Evans (business) shared this perspective and offered clarification of the importance of dual criteria: both outcome measures and comfort with the consultant:

> One kind of feedback is, how comfortable were you about the individual and the person's attitude, and how the person approached the client or situation? The other kind of feedback

is, what were the outcomes? You can have a nice consultant who was just great and friendly and wonderful, but you had the feeling that nothing happened. An athlete I know recently told me, "Hell, the psychologist was okay and interesting, but I don't think I've gone anywhere." As a result of that, the individual really didn't want to see anybody. [But on the other hand], you can get somebody like a Bobby Knight where everybody says, "yeah, but look at his outcomes." So you've got to deal with the other aspect: Not only are there performance outcomes, but how comfortable and how reasonable is the person?

EXPERIENCE

To assess competence, a number of consultants would also want to know the amount of experience the person had in this particular field with these particular kinds of performers. For example, although formal, structured training might be optimal, Dr. Alice Austin (business) suggested various other routes by which someone might become a performance consultant. It can take two to five years for someone to become a capable and competent organizational developmental psychologist, but a person might be sufficiently qualified to engage in executive coaching if he or she had a business background as an engineer or in marketing and then obtained skills in counseling and coaching.

Dr. Desmond (dance) emphasized that merely attending a workshop or reading a book would not be sufficient experience to gain competency. To determine competence, she would require a review of the consultant's training, background, and experience in working with performers and dancers, as well as an interview with them.

PERSONAL CHARACTERISTICS

Several consultants mentioned the importance of taking personal characteristics into account when assessing competence. Dr. Andrew Adams (business), for example, noted that formal criteria do not always determine competency. In several instances, he has found that self-educated people, without formal degrees, have been great contributors. Dr. Gates (high-risk) commented on the relative merits of being personally acquainted with professionals to whom he refers others, as compared with knowing them on paper only: "I would much rather refer to a person than I would a certification. But I would much rather refer to a person with certification than one without."

Dr. Dean (business) suggested that a general assessment of personal characteristics be a component of evaluating competence: "I would look at some of the personal factors. I'd assess their personal characteristics, their training, their intelligence, their flexibility, their confidence, their follow-through, whether they respond promptly to e-mail and phone messages—things like that."

Given the various routes to working in performance consulting and the ways in which individuals may decrease cognitive dissonance by accepting the validity of their own path, perhaps the most honest comment was expressed by Dr. Owen Osborne (theatre): "I have to say I really would find it difficult to know what to look for. I mean, actually I'd look for somebody just like me."

Additional Ethical Concerns

The APA Ethics Code applies to psychologists' practice. Beyond issues of competence and the maintenance of expertise, many of the other standards are broadly applicable to the field of performance psychology. That this is a relatively new field doesn't exempt the practitioner from these standards; however, the manner in which the standards apply may differ from more established areas, such as clinical psychology, organizational consulting, or research.

Standards that pertain to scientific professional judgment, the nature of psychological services, evaluation and assessment, privacy and confidentiality, and avoiding harm may all be relevant. Here, we discuss these and other concerns in terms of multiple role relationships, informed consent, confidentiality, and organizational issues.

MULTIPLE ROLE RELATIONSHIPS

The ethical performance consultant must be especially aware of the complex area of multiple relationships. Expectations concerning consultation may vary from one performance culture to another and even within performance settings. Where there is potential for blurring of roles, problems can arise.

This issue of multiple relationships has been discussed in sport psychology (e.g., Ellickson & Brown, 1990; Whelan et al., 2002). Role confusion may occur because of a variety of circumstances: Sport psychologists may have various roles within a system or may, because of their knowledge base, have several areas of expertise. For example, a sport psychologist may have expertise in both performance enhancement and the treatment of eating disorders. Would it be ethical for that person to treat the eating disorder of a team member while providing services to the team? The identical dilemma may confront a consultant to a dance company. How should the participant–client and the consultant–therapist relate to each other in the two situations?

Or consider the pragmatics and dangers of the following situation: Suppose that a performance organization has obtained funding for a public relations coordinator. They learn of the possible benefits of working with a performance consultant and they would like to, but they have no funding. A performance consultant has an undergraduate degree in communications and worked in public relations prior to returning to graduate school for training as a psychologist. The organization would like to hire the person to handle both public relations and serve as a performance resource for the organization. Is it ethical for one person to perform both of these complex roles?

As another example of different norms, again using the world of sports: It is common practice for a sport psychologist to travel with a team, often sharing meals and lodging, with consequent frequent informal interactions with the athletes. Many consultants describe these moments of informal interaction as their most effective opportunities for intervention. As the athlete comes to know the consultant on a daily basis and sees the sport psychologist's responses to a variety of life situations, the consultant gains credibility and respect (Van Raalte, 1998). How does one balance the potential for role confusion in such circumstances?

Psychology has traditionally advocated fairly rigid standards regarding multiple role relationships. The norm for conventional therapy restricts interactions to the four walls of the consulting office. It is difficult to imagine an ethical psychotherapist suggesting he or she accompany a client to a ski resort to observe the client's interactions and offer immediate "therapy on the slopes." Likewise, it is considered unethical for a psychologist to act in the dual roles of therapist and supervisor to an individual; it would generally be considered unethical to provide therapy services to a friend. Suppose this friend is an emotionally healthy, world-class performer, interested in becoming better at the process of auditions. Would it be unethical to provide performance consultation? Few if any other professions expect such a stringent restriction of interaction between provider and client.

Newman, Robinson-Kurpius, and Fuqua (2002) have suggested that in the field of consulting psychology, multiple relationships contain the potential for loss of objectivity as well as exploitation of clients. Yet, within consulting psychology, "dual relationships . . . [may] be more the norm than the exception" (p. 740). The very nature of extensive interactions between professionals, each operating within his or her particular domain of expertise, may lead to the consultative relationship in the first place or may be necessary in order for effective consultation to occur.

The issue of the appropriateness of a dual relationship hinges on whether it either (a) impairs a consultant's objectivity, competence, or effectiveness in delivering services; or (b) exploits or harms the client in any way. The APA (2002) Ethics Code is explicit in declaring that "multiple relationships that would not reasonably be expected to cause impairment or risk exploitation or harm are not unethical" (p. 1065). In each of the examples above, the ethical practitioner must weigh the merits of a given situation against these standards.

Perhaps even more challenging is this question: "Can a practitioner ethically provide both psychotherapy and performance consulting services to an individual?" As with most ethical dilemmas, the issues involved are complex and delicate.

For example, consider a situation in which a therapist is working with an individual who is diagnosed as having a narcissistic personality disorder. The individual routinely encounters difficulties in interpersonal relations both at home and at work. Although the initial referral and focus of therapy center on difficulty in social situations, the client is aware that the therapist also provides performance coaching and specifically asks for assistance at work. Can the therapist ethically provide both therapy and coaching? The answer hinges on whether the practitioner is at risk of exploiting the client.

The content of services is not at issue. Many forms of therapy, such as strategic and solution-focused approaches, concentrate on improving one's performance in social and business settings. If a therapist has the appropriate training and expertise, expanding the focus of treatment to include formal work on performance would seem both appropriate and prudent. The focus is the same whether it is called "performance coaching" or "an extension of therapy."

The risk of ethical impropriety occurs, however, if the practitioner uses a different fee structure for "consultation." Consultants typically charge higher hourly rates than do therapists. Shifting charges for services that might equally be seen as falling under the purview of therapy can be interpreted as exploitation of the client (Eric Harris, personal communication, January 28, 2003)

A coaching relationship is typically viewed as a business contract. In marked contrast, a therapeutic relationship entails a special trust on the part of the client and a corresponding responsibility of the therapist to protect the client. The vulnerability of the client arises from two different aspects: the client's emotional fragility and imbalances of power. This imbalance of power can leave the client susceptible to undue influence by the therapist. The ethical therapist is committed not to take advantage of that trust. If there is a therapeutic relationship, one can never be certain if a client's acceptance of a coaching contract is influenced by not wanting to disappoint the therapist. In such circumstances, the therapist is advised to either address the performance concerns as a part of the therapy services or refer the client to another person for coaching–consulting services.

What about providing psychotherapy to a person for whom one provided performance consultation? There would seem to be little risk of exploitation in shifting from consultation to therapy. However, the ethical therapist must consider whether his or her functioning would be impaired by doing so: If I establish a special therapeutic relationship with this individual, can I still function with objectivity, competence, and effectiveness as a performance consultant? Will the client be able to receive performance feedback as effectively once the more intense therapy relationship is established?

Our personal experience is that having a breadth of skills and expertise can be an asset in both consulting and therapy. There have been times when it was difficult to distinguish between the process of performance consulting and therapy. There have also been times when clients have clearly preferred keeping performance consultation and therapy separate. When in doubt, therapists are urged to err on the side of caution (in this case, separation of services).

Whether therapy and consultation relationships actually differ is undoubtedly a subject for debate among professionals. Psychologists are advised that even if there is no fee differential, engaging in both activities simultaneously may put one at risk of being the subject of an ethical complaint by a disgruntled patient. The more vulnerable the patient is, the greater the risk. This does not necessarily mean that one has acted unethically; however, the exposure to criticism would be greater.

INFORMED CONSENT, CONFIDENTIALITY, AND SERVICES PROVIDED TO ORGANIZATIONS

The intent of informed consent is to keep clients from feeling betrayed. When providing any services—therapy, assessment, counseling, or consultation—an ethical practitioner makes known the reasonable risks, benefits, and expectations, so the consumer can make an informed decision in agreeing to services. This issue is covered by Standard 3.10.

> 3.10 When psychologists conduct research or provide
> assessment, therapy, counseling, or consulting services in
> person or via electronic transmission or other forms of
> communication, they obtain the informed consent of the

individual or individuals using language that is reasonably understandable to that person or persons except when conducting such activities without consent is mandated by law or governmental regulation or otherwise provided in this Ethics Code.

The consultant and client should be clear as to what services are being provided, the financial charges, expectations regarding payment, and guidelines for confidentiality. By being explicit about expectations, a consultant establishes the foundation on which a trusting, collaborative relationship is developed. Guidelines proposed by the APA Insurance Trust, an organization designed to meet the insurance and financial security needs of APA members, recommend that informed consent include a definition of the goals and methods of consultation as well as a method of measuring the outcome of these efforts (Harris, 2002a).

An additional complication in consulting relationships is the question of who is consenting to the services. "A distinguishing feature of consulting relationships is their triadic nature" (Newman et al., 2002, p. 733). Across domains, many consultative relationships involve decisions made by one party or entity in power (e.g., a manager, director, or supervisor) about services offered by the consultant to another person or part of the system. The specific APA standards regarding confidentiality (Standard 4) most clearly pertain to relations between two individuals: the psychologist and a client or research participant. In many performance consultation circumstances, however, the "triadic nature" of the setting and the situation involves a delicate balance that necessitates spelling out the nature and limits of confidentiality. Furthermore, as mentioned in the context of multiple role relationships, different domain cultures may have markedly different attitudes, beliefs, and practices regarding confidentiality than those understood by psychologists (Whelan et al., 2002). For example, a military officer may expect a consultant to disclose any condition that might negatively affect a soldier's performance and thereby put other team members at risk, whereas a conductor might be appalled if any information about consultation with a member of the orchestra were disclosed. It is crucial for the psychologist to clarify the exact nature of confidentiality prior to engaging in the consultation process.

The ethical practitioner must consider complexities of power differential, payment, and, especially, confidentiality. Ethical practice in such circumstances involves explicit definition of the nature, expectations, and boundaries of the consulting relationship, as stated in Standard 3.11(a), Psychological Services Delivered to or Through Organizations:

3.11(a) Psychologists delivering services to or through organizations provide information beforehand to clients and when appropriate those directly affected by the services about (1) the nature and objectives of the services, (2) the intended recipients, (3) which of the individuals are clients, (4) the relationship the psychologist will have with each person and the organization, and (5) limits of confidentiality. As soon as feasible, they provide information about the results and conclusions of such services to appropriate persons.

ADVERTISING

The issue of advertising is also relevant in a developing field. Standard 5.01 pertains to the Avoidance of False or Deceptive Statements. In particular, Standard 5.01 (b) states:

> 5.01 (b) Psychologists do not make false, deceptive, or fraudulent statements concerning (1) their training, experience, or competence; (2) their academic degrees; (3) their credentials; (4) their institutional or association affiliations; (5) their services; (6) the scientific or clinical basis for, or results or degree of success of, their services; (7) their fees; or (8) their publications or research findings.

This standard applies to all areas of practice, although it may be difficult to determine compliance in a field where specific standards have yet to be established. From a legal perspective, psychologists cannot be accused of misleading others if they actually provide the services they claim to provide and if their expertise is credible.

Dr. Franklin Fiske (business) expressed concern about the flashy executive coach or the motivational speaker who promises a quick fix:

> Companies bring these people in as motivators, they tell great stories, they're entertaining, they get people psyched up, they'll be in the room going, "Yes, let's go, let's go." The problem is the next day the participants wake up and then it's business as usual because they didn't give them any tools. You can't expect change in a two-hour workshop.

APPLICABILITY

Some practitioners have suggested that because their practice is, for example, executive coaching rather than psychotherapy, the Ethics Code does not apply to them or their activities. In fact, the Ethics Code is explicit in distinguishing not only between psychologists' roles but also between psychologists' public and private selves. The second paragraph of the Ethics Code (APA, 2002) states:

This Ethics Code applies only to psychologists' activities that are part of their scientific, educational, or professional roles as psychologists. Areas covered include but are not limited to the clinical, counseling, and school practice of psychology; research; teaching; supervision of trainees; public service; policy development; social intervention; development of assessment instruments; conducting assessments; educational counseling; organizational consulting; forensic activities; program design and evaluation; and administration. This Ethics Code applies to these activities across a variety of contexts, such as in person, postal, telephone, Internet, and other electronic transmissions. These activities shall be distinguished from the purely private conduct of psychologists, which is not within the purview of the Ethics Code.

By virtue of being licensed and members of APA, psychologists are subject in all of their professional actions to the Ethics Code, even if, in a particular role, they are not referring to themselves as psychologists. This does not mean that psychologists *must* refer to themselves as psychologists. They can describe themselves, for example, as performance consultants. The Ethics Code, nonetheless, applies to them and their activities. As there is variability among insurance companies, consultants should carefully review their practice liability policies with regard to coverage for their coaching and consulting practices.

Putting It All Together

To fully explore training, competence, and ethics in this chapter, we have partitioned these different aspects of performance consulting into separate components. Although this yields a clearer understanding of the different parts, it is in fact the gestalt, the totality, that creates the trained, competent, ethical practitioner.

To end this section, we share vignettes of specific work done by three of our consultants. Each brings his own background and training to work with diverse populations. Each illustrates the diverse ways in which practitioners are moving from their already established areas of expertise into new arenas of performance consulting.

Dr. Gates exemplified a sports sciences professor whose expertise as a sport psychology consultant led to work in high-risk sports. In his "day job," Dr. Norris provided therapy in a university counseling center. He also consulted with rock bands. The training staff of a few organizations with high-risk professionals pursued Dr. Jarrett, trained in psychology with a subsequent career in sport psychology consulting, to apply those skills to their domain.

With a doctoral degree in sports sciences and training in counseling techniques, Dr. Gordon Gates has extensive experience in both research and practice. University-based, he has consulted with elite athletic teams, individuals, and organizations for nearly 20 years. About seven years ago, he began working with auto racing drivers and pit crews. His pragmatic, nonpretentious style and recognition of his limitations have been central to his success. He provided the following example of the interplay of these elements from his consultation with a NASCAR team whose driver had difficulty performing after his wife left him:

> We went to dinner one night and we kind of talked about it. I said I am not a clinician, blah, blah, blah. At one point he went off to the restroom. He came out with wet hands—there were no towels—and he didn't know what to do. And he ended up finally giving up and just wiped them on his jeans. And I made a comment to them like, "Oh, we can dress him up, but we can't take him anywhere." He later told the other guys that the reason I got hired was because I treated him like just a normal guy and he felt pretty comfortable with that.
>
> I worked really hard with him, and I think I was effective. We practiced thought stopping. We did affirmations. Centering. And I was pretty scared because at that point I hadn't worked in auto racing. I just had these visions of him hitting the wall. But I was pretty smart with it. I talked to him about it and for instance when we did thought stopping, I would tell him the technique, but then I would ask him "Could you do that in the car?" And then we talked about it and then he tried it, just taking it for a few laps. Then he tried it in a time trial. Then he tried it in a race.
>
> We did a pilot testing protocol for almost all of the stuff we did in the car. We did most of the stuff that you do with a normal athlete who was having task-interfering thoughts.
>
> I didn't have any illusions that we were solving the problem. We were doing triage, Band-Aids—but he owned the team and he couldn't quit, or 50 people would have been out of work. We had to help him get his head right in the car.
>
> He was able to get in the car and not kill anybody. I got him past the impasse of dealing with his wife. There is no doubt in my mind that I helped him there. But I couldn't help him on the bigger issue. I ended up getting him back in counseling with a marriage and family therapist.

Dr. Nick Norris obtained a doctorate in counselor education 30 years ago. Professionally, he is based in a university counseling center, but over the years he has been involved in outreach to the music department of his university. Through his involvement in presentations at music conferences, he has also become known to a network of musicians:

If you get beyond the individual performer, whether it's a flute section or any musical group, you've got to take a look at "How do we gel musically?" and then "How do we gel professionally, from a business perspective?" because those two go hand-in-hand if you're going to be successful out in the real musical world. I take kind of a goal-setting, problem-solving, communication approach. And then as I work with a group along those lines, I start to see all this other stuff. Individual, personal, mental health problems of a wide variety. Individual personal performance problems, stage fright, and so on.

One of my better consulting jobs has been with a Grammy-winning group. That's just something that's evolved over time. It really has always been focused on helping them as a band, as a functioning musical performing group, learn how to identify goals, and how to do problem solving, and how to be a community, on an organizational–business, as well as creative, level.

I haven't worked with them as a group now probably for a year. But there's intermittent contact. Just last night I probably spent 20 minutes on the phone with one of their major players, helping him, coaching him. It's like a corporate coaching concept: coaching him as to "okay you've got this communication problem, how in the hell are you going to solve it?" We brainstormed, and he came up with a way to approach the rest of the group. But I also recognized that he was really in a depressive kind of crisis. And knowing his long-term history and stuff, I was able not only to help him personally but also to help him figure out how to take this performance issue, business-related, back to the group where he was just stopped solid.

What I find really satisfying is seeing them take what I've coached them on and put it into practice without me. So it might be about communication, which gets all the way down to paraphrasing and "I" statements and no assumption making. Or goal setting. Or problem solving, in which you coach them on the process, and they put that into action in their rehearsals or business meetings or performances. And to know that they're also becoming increasingly more sensitive about the interpersonal stuff that goes with being a musical group, where they can be sensitive to each other, not just as musicians, as band-mates, as business partners, but also as people.

Shortly after obtaining his doctorate in counseling psychology 15 years ago, Dr. John Jarrett became one of the first of the current wave of psychologist practitioners hired for a permanent position working with elite athletes. Approached by administrators in high-risk professions to adapt some of his sport psychology work to their areas, he has now developed expertise in working with airline pilots, SWAT teams, and nuclear energy workers:

> I've been focusing on getting nuclear energy technicians and engineers ready for an exam that is pretty rigorous in terms of the quantity of the material that they study and the quality of their knowledge. They've been adopting a different perspective where certainly the content is still of paramount importance, but also a lot of attention is paid to training them for the exam process.
>
> They have training facilitates at these places that are just unbelievable. They could simulate the control room; they had complete mock re-creations of the room that the nuclear engineers sit in when they are monitoring the plant. It goes right down to the same indicators and visual feedback mechanisms and all the dials and knobs and buttons, they're all there. In terms of simulation, it's even better than what we would usually have available even for elite athletes. We didn't have to rely nearly as much on imagery work; we could just walk into these re-creations.
>
> What was really interesting to me was they have these fantastic resources for concentrating upon the emotional, cognitive preparation of the individuals, but they didn't use it for that. They used it for two purposes: They gave them as complicated scenarios as they could to challenge them all the time, to keep testing their knowledge. Also, there was supposed to be a general understanding that "Let's make it as stressful as we can; the more stress we put them under, the better they will be prepared for the exam." But without the connection of: Let's give them coping skills as well, so that with the high level of stress we're putting them under, we're also teaching them how to handle it.
>
> A lot of my work has really involved changing their training program. It's sometimes not as immediately gratifying as the sport psychology work, because you have to know the situation in an organization fairly well before you can start

being effective. But the work I've done over the years with the nuclear energy industry is something that I've felt really good about. I certainly know they've been extremely pleased with the results.

Recommendations to Consultants

Based on the comments of our expert consultants, our expert performers (as described in earlier chapters), and our own experience, we would make the following specific observations and recommendations with regard to training, competence, and ethics in performance psychology:

- Successful performance consultants identify the following elements as central to becoming competent in the field: formal academic training, structured postdegree training, performance experience, informal training (e.g., reading, being mentored, peer consultation or volunteering in the performance domain), and formative life experiences.
- Until the advent of specific graduate programs in performance psychology, it is unlikely that any current graduate training will provide the breadth of knowledge required for competent practice. Individuals should assess their areas of competency and seek supplemental training to remedy any deficits.
- Performance experience, whether in the relevant domain or transferred from a different domain, is helpful.
- Knowledge of the relevant domain, whether through experience or learning, is essential.
- At present, no formal standards exist for assessing competence in performance consulting. Informal standards by which others weigh competency and credibility include one's formal academic and postdegree training, direct observation of one's work and interactions with others, the outcome of one's consulting efforts, the experience and personal characteristics that one brings to the consulting context, and professional affiliation with an organization that maintains a code of ethics for practice. It is especially important to recognize the limits of one's abilities and not to practice beyond one's area of competence.
- Documentation of training and the means by which one establishes competency are important, not only to ensure quality of service, but also for effective risk management. Substantiated training and knowledge can set the context for recognizing the consultant's competence.

■ Until specific guidelines for performance consulting are established, the reasonable steps and relevant education required are defined by the "prevailing professional judgment of psychologists engaged in similar activities in similar circumstances" (APA, 2002, p. 1061). In this regard, the experience and education of other performance consultants, not merely one's generalist peers, would form the relevant reference group.

■ Interaction between performance consultants and clients may occur in a variety of settings other than an office. Practitioners are advised to be particularly attuned to issues of confidentiality and multiple role relationships. In considering a change of venue, shift in focus, or any variation of interactions that may alter the relationship with the client, one must ensure that the change neither (a) impairs or diminishes one's professional functioning nor (b) possibly exploits or harms the client.

■ Engaging simultaneously in psychotherapy and performance consultation with an individual is not unethical as long as the above conditions are met. Nonetheless, practitioners should be advised that such action may put them at greater risk for a complaint by a discontented client. The amount of risk is directly related to the emotional vulnerability of the client.

■ Performance consultants should prepare written explanations of practices, fees, and policies to clients as a matter of informed consent.

■ When consultation involves third parties, such as a referring manager or supervisor, the guidelines for confidentiality should be explicitly defined and clarified with all parties prior to commencing services.

■ As practitioners vie for business in this new and still evolving area, special attention is required to accurately represent one's skills, abilities, and experience.

■ Whether they provide consultation, coaching, or therapy, psychologists are subject to all aspects of the APA Ethics Code, in all aspects of their professional work.

The Consultant as Performer $\Big|$ 16

It is not what you know that is important; it is what people do with what you know.

—Old grandfather saying

Throughout the process of interviewing participants and then writing this book, we have reflected on the idea—both metaphor and actuality—that the consultant is a performer in his or her own right. As we came to understand the experiences of both performers and consultants, we were increasingly aware that the information which focused on those we designated as performers was equally applicable to those who take on the role of performance consultant. In this final chapter, we attempt to synthesize and reflect on some of the primary observations that have been gathered through the course of our work.

Successful performance consulting poses a special challenge. As an evolving field, it requires three levels of knowledge (Terenzini, 1993): foundational or basic knowledge; specific knowledge of the performance domain; and contextual intelligence.

These levels of knowledge to some degree move from general to specific competencies. Among the foundational skills, we have identified five essential areas of knowledge that consultants learn through formal coursework and training: relationship skills, change skills, knowledge of performance excellence, knowledge of the physiological aspects of performance, and knowledge of systems consultation. Domain-specific knowledge must be built on this foundational knowledge. One also must have "contextual intelligence" to understand the systemic principles and interactions within a specific consultation situation.

Knowledge and skills in these three core areas are not sufficient, however; consultants must also have a number of the performance skills and competencies that we have discussed in the preceding chapters: They must be able to present themselves effectively and efficiently to apply the knowledge that they have. They must be excellent performers themselves.

Foundational Skills

The five foundational skills described below are gained through graduate training or supplementary learning. Learning can occur through formal classroom lectures, readings, or on-line resources. Some of the skills should be actively practiced under supervision in order for the consultant to become competent.

BASIC RELATIONSHIP OR COUNSELING SKILLS

Relationship skills are essential to develop rapport. It is important to be able to listen and convey empathy and support. Research has indicated that the quality of counselor–client relationship is the best single predictor of outcome in counseling and therapy (Whiston & Sexton, 1993). We conclude that these skills are critical to effective consulting as well.

One of the most succinct descriptions of this issue that we heard was from Dr. Jarrett. He reflected on situations in which he had been called in, following unsuccessful work by another consultant:

> Sometimes I get caught in situations where another psychologist has already been in there and failed. A common thread of why they failed often seems to be that they didn't establish a human relationship with people. They were aloof or noncommunicative or unresponsive to the needs of the people whom they were working with. I've usually heard, "Oh, such a smart person; he really knew his stuff, but we just couldn't work with him."

A successful consultant must be able to identify both the strengths and the nature of difficulties the client wants to address. In some situations, this assessment may require formal evaluation, including the use of a battery of instruments. For others, observation and interview provide adequate information for thorough assessment. In all cases, this evaluation should be rapid, thorough, and efficient. Depending on the particular area of performance, it will be critically important to differentiate between difficulties caused by basic limitations (e.g., anatomy or ability) and those related to mental or emotional factors.

Basic counseling skills are a cornerstone of consulting. Three skills are especially important: being able to successfully establish a positive, trusting relationship; being able to accurately assess a given situation; and being able to design interventions to help bring about change.

SKILLS FACILITATING CHANGE

The combination of basic counseling skills and accurate assessment provides a foundation for designing and implementing interventions. Consultation is premised on the assumption that an individual or group intends to effect change in order to improve. Understanding the processes of change (Prochaska, Norcross, & DiClemente, 1994) provides the consultant a framework for assisting others. Although it is not impossible for a performance consultant to think in psychodynamic terms or use a nondirective style, feedback from successful consultants and performers alike suggests that directive, solution-oriented models fit more readily with the needs of performance consultation. Training in cognitive approaches is especially helpful, as is a grounding in the principles of positive psychology.

KNOWLEDGE OF PERFORMANCE EXCELLENCE

Our interviews suggest that the knowledge base of literature, research, and principles of applied performance enhancement interventions with athletes is widely applicable to nonathletic areas of performance. Although sports analogies may not be appropriate in every domain and venue, the core concepts and the extensive and systematic research in applied sport psychology are simply too valuable to ignore. Historically, this knowledge base has not been part of the training of psychologists. Psychology has focused more on the diagnosis and treatment of psychopathology. This deficit focus provides both a markedly different information base and perspective from that of attending to and nurturing excellence.

Knowledge of performance enhancement has evolved primarily in departments of kinesiology, physical education, and sport and exercise sciences. Rather than attempting to "re-invent the wheel," or worse, inappropriately apply pathology-based concepts, consultants are advised to do their homework and become familiar with the available literature. Not to do so is at best naïve—and more likely, inappropriately arrogant.

KNOWLEDGE OF PHYSIOLOGICAL ASPECTS OF PERFORMANCE

Psychology as well as the other counseling professions typically maintains the Cartesian mind–body dichotomy. Knowledge of relevant aspects of the physiology of performance is a critical skill for consultants. Maslow (1968) recognized the hierarchy of needs on which human functioning rests. As we have described here, neither a surgeon nor a talk show host can perform optimally without sufficient sleep; issues such as the grip on one's violin or the possibility of correct "turn-out" in ballet are rooted in our anatomy. A competent performance consultant should have a basic working knowledge of physiology germane to the performance setting and seek additional consultation as needed.

KNOWLEDGE OF SYSTEMS CONSULTATION

Performers do not act in isolation. It is the individual in the context of his or her particular performance milieu that is of relevance to the consultation interaction. Consultants may gain a general understanding of the interaction between the individual and the system through knowledge of family systems, or through theories and practices of consultation or coaching.

Recently, personality theorists have begun to address this complex area as well. In particular, Mischel and Shoda (1995) developed a framework, the cognitive-affective personality system (CAPS), to describe the interactive quality of person and system. They suggested that there are predictable elements to individuals' perceptions, expectancies and beliefs, affects, goals and values, and self-regulatory processes. This "if–then" interaction of Person × Situation allows for a particular "behavioral signature." Sport psychologist Ronald Smith (2002) has looked at the CAPS perspective in relation to the sport environment. He has considered applications that pertain to sport performance anxiety, burnout, achievement goal theory, and understanding of the individual athlete. The CAPS model offers another framework for consultants attempting to navigate the intricacies of performance settings.

Domain-Specific Knowledge

Domain-specific knowledge is acquired in a variety of ways: through one's own active involvement in the domain or through absorption of the culture by means of formal or informal learning. Knowledge of consultation skills in specific domains varies widely: Considerable information exists about executive coaching, whereas information on consulting with modern dancers is at best nascent.

Among the people we interviewed, there was not a consensus as to how much knowledge of a specific performance domain is required in order to establish credibility. Most performers, though not all, would want a consultant who had actually worked either in their specific domain or a comparable performance domain. On the other hand, some of our consultants felt that performance was universal and that domain-specific knowledge was not necessary. Having participated in a particular performance domain may not be required, but three things are critical:

First, an effective consultant must at the very least have an appreciation for and interest in the particular performance domain. A pacifist attempting to consult with the military, or an individual who finds ballet a waste of time, will have a short-lived career consulting in those areas.

Second, the consultant must have respect for performers in the specific domain. Respect moves beyond appreciation and interest. It means acknowledgement of the challenges and difficulties that the performer faces on a daily basis. This is a cornerstone of being able to develop empathy with any individual. Respect also encompasses an understanding of the domain in addition to the person.

Third, for success it is critical to be able to speak the language of the specific domain. Each domain has a history, language, and culture. Consulting can be considered an experience in cultural immersion. The effective consultant makes the effort to learn the language and take responsibility for effective communication, rather than expecting the performer to learn the consultant's language.

Contextual Intelligence

Successful consultation involves more than knowledge of technical skills and techniques. It includes knowledge of the implementation of change within a given system. It requires an understanding of the context in which one operates—knowing what works with which persons in what situations. It is more than *knowing what* to do; it is *knowing how* to get it done. Contextual intelligence is both a sensitivity to the uniqueness of the particular situation and an acquired skill.

Institutional researchers (Terenzini, 1993) and contemporary intelligence theorists (Davidson & Downing, 2000; Sternberg, 1985, 1997; Wagner, 2000) have associated contextual intelligence with "practical know-how that rarely is formally described or taught directly" (Wagner, 1987, p. 383). It is the skill that is most closely associated with wisdom and practical knowledge, and it has been shown to be the best predictor of success in actual performance situations (Sternberg, 2000). It reflects "organizational savvy and wisdom" (Terenzini, 1993, p. 6).

Successful consultants recognize the importance of knowing both the formal and informal structure of an organization—that is, knowing who has the power to influence decisions and "the way the system works."

Understanding the system is critical for interventions, whether with individuals, groups, or systems.

An example of the application of contextual intelligence relates to the issue of domain-specific information. The savvy consultant treats each domain as unique and goes through a process of inquiry and learning. Even if little or no new information is anticipated, it is still important to go through the process, because *performers* generally believe it is important. Regardless of whether new information is gained—and usually, it will be—the performer will be more receptive to feedback and suggestions if he or she feels that the unique aspects of the situation have been fully considered and appreciated.

Gaining contextual intelligence has often been considered a tacit process, learned indirectly through experience. Systems theory (Bateson, 1972; Brown & McDaniel, 1995; Wynne et al., 1986) offers a model for assessing organizations and developing contextual "maps," thereby hastening the learning curve. A consultant is well on the way to developing contextual intelligence if he or she learns the language within the system; the structure, processes and patterns; the means of influence within the system; and basic attitudes and values.

You're On

Merely having knowledge is not necessarily equivalent to good consultation. A consultant must be able to engage the client and deliver advice in a fashion such that the client wants to participate in the process. When a consultant enters the arena, he or she is essentially an unknown quantity to whom attributes will rapidly be ascribed. The client is likely to impute certain characteristics on the basis of prior conceptions or experience with consultants. These assumptions usually are re-evaluated throughout the initial contact. They can easily make or break the consult.

As superficial as it may seem, one's physical appearance and presentation set the stage for either effective or ineffective consultation. Often, initial appearance creates an instantaneous impression related to the client's assumption of credibility. A casually attired consultant may bomb in a business setting. Wearing a conservative three-piece suit can be equally disastrous for consulting in the creative world of radio. Dr. Gates's informal, humorous put-down of a stock car racer created the opportunity for effective, trusting consultation. A performer from another setting might feel offended and "dissed."

Other consultant characteristics also were considered important, at least in terms of initial impression. The performers we interviewed universally agreed that older consultants are generally perceived as more experienced and more credible. Having a "good voice" is important. Attitude is a crucial factor, as one wants to be alert, attentive and listen with respect. Being able to "speak" the language and engage in a collaborative fashion—fundamentals of good consultation method—were highlighted by performers. Our interviews indicated that it is important to present a pragmatic attitude that dispels the traditional image of a psychologist. An action and solution-oriented attitude is a plus; psychodynamic interpretations, solicitous "mmm-hmms", and nondirective reflection may be of little benefit or even damaging.

It is important to come across as knowledgeable and confident, yet equally important to admit what one does not know. It is far more acceptable to confess ignorance than attempt to bluff, deceive, or "oversell" one's knowledge and abilities. The client will soon recognize the deception, at which point all credibility is lost.

Integrity is essential for credibility and, hence, effective consultation. This means behaving in a fashion that is isomorphic with the principles and models that one proposes. This point—practicing what one preaches—was recognized and emphasized by consultants more often than by performers. If you advocate applying specific mental skills for peak performance, you want to have clear goals and a specific game plan. You will use imagery to prepare for the consultation, practice relaxation techniques to manage your own physical activation, notice and direct your concentration, and assess and manage your self-talk. If you advocate balancing work and personal life, your life should reflect a comparable equilibrium. Business consultation often focuses on the style of interactions that the client has with co-workers or subordinates. Thus, the consultant's isomorphic behavior may be especially crucial for business consultants.

Engaging the client is the essence of your performance as a consultant. It is a dance in which all of your knowledge, all of your skills, and the essence of being intermingle and interact within the encounter with your client. It is the moment when you're on, consulting for peak performance.

Appendix

List of Participants | A

Performer Participants

BUSINESS DOMAIN

Anna, lawyer
Arthur, lawyer
Barry, advertising executive
Charles, insurance executive
David, banker

HIGH-RISK DOMAIN

Eric, neurosurgeon
Frederick, emergency room physician
George, Special Forces medic; police sniper

PERFORMING ARTIST DOMAIN

Harold, choral conductor
Ian, broadcaster, actor
Jerry, ballet dancer
Brenda, actor
Charlotte, ballet dancer; arts administrator

Diane, orchestral violinist
Keith, actor
Ellen, violinist; chamber orchestra conductor
Faith, singer
Grace, broadcaster
Helena, modern dancer
Larry, actor
Michael, orchestral conductor
Ilene, pianist; arts administrator
Norman, cellist

Consultant Participants

BUSINESS DOMAIN

Dr. Andrew Adams, former professor of organizational development; business consultant and best-selling author; owns a large corporation

Dr. Alice Austin, counseling psychologist; sport psychology training; business training; independent consultant

Dr. Brian Bell, clinical and family–systems psychologist; retired dean of school of psychology; independent consultant

Dr. Barbara Benton, doctoral degree in sport science; training and employment by major business training group

Dr. Colin Cross, doctoral degree in sport science; former coach and administrator; independent business consultant

Dr. Claire Crown, clinical psychologist; training in business consultation; independent business consultant

Dr. Daniel Dean, clinical psychologist; employed by major sport organization as sport psychology consultant; training by and part-time consultant with a major business training group

Dr. Edward Evans, clinical psychologist; retired psychology department chair

Dr. Franklin Fiske, doctoral degree in social psychology; independent sport psychology and business consultant

HIGH-RISK DOMAIN

Dr. Gordon Gates, doctoral degree in sport science; university professor; independent sport psychology and business consultant

Dr. Irving Ingram, doctoral degree in industrial–organizational psychology; owns independent forensic consulting practice

Dr. John Jarrett, clinical psychologist; university professor; independent consultant; former sport psychology consultant to a major national organization

Dr. Kenneth King, clinical psychologist; sport and business psychology consultant; military consultant

Dr. Leo Lindsay, doctoral degree in sport science; university professor; consultant to Navy SEALS

PERFORMING ARTS DOMAIN

Dr. Donna Desmond, clinical psychologist; retired ballet dancer

Dr. Marc Martin, musician; composer; additional counseling training

Dr. Nick Norris, doctoral degree in counseling education; university counseling center staff; independent music consulting

Dr. Owen Osborne, doctoral degree in personality psychology; postdoctorate clinical training; independent psychology coach for actors

Interview Questions for Performers | B

Basic Information–Joining

1. Let me check the spelling of your name. What is your age? What is your current location and affiliation?
2. How long have you been in your field?
3. Please describe your current level of involvement in your field.
4. Can you describe a few performance moments that felt especially memorable? (If positive, ask for negative; if negative, ask for positive.)

Initial Information on Mental Processes (Maintain reference to best–peak performance)

1. What are the mental, psychological, and emotional factors that influence successful performance in your field?
2. What kind of mental preparation do you find useful for performance?
3. How and where did you learn it?
4. What about it is helpful to you?
5. How do you cope with stress?

6. What are the mental, psychological, and emotional factors involved in preparing for a performance (working) with others in contrast to preparing for a solo performance (working alone)?

Introduction of Concept of Performance Psychology

"I am particularly interested in speaking with you today about performance psychology and performance psychologists. This area focuses on the ways in which, from a mental or emotional perspective, performance can be improved."

Questions After Introducing the Concept of Performance Psychology

1. Have you ever known someone who used a performance enhancement consultant? For what kinds of issues? What did they do? Was it helpful?
2. What kind of information about [your particular field] would be critically important for the consultant to know (e.g., setting, stresses, technical knowledge)?
3. What mental and emotional aspects of performance do you consider unique to your field?
4. When you think of the ideal consultant, what type(s) of assistance and skills would the consultant provide?
5. What kind of personal characteristics would you look for in such a consultant? How important is age, gender, or ethnicity?
6. How important might age, gender, or ethnicity be to other performers in your field?
7. What kinds of services or efforts might actually hinder your performance?
8. What would you consider an ideal consultation setting for performance enhancement (e.g., meeting with a consultant one on one or in a small or large group setting; meeting at your place of work–rehearsal or away from that locale)?
9. If you were working with a performance consultant, would you be concerned about others (e.g., your agent, coach, or peers)

knowing that you were working with someone and what issues you were addressing? Would this be similar to or different from concerns you might have about someone knowing you were in psychotherapy?

Checklist

A performance enhancement specialist might provide the following services. What kinds of services might you find helpful? In what situations? For what circumstances?

- goal setting
- imagery
- thought stopping
- arousal management
- performance strategies
- pre-performance mental readying routines
- re-focusing skills
- dealing with injury
- dealing with career transition
- relationship issues
- confidence
- getting along with other performers (cohesion, harmony, teamwork, etc.)
- dealing with media
- time management
- dealing with fears

Appendix

Interview Questions for Consultants | C

Basic Information–Joining

1. How long have you been in your field? How long have you been consulting with performers? With what kinds of performers do you work? (Note to interviewers: If more than one, begin interview with focus on primary one, then return to significant questions after going through each of the major sections.)
2. What were some of your best consulting experiences? What about them made them "best"? When have you felt most effective? (Be specific.)
3. Are there other (specific) consulting experiences that have been especially memorable in some way?

Initial Information on Mental Processes (Maintain reference to best–peak performance)

1. What are the mental, psychological, and emotional factors that influence successful performance (in designated field)?
2. What kind of mental preparation do you find useful for performance? How and where do you teach it? How is it helpful?

3. Is the process of teaching mental skills different when you are working with a solo performer as compared with a group?

Introduction of Concept of Performance Psychology

"I am particularly interested in speaking with you today about performance psychology and performance psychologists. This area focuses on the ways in which, from a mental or emotional perspective, performance can be improved."

Questions After Introducing the Concept of Performance Psychology:

1. As a consultant, what kinds of issues have you addressed? What did you do? Was it helpful?
2. What kind of information about [your particular field] would be critically important for the consultant to know (e.g., setting, stresses, technical knowledge)?
3. What do you consider unique (competencies, risks) to this field?
4. When you think of the ideal consultant, what type(s) of assistance and skills would the consultant provide?
5. What kind of personal characteristics would you look for in such a consultant?
6. How important is age, gender, or ethnicity?
7. What kinds of services or efforts might actually hinder a performer?
8. What would you consider an ideal consultation setting for performance enhancement (e.g., meeting with a client one on one or in a small or large group setting; meeting at their place of work–rehearsal or away from that locale, such as your office)?
9. What do performers want regarding confidentiality? Are there ways in which this is similar to or different from concerns clients have about confidentiality in psychotherapy?

Questions About Training and Competence

1. What type of training or experience has best prepare you for working with performers?
2. How would you assess whether a colleague was competent to provide such services?

Checklist

A performance enhancement specialist might provide the following services. Which have you found helpful? In what situations? For what circumstances?

- goal setting
- imagery
- thought stopping
- arousal management
- performance strategies
- pre-performance mental readying routines
- re-focusing skills
- dealing with injury
- dealing with career transition
- relationship issues
- confidence
- getting along with other performers (cohesion, harmony, teamwork, etc.)
- dealing with media
- time management
- dealing with fears

References

Abramowitz, R. (2000). *Is that a gun in your pocket?* New York: Random House.

Alexander, D. A., Walker, L. G., Innes, G., & Irving, B. L. (1993). *Police stress at work*. London: Police Foundation.

American Psychological Association. (1992). Ethical principles of psychologists and code of conduct. *American Psychologist, 47,* 1597–1611.

American Psychological Association. (2002). Ethical principles of psychologists and code of conduct. *American Psychologist, 57,* 1060–1073.

American Psychological Association. (n.d.). *About Division 47: Division Projects*. Retrieved March 11, 2003, from http://www.psyc.unt.edu/apadiv47/about_divprojects.html

American Psychological Association, Society of Consulting Psychology, Education and Training Committee. (2000). Principles for education and training at the doctoral and post-doctoral level in consulting psychology. *Organizational Consulting Psychology*. Retrieved November 17, 2002, from http://www.apa.org/divisions/div13/

Andersen, M. B. (Ed.). (2000a). *Doing sport psychology: Process and practice*. Champaign, IL: Human Kinetics.

Andersen, M. B. (2000b). Introduction. In M. B. Andersen (Ed.), *Doing sport psychology: Process and practice* (pp. xiii–xvii). Champaign, IL: Human Kinetics.

Andersen, M. B., Van Raalte, J. L., & Brewer, B. W. (2001). Sport psychology service delivery: Staying ethical while keeping loose.

Professional Psychology: Research and Practice, 32, 12–18.

Aronson, E. (1994). *The social animal*. San Francisco: Freeman.

Aronson, E., Wilson, T. D., & Alpert, R. M. (1994). *Social psychology*. New York: Harper Collins.

Baillie, P. H. F., & Danish, S. J. (1992). Understanding the career transition of athletes. *The Sport Psychologist, 6,* 77–98.

Bandura, A. (1977). Self-efficacy: Toward a unifying theory of behavioral change. *Psychology Review, 84,* 191–215.

Bandura, A. (1986). *Social foundation of thought and action: A social cognitive theory*. Englewood Cliffs, NJ: Prentice-Hall.

Bateson, G. (1972). *Steps to an ecology of mind*. London: Jason Aronson.

Beisser, A. (1977). *The madness in sport*. Bowie, MD: Charles Press.

Benjamin, G. A., Darling, E. J., & Sales, B. (1990). The prevalence of depression, alcohol abuse, and cocaine abuse among United States lawyers. *International Journal of Law and Psychiatry, 13,* 233–246.

Benjamin, G. A., Sales, B. D., & Darling, E. (1992). Comprehensive lawyer assistance programs: Justification and model. *Law and Psychology Review, 16,* 113–136.

Biggam, F. H., Pwer, K. G., MacDonald, R. R., Carcary, W. B., & Moodie, E. (1997). Self-perceived occupational stress distress in a Scottish police force. *Work and Stress, 11,* 118–133.

Bloom, B. S. (Ed.). (1985). *Developing talent in young people*. New York: Ballantine.

Boring, E. G. (1950). *A history of experimental psychology*. New York: Appleton-Century-Crofts.

Brandfonbrener, A. G. (1999). Theatrical patients in a performing arts practice. *Medical Problems of Performing Artists, 14*, 21–24.

Brandt, N. (1993). *Con brio: Four Russians called the Budapest String Quartet*. New York: Oxford University Press.

Brewer, B., & Van Raalte, J. (2002). Introduction to sport and exercise psychology. In J. L. Van Raalte & B. W. Brewer (Eds.), *Exploring sport and exercise psychology* (pp. 3–9). Washington, DC: American Psychological Association.

Brown, C. H. (2001). Clinical cross-training: Compatibility of sport and family systems psychology. *Professional Psychology: Research and Practice, 32*, 19–26.

Brown, C. H., & McDaniel, S. (1995, Summer). Spam and bagels: Recipes for healthy consultations. *The Family Psychologist, 11*, 14–15.

Brown, J. M., & Campbell, E. A. (1990). Sources of occupational stress in the police. *Work and Stress, 4*, 305–318.

Brown, J. M., & Campbell, E. A. (1994). *Stress and policing: Sources and strategies*. Chichester, England: Wiley.

Burton, D. (1989). Winning isn't everything: Examining the impact of performance goals on collegiate swimmers' cognitions and performance. *The Sport Psychologist, 12*, 404–418.

Caironi, P. C. (2002). Coaches coach, players play, and companies win. *The Industrial–Organizational Psychologist, 40*, 37–44.

Carr, C. M., & Murphy, S. M. (1995). Alcohol and drugs in sport. In S. M. Murphy (Ed.), *Sport psychology interventions* (pp. 283–306). Champaign, IL: Human Kinetics.

Carron, A. V. (1993). Toward the integration of theory, research, and practice in sport psychology. *Journal of Applied Sport Psychology, 5*, 207–221.

Cassell, E. J. (1985). *Talking with patients: Vol. I. The theory of doctor–patient communication*. Cambridge, MA: MIT Press.

Clarkson, M. (1999). *Competitive fire*. Champaign, IL: Human Kinetics.

Clavell, J. (Ed.). (1983). *The art of war by Sun Tzu*. New York: Delta.

Cogan, K. D. (1998). Putting the "clinical" into sport psychology consulting. In K. F. Hays (Ed.), *Integrating exercise, sports, movement, and mind: Therapeutic unity* (pp. 131–143). Binghamton, NY: Haworth.

Cole, W. (2000, October 16). The (un)therapists. *Time*

Conroy, D. E., Poczwardowski, A., & Henschen, K. P. (2001). Evaluative criteria and consequences associated with failure and success for elite athletes and performing artists. *Journal of Applied Sport Psychology, 13*, 300–322.

Covey, S. R. (1989). *The 7 habits of highly effective people*. New York: Simon & Schuster

Covey, S. R., Merrill, A. R., & Merrill, R. R. (1994). *First things first*. New York: Simon & Schuster.

Cox, T., & Ferguson, E. (1991). Individual differences, stress and coping. In C. L. Cooper & R. Payne (Eds.), *Personality and stress: Individual differences in the stress process* (pp. 7–30).Chichester, England: Wiley.

Csikszentmihalyi, M. (1990). *Flow: The psychology of optimal experience*. New York: Harper & Row.

Csikszentmihalyi, M., Rathunde, K., & Whalen, S. (1993). *Talented teenagers: The roots of success and failure*. New York: Cambridge University Press.

Danish, S. J., Petitpas, A. J., & Hale, B. D. (1993). Life development intervention for athletes: Life skills through sport. *The Counseling Psychologist, 21*, 352–385.

Davidson, J. E., & Downing, C. L. (2000). Contemporary models of intelligence. In R. Sternberg (Ed.), *Handbook of intelligence* (pp. 34–49). New York: Cambridge University Press.

Dean, B. (2001, January/February). The sky's the limit. *Family Therapy Networker*, 36–44.

Deming, W. (1982). *Out of the crisis*. Cambridge, MA: MIT, Center for Advanced Engineering Study.

De Shazer, S. (1982). *Patterns of brief family therapy: An ecosystemic approach*. New York: Guilford.

De Shazer, S. (1985). *Keys to solution in brief therapy*. New York: Norton.

Drogin, E. (1991). Alcoholism in the legal profession: Psychological and legal perspectives and interventions. *Law and Psychology Review, 15*, 117–162.

Duda, J. (1992). Motivation in sport settings: A goal perspective approach. In G. C. Roberts (Ed.), *Motivation in sport and exercise* (pp. 57–91). Champaign, IL: Human Kinetics.

Dunkel, S. E. (1989). *The audition process: Anxiety management and coping strategies*. Stuyvesant, NY: Pendragon.

Durand-Bush, N., & Salmela, J. H. (2001). The development of talent in sport. In R. N.

Singer, H. A. Hausenblas, & C. M. Janelle (Eds.), *Handbook of sport psychology* (pp. 269–289). New York: Wiley.

Ellickson, K. A., & Brown, D. R. (1990). Ethical considerations in dual relationships: The sport psychologist–coach. *Journal of Applied Sport Psychology, 2,* 186–190.

Endler, N. S., & Parker, J. D. A. (1990). Multidimensional assessment of coping: A critical evaluation. *Journal of Personality and Social Psychology, 58,* 844–854.

Engel, G. L. (1977). The need for a new medical model: A challenge for biomedicine. *Science, 196,* 129–136.

Ericsson, K. A., Krampe, R. T., & Tesch-Römer, C. (1993). The role of deliberate practice in the acquisition of expert performance. *Psychological Review, 100,* 363–406.

Foster, S. (1996). Healing work-related trauma. *At Work, 5,* 7–9.

Foxhall, K. (2002, April). More psychologists are attracted to the executive coaching field. *Monitor on Psychology,* pp. 52–53.

Gawande, A. (2002, January 28). The learning curve. *The New Yorker,* pp. 52–61.

General Motors. (1998, February). Team Monte Carlo and NASCAR ride high on explosive growth. *News and Events: News from GM* [Online press release]. Retrieved August 5, 2003, from http://media.gm.com/chevy/98news/c980215b.htm.

Gill, D. L. (1986). *Psychological dynamics in sport.* Champaign, IL: Human Kinetics.

Glass, R. M. (1996). The patient–physician relationship: JAMA focuses on the center of medicine. *Journal of the American Medical Association, 275,* 147–148.

Goleman, D. (1995). *Emotional intelligence.* New York: Bantam Books.

Gould, D. (2002). Moving beyond the psychology of athletic excellence [Special issue]. *Journal of Applied Sport Psychology, 14*(4).

Gould, D., & Damarjian, N. (1998). Insights into effective sport psychology consulting. In K. F. Hays (Ed.), *Integrating exercise, sports, movement, and mind: Therapeutic unity* (pp. 111–130). Binghamton, NY: Haworth.

Gould, D., Dieffenbach, K., & Moffett, A. (2002). Psychological characteristics and their development in Olympic champions. *Journal of Applied Sport Psychology, 14,* 172–204.

Gould, D., Eklund, R. C., & Jackson, S. A. (1993). Coping strategies used by U.S. Olympic wrestlers. *Research Quarterly for Exercise and Sport, 64,* 83–93.

Gould, D., Guinan, D., Greenleaf, C., Medbery, R., & Peterson, K. (1999). Factors affecting Olympic performance: Perceptions of athletes and coaches from more and less successful teams. *The Sport Psychologist, 13,* 371–394.

Gould, D., & Pennisi, N. S. (2002, August). Adaptive and maladaptive perfectionism: Helping the dancer–athlete achieve personal excellence. In L. H. Hamilton (Chair), *Psychology of the dancer/athlete: Pushing beyond physical and mental limitations.* Symposium conducted at the Annual Convention of the American Psychological Association, Chicago.

Gould, D., & Pick, S. (1995). Sport psychology: The Griffith era. *The Sport Psychologist, 9,* 391–405.

Gould, D., Tammen, V., Murphy, S., & May, J. (1989). An examination of U.S. Olympic sport psychology consultants and the services they provide. *The Sport Psychologist, 3,* 300–312.

Gould, D., Udry, E., Tuffey, S., & Loehr, J. (1996). Burnout in competitive junior tennis players. I: A quantitative psychological assessment. *The Sport Psychologist, 10,* 322–340.

Gould, D., Weiss, M., & Weinberg, R. S. (1981). Psychological characteristics of successful and nonsuccessful Big Ten wrestlers. *Journal of Sport Psychology, 3,* 69–81.

Greben, S. E. (1999). Problems, challenges, and opportunity through aging of performing artists. *Medical Problems of Performing Artists, 14,* 85–86.

Greenleaf, C., Gould, D., & Dieffenbach, K. (2001). Factors influencing Olympic performance: Interviews with Atlanta and Nagano U.S. Olympians. *Journal of Applied Sport Psychology, 13,* 154–184.

Greenspan, M. J., & Feltz, D. F. (1989). Psychological interventions with athletes in competitive situations: A review. *The Sport Psychologist, 3,* 219–236.

Haber, S., Rodino, E., & Lipner, I. (2001). *Saying good-bye to managed care: Building your independent psychotherapy practice.* New York: Springer.

Haley, J. (1987). *Problem-solving therapy.* San Francisco: Josey-Bass.

Hamilton, L. H. (1997). *The person behind the mask: A guide to performing arts psychology.* Greenwich, CT: Ablex.

Hamilton, L. H. (1998). *Advice for dancers: Emotional counsel and practical strategies.* San Francisco: Jossey-Bass.

Hamilton, L. H. (2002, August). Implications for treating maladaptive perfectionism: A case presentation. In L. H. Hamilton (Chair),

Psychology of the dancer/athlete: Pushing beyond physical and mental limitations. Symposium conducted at the Annual Convention of the American Psychological Association, Chicago.

Hamilton, L. H., & Hamilton, W. G. (1991). Classical ballet: Balancing the costs of artistry and athleticism. *Medical Problems of Performing Artists, 6,* 39–43.

Hamilton, L. H., & Hamilton, W. G. (1994). Occupational stress in classical ballet: The impact in different cultures. *Medical Problems of Performing Artists, 9,* 35–38.

Hamilton, L. H., Hamilton, W. G., & Meltzer, J. D. (1989). Personality, stress, and injuries in professional ballet dancers. *American Journal of Sports Medicine, 17,* 263–267.

Hamilton, L. H., Hamilton, W. G., Warren, M. P., Keller, K., & Molnar, M. (1997). Factors contributing to the attrition rate in elite ballet students. *Journal of Dance Medicine & Science, 1,* 131–138.

Hanin, Y. (2000). Individual zones of optimal functioning (IZOF) model: Emotion–performance relationships in sport. In Y. Hanin (Ed.), *Emotions in sport* (pp. 65–89). Champaign, IL: Human Kinetics.

Hardy, L. (1990). A catastrophe model of anxiety and performance. In J. G. Jones & L. Hardy (Eds.), *Stress and performance in sport* (pp. 81–106). Chichester, England: Wiley.

Hardy, L., Jones, G., & Gould, D. (1996). *Understanding psychological preparation for sport: Theory and practice of elite performers.* New York: Wiley.

Harris, E. (2002a, November). *Legal and ethical risk management in professional psychological practice—Sequence I: General risk management strategies.* Workshop presented by the American Psychological Association Insurance Trust and the North Carolina Psychological Center, Chapel Hill, NC.

Harris, E. (2002b). *Risk management for therapists who coach.* Retrieved September 3, 2003 from www.MentorCoach .com

Hays, K. F. (2002). The enhancement of performance excellence among performing artists. *Journal of Applied Sport Psychology, 14,* 299–312.

Hays, K. F. (2003, February). Performers: When perfect is the only thing. In K. F. Hays (Chair), *Perfectionism: Good, bad, or always ugly?* Symposium conducted at the Annual Convention of the Ontario Psychological Association, Toronto.

Hays, K. F., & Smith, R. J. (2002). Incorporating sport and exercise psychology into clinical practice. In J. L. Van Raalte & B. W. Brewer (Eds.), *Exploring sport and exercise psychology* (2nd ed.; pp. 479–502). Washington, DC: American Psychological Association.

hooks, b. (1996). *Reel to real: Race, sex, and class at the movies.* New York: Routledge.

Horowitz, I. A. (1980). Juror selection: A comparison of two methods in several criminal cases. *Journal of Applied Social Psychology, 10,* 86–99.

International Coach Federation. (2002). Coaching core competencies. Retrieved July 11, 2003, from http://www.coachfederation. org/credentialing/en/core.htm <http:// www.coachfederation.org/credentialing/ en/core.htm>

Jackson, S., Thomas, P., Marsh, H., & Smethurst, C. (2001). Relationship between flow, self-concept, psychological skills and performance. *Journal of Applied Sport Psychology, 13,* 129–153.

Jackson, S., & Csikszentmihalyi, M. (1999). *Flow in sports.* Champaign, IL: Human Kinetics.

Johnson, L. A. (2003, February 2). Malpractice insurance crisis heats up. *The Charlotte Observer,* p. A4.

Jones, G. (2002). Performance excellence: A personal perspective on the link between sport and business. *Journal of Applied Sport Psychology, 14,* 268–281.

Jowitt, D. (2001). Focus on excellence. In D. Jowitt, R. Alston, K. Kain, J. Kylian, & R. Philp (Eds.), *Not just any body: Advancing health, well-being and excellence in dance and dancers* (pp. 3–4). Owen Sound, Ontario, Canada: The Ginger Press.

Kain, K. (1994). *Movement never lies: An autobiography.* Toronto: McClelland & Stewart.

Kampa-Kokesch, S., & Kilburg, R. R. (2001). Executive coaching: A comprehensive review of the literature. *Consulting Psychology Journal: Practice and Research, 53,* 139–153.

Katz, P. (1999). *The scalpel's edge: The culture of surgeons.* Boston: Allyn & Bacon.

Kaye, E. (1998, May 24). At the end of a brief, brilliant turn. *The New York Times,* pp. AR1, AR27.

Kilburg, R. R. (Ed.). (1996). Executive coaching [Special issue]. *Consulting Psychology Journal, 48* (2).

Kilburg, R. R. (2000). *Executive coaching.* Washington, DC: American Psychological Association.

Kogan, J. (1989). *Nothing but the best: The struggle for perfection at the Juilliard School.* New York: Limelight.

Kogan, N. (2002). Careers in the performing arts: A psychological perspective. *Creativity Research Journal, 14*, 1–16.

Krasnow, D., Mainwaring, L., & Kerr, G. (1999). Injury, stress, and perfectionism in young dancers and gymnasts. *Journal of Dance Medicine & Science, 3*, 51–58.

Lanchester, J. (2003, January 6). High style: Writing under the influence. *The New Yorker*, 80–84.

Lazarus, R. S., & Folkman, S. (1984). *Stress appraisal and coping*. New York: McGraw-Hill.

Leonard, H. S., & Freedman, A. M. (2000). From scientific management through fun and games to high-performing teams: A historical perspective on consulting to team-based organizations. *Consulting Psychology Journal: Practice and Research, 52*, 3–19.

Le Scanff, C., Bachelard, C., Cazes, G., Rosnet, E., & Rivolier, J. (1997). Psychological study of a crew in long-term space flight simulation. *International Journal of Aviation Psychology, 7*, 293–309.

Le Scanff, C., & Taugis, J. (2002). Stress management for police special forces. *Journal of Applied Sport Psychology, 14*, 330–343.

Lesyk, J. J. (1998). *Developing sport psychology within your clinical practice: A practical guide for mental health professionals*. San Francisco: Jossey-Bass.

Levinson, H. (1996). Executive coaching. *Consulting Psychology Journal, 48*, 115–123.

Levinson, W., Roter, D. L., Mullooly, J. P., Dull, V. T., & Frankel, R. M. (1997). Physician-patient communication: The relationship with malpractice claims among primary care physicians and surgeons. *Journal of the American Medical Association, 277*, 553–559.

Lincoln, Y. S., & Guba, E. G. (1985). *Naturalistic inquiry*. Newbury Park, CA: Sage.

Linder, D. E., Pillow, D. R., & Reno, R. R. (1989). Shrinking jocks: Derogation of athletes who consult a sport psychologist. *Journal of Sport & Exercise Psychology, 11*, 270–280.

Littler, W. (2003, January 20). The new guy at the TSO has work cut out for him. *The Toronto Star*, E4.

Locke, E. A., & Latham, G. P. (1990). *A theory of goal setting and task performance*. Englewood Cliffs, NJ: Prentice-Hall.

Locke, E. A., Shaw, K. N., Saari, L. M., & Latham, G. P. (1981). Goal setting and task performance (1969–1980). *Psychological Bulletin, 96*, 125–152.

Mahoney, M. J., & Avener, M. (1977). Psychology of the elite athlete: An exploratory study. *Cognitive Therapy and Research, 1*, 135–142.

Mahoney, M. J., Gabriel, T. J., & Perkins, T. S. (1987). Psychological skills and exceptional athletic performance. *The Sport Psychologist, 1*, 181–199.

Mandel, S. (1993). *Effective presentation skills* (Rev. ed.). Menlo Park, CA: Crisp Publications.

Marchant-Haycox, S. E., & Wilson, G. D. (1992). Personality and stress in performing artists. *Personality and Individual Differences, 13*, 1061–1068.

Martin, J. J., & Cutler, K. (2002). An exploratory study of flow and motivation in theater actors. *Journal of Applied Sport Psychology, 14*, 344–352.

Maslow, A. H. (1968). *Towards a psychology of being* (2nd ed.). Princeton, NJ: VanNostrand.

Mayo, E. (1933). *Human problems of an industrial civilization*. New York: Macmillan.

McCann, S. (1995). Overtraining and burnout. In S. M. Murphy (Ed.), *Sport psychology interventions* (pp. 347–368). Champaign, IL: Human Kinetics.

McGrath, J. E. (1970). A conceptual formation for research on stress. In J. E. McGrath (Ed.), *Social and psychological factors in stress* (pp. 19–49). New York: Holt, Rinehart and Winston.

McGregor, D. (1960). *The human side of enterprise*. New York: McGraw Hill.

Meyers, A. W. (1995). Ethical principles of the Association for the Advancement of Applied Sport Psychology. *AAASP Newsletter, 10*, pp. 15, 21.

Meyers, A. W., Coleman, J., Whelan, J., & Mehlenbeck, R. (2001). Examining careers in sport psychology: Who is working and who is making money? *Professional Psychology: Research & Practice, 32*, 5–11.

Meyers, A. W., Whelan, J. P., & Murphy, S. (1995). Cognitive behavioral strategies in athletic performance enhancement. In M. Hersen, R. M. Eisler, & P. M. Miller (Eds.), *Progress in behavior modification* (pp. 137–164). Pacific Grove, CA: Brooks/Cole.

Miller, P. S., & Kerr, G. A. (2002). Conceptualizing excellence: Past, present, and future. *Journal of Applied Sport Psychology, 14*, 140–153.

Mischel, W., & Shoda, Y. (1995). A cognitive-affective system theory of personality: Reconceptualizing situations, dispositions, dynamics, and invariance in personality structure. *Psychological Review, 102*, 246–268.

Mishra, R. (2003, February 5). Repetition makes best surgeons, studies find. *Boston Globe,* p. A1.

Murphy, S. M. (1995). Introduction to sport psychology interventions. In S. M. Murphy (Ed.), *Sport psychology interventions* (pp.1–15). Champaign, IL: Human Kinetics.

Naisbitt, J. (1982). *Megatrends: Ten new directions transforming our lives.* New York: Warner.

Newburg, D., Kimiecik, J., Durand-Bush, N., & Doell, K. (2002). The role of resonance in performance excellence and life engagement. *Journal of Applied Sport Psychology, 14,* 249–267.

Newman, J. L., Robinson-Kurpius, S. E., & Fuqua, D. R. (2002). Issues in the ethical practice of consulting psychology. In R. L. Lowman (Ed.), *The California School of Organizational Studies handbook of organizational consulting psychology: A comprehensive guide to theory, skills, and techniques* (pp. 733–758). San Francisco: Jossey-Bass.

Nicholls, J. G. (1992). The general and the specific in the development and expression of achievement motivation. In G. C. Roberts (Ed.), *Motivation in sport and exercise* (pp. 31–56). Champaign, IL: Human Kinetics.

Nideffer, R. (1976). Test of attentional and interpersonal style. *Journal of Personality and Social Psychology, 34,* 394–404.

Nideffer, R. (1981). *The ethics and practice of applied sport psychology.* Ithaca, NY: Mouvement.

Nideffer, R. (1985). *Athletes' guide to mental training.* Champaign, IL: Human Kinetics.

Nolen, W. (1970). *The making of a surgeon.* New York: Pocket Books.

Null, G. (1993). *Black Hollywood: From 1970 to today.* Secaucus, NJ: Carol Publishing.

Obrecht, S., & Telson, H. (1992). On the road again: Alternatives for maintaining psychotherapeutic continuity with actors. *Medical Problems of Performing Artists, 7,* 69–75.

O'Donovan-Polten, S. (2001). *The scales of success: Constructions of life-career success of eminent men and women lawyers.* Toronto: University of Toronto Press.

Ogilvie, B., & Tutko, T. (1966). *Problem athletes and how to handle them.* London: Pelham.

O'Hanlon, W. H. (1987). *Taproots: Underlying principles of Milton Erickson's therapy and hypnosis.* New York: Norton.

Orlick, T. (1986). *Psyching for sport: Mental training for athletes.* Champaign, IL: Leisure Press.

Orlick, T., & Partington, J. (1987). The sport psychology consultant: Analysis of critical components as viewed by Canadian Olympic athletes. *The Sport Psychologist, 1,* 4–17.

Ostwald, P. F. (1992). Psychodynamics of musicians: The relationship of performers to their musical instruments. *Medical Problems of Performing Artists, 7,* 110–113.

Patton, M. (1990). *Qualitative evaluation and research methods.* Newbury Park, CA: Sage.

Perrott, L. A. (1999). *Reinventing your independent practice as a business psychologist: A step-by-step guide.* San Francisco: Jossey-Bass.

Peters, T. J., & Waterman, R. H. (1982). *In search of excellence.* New York: Harper & Row.

Petitpas, A., Giges, B., & Danish S. (1999). The sport psychologist–athlete relationship: Implications for training. *The Sports Psychologist, 13,* 344–357.

Petrie, T. A. (1998). Anxiety management and the elite athlete: A case study. In K. F. Hays (Ed.), *Integrating exercise, sports, movement, and mind: Therapeutic unity* (pp. 161–173). Binghamton, NY: Haworth.

Petrie, T. A., & Diehl, N. S. (1995). Sport psychology in the profession of psychology. *Professional Psychology: Research and Practice, 26,* 288–291.

Poczwardowski, A., & Conroy, D. E. (2002). Coping responses to failure and success among elite athletes and performing artists. *Journal of Applied Sport Psychology, 14,* 313–329.

Poczwardowski, A., Sherman, C. P., & Henschen, K. P. (1998). A sport psychology service delivery heuristic: Building on theory and practice. *The Sport Psychologist, 12,* 191–207.

Pope, K. S., & Vasquez, M. J. T. (1998). *Ethics in psychotherapy and counseling: A practical guide* (2nd ed.). San Francisco: Jossey-Bass.

Privette, G., & Bundrick, C. M. (1991). Peak experience, peak performance, and flow: Personal descriptions and theoretical constructs. *Journal of Social Behavior and Personality, 6,* 169–188.

Prochaska, J. O., & DiClemente, C. C. (1983). Stages and processes of self-change of smoking: Toward an integrative model of change. *Journal of Consulting and Clinical Psychology, 51,* 390–395.

Prochaska, J. O., Norcross, J. C., & DiClemente, C. C. (1994). *Changing for good.* New York: William Morrow.

Quill, T. E. (1983). Partnership in patient care: A contractual approach. *Annals of Internal Medicine, 98,* 228–234.

Raglin, J. S. (1993). Overtraining and staleness: Psychometric monitoring of endurance athletes. In R. B. Singer, M. Murphey, & L. K. Tennant (Eds.), *Handbook of research on sport psychology* (pp. 840–850). New York: Macmillan.

Ravizza, K. (1977). Peak experience in sport. *Journal of Humanistic Psychology, 17,* 35–40.

Ravizza, K. (1988). Gaining entry with athletic personnel for season-long consulting. *The Sport Psychologist, 2,* 243–274.

Sachs, M. L. (1993). Professional ethics in sport psychology. In R. N. Singer, M. Murphey, & L. K. Tennant (Eds.), *Handbook of research on sport psychology* (pp. 921–932). New York: Macmillan.

Sarason, S. B. (1967). Towards a psychology of change and innovation. *American Psychologist, 22,* 227–233.

Schoen, C., & Estanol-Johnson, E. (2001, May). *Assessment of the applicability of sport psychology implementation to ballet and dance.* Paper presented at the 10th World Congress of Sport Psychology, Skiathos, Greece.

Seashore, C. E. (1967). *Psychology of music.* New York: Dover. (Original work published 1938)

Seligman, M., & Csikszentmihalyi, M. (2000). Positive psychology. *American Psychologist, 55,* 5–14.

Selye, H. (1975). *Stress without distress.* New York: Signet.

Sheldon, K. M., & King, L. (2001). Why positive psychology is necessary. *American Psychologist, 56,* 216–217.

Sidimus, J. (1998, April). *The artist in society: Prejudices, myths and misconceptions.* Paper presented at The Dance Goes On Conference, Toronto.

Simons, J. P., & Andersen, M. B. (1995). The development of consulting practice in applied sport psychology: Some personal perspectives. *The Sport Psychologist, 9,* 449–468.

Singer, R. N. (1989). Applied sport psychology in the United States. *Journal of Applied Sport Psychology, 1,* 61–80.

Smith, R. E. (2002, October). *Understanding the athlete: Toward a social cognitive-affective processing model.* Coleman Griffith Lecture presented at the Annual Conference of the Association for the Advancement of Applied Sport Psychology, Tucson, AZ.

Smith, R. R., & Christensen, D. S. (1995) Psychological skills as predictors of performance and survival in professional baseball. *Journal of Sport and Exercise Psychology, 17,* 399–415.

Stapp, J. (1996). *An unusual career in psychology: Trial consultant* [On-line article]. Retrieved from http://www.apa.org/psa/janfeb96/alt.html

Steinhardt, A. (1998). *Indivisble by four: A string quartet in pursuit of harmony.* New York: Farrar, Straus & Giroux.

Sternberg, R. J. (1985). *Beyond IQ: A triarchic theory of human intelligence.* New York: Cambridge University Press.

Sternberg, R. J. (1997). *Successful intelligence.* New York: Plume.

Sternberg, R. J. (2000). Intelligence and wisdom. In R. Sternberg (Ed.), *Handbook of intelligence* (pp. 631–649). New York: Cambridge University Press.

Strauss, G. (2001, March 6). "Corporate athletes" hit the mat: LGE Performance applies sports-style training principles to business. *USA Today,* 18.

Terenzini, P. T. (1993). On the nature of institutional research and the knowledge and skills it requires. *Research in Higher Education, 34,* 1–10.

Tobias, L. L. (1996). Coaching executives. *Consulting Psychology Journal, 48,* 87–95.

U.S. Army. (2002). Enlisted careers—General enlistment requirements. Retrieved July 11, 2003, from http://www.army-military.org/enlistmentrequirements.htm

Van Raalte, J. L. (1998). Working in competitive sport: What coaches and athletes want psychologists to know. In K. F. Hays (Ed.), *Integrating exercise, sports, movement, and mind* (pp. 101–110). Binghamton, NY: Haworth.

Van Raalte, J. L., & Brewer, B. W. (Eds.). (2002). *Exploring sport and exercise psychology* (2nd ed.). Washington, DC: American Psychological Association.

Van Raalte, J. L., Brewer, B. W., Rivera, P. M., & Petipas, A. J. (1994). The relationship between observable self-talk and competitive Junior tennis players' match performances. *Journal of Sport and Exercise Psychology, 16,* 400–415.

Wagner, R. K. (1987). Tacit knowledge in everyday intelligent behavior. *Journal of Personality and Social Psychology, 52,* 1236–1247.

Wagner, R. K. (2000). Practical intelligence. In R. Sternberg (Ed.), *Handbook of intelligence* (pp. 380–395). New York: Cambridge University Press.

Walfish, S. (2001, August). *Clinical practice strategies outside the realm of managed care.* Paper presented at the Annual Convention of the American Psychological Association, San Francisco.

Weinberg, R., Butt, J., & Knight, B. (2001). High school coaches' perceptions of the process of goal setting. *The Sport Psychologist, 15,* 20–47.

Weinberg, R., & Gould, D. (1995). *Foundations of sport and exercise psychology.* Champaign, IL: Human Kinetics.

Weinberg, R., & McDermott, M. (2002). A comparative analysis of sport and business organizations: Factors perceived critical for organizational success. *Journal of Applied Sport Psychology, 14*, 282–298.

Whelan, J. P., Meyers, A. W., & Elkin, T. D. (2002). Ethics in sport and exercise psychology. In J. L. Van Raalte & B. W. Brewer (Eds.), *Exploring sport and exercise psychology* (2nd ed., pp. 503–523). Washington, DC: American Psychological Association.

Whiston, S. C., & Sexton, T. L. (1993). An overview of psychotherapy outcome research: Implications for practice. *Professional Psychology: Research & Practice, 24*, 43–51.

Wildenhaus, K. J. (1997). Sport psychology services in a clinical practice. In L. VandeCreek, S. Knapp, & T. L. Jackson (Eds.), *Innovations in clinical practice: A source book* (Vol. 15, pp. 365–383). Sarasota, FL: Professional Resource Press.

Williams, G., Frankel, R., Campbell, T., & Deci, E. (2000). Research on relationship-centered care and healthcare outcomes from the Rochester Biopsychosocial Program: A self-determination theory integration. *Families, Systems & Health, 18*, 79–90.

Williams, J., & Krane, V. (1997). Psychological characteristics of peak performance. In J. Williams (Ed.), *Applied sport psychology: Personal growth to peak performance* (pp. 137–147). Mountain View, CA: Mayfield.

Winner, E. (1996). The rage to master: The decisive role of talent in the visual arts. In K. A. Ericsson (Ed.), *The road to excellence: The acquisition of expert performance in the arts and sciences, sports and games* (pp. 271–301). Mahwah, NJ: Erlbaum.

Witherspoon, R., & White, R. P. (1996). Executive coaching: A continuum of roles. *Consulting Psychology Journal, 48*, 124–133.

Wolfe, T. (1979). *The right stuff*. New York: Farrar, Straus and Giroux.

Wootten, C. (2001). Gender-based and relationship issues. In D. Jowitt, R. Alston, K. Kain, J. Kylian, & R. Philp (Eds.) *Not just any body: Advancing health, well-being and excellence in dance and dancers* (pp. 58–62). Owen Sound, ON, Canada: The Ginger Press.

Wynne, L. C., McDaniel, S. H., & Weber, T. T. (1986). *Systems consultation: A new perspective for family therapy*. New York: Guilford.

Author Index

Abramowitz, R., 62, 63, 70
Albert, R. M., 95
Alexander, D. A., 47
American Psychological Association (APA), 252, 253, 255, 271, 274, 280
Andersen, M. B., 8, 217, 220, 237, 240, 242, 252
Aronson, E., 95
Avener, M., 114

Bachelard, C., 55
Baillie, P. II. F., 83
Bandura, A., 83, 106
Bateson, G., 286
Beisser, A., 16
Benjamin, G. A., 34
Biggam, F. H., 47
Bloom, B. S., 91
Boring, E. G., 7
Brandfonbrener, A. G., 73
Brandt, N., 207
Brewer, B. W., 7, 8, 114, 252
Brown, C. H., 8, 17, 252, 286
Brown, D. R., 269
Brown, J. M., 47
Bundrick, C. M., 172
Burton, D., 106
Butt, J., 23

Caironi, P. C., 12
Campbell, E. A., 47
Campbell, T., 46
Carcary, W. B., 47
Carr, C. M., 63
Carron, A. V., 7
Cassell, E. J., 46

Cazes, G., 55
Christensen, D. S., 8
Clarkson, M., 142
Clavell, J., 53
Cogan, K. D., 8
Cole, W., 12, 13
Coleman, J., 9
Conroy, D. E., 10, 19, 24, 131, 152
Covey, S. R., 36, 93
Cox, T., 152
Csikszentmihalyi, M., 15, 92, 93, 132, 133, 171, 172, 181, 193, 251
Cutler, K., 10

Damarjian, N., 16, 220, 242
Danish, S. J., 15, 33, 83
Darling, E. J., 34
Davidson, J. E., 285
Dean, B., 11, 12, 13
Deci, E., 46
Deming, W., 38
De Shazer, S., 16
DiClemente, C. C., 93, 283
Dieffenbach, K., 66, 100
Diehl, N. S., 7
Doell, K., 10
Downing, C. L., 285
Drogin, E., 34
Duda, J., 83
Dull, V. T., 46
Dunkel, S. E., 64, 108, 136
Durand-Bush, N., 10, 91, 92

Eklund, R. C., 24
Elkins, T. D., 252

309

Subject Index

AAASP (Association for the Advancement of
  Applied Sport Psychology), 8
  Code of Ethics of, 252
Abilities, basic, 82–83
Academic training, formal, 257–259
Access, on part of consultants, 239
Activation, 110
Activation management, 110–111
  imagery for, 114
Active intentional learning, 97–101
  and goal setting, 107
Actors
  as assuming personalities, 65
  and family disruption, 69–70
  and goal setting, 108
  individualism of, 68–69
  and injury, 73
  with intuitive sense of self, 85
  and mind-body relationship, 67
  and relaxation techniques, 67, 77
  and research interviews, 21
  technical preparation for, 97
  uncertainty in careers of, 59, 108
  unemployment among, 63, 108
  and use of routines, 75
  and willingness to risk, 181–182
"Adams, Dr. Andrew" (consultant, business)
  on assessing competence, 268
  on consultants' milieu, 31
  on empathy, 218
  on gender and ethnicity, 228
  on life experiences, 263
  on psychologists' understanding, 257
Advertising, 274
Aerobic exercise, 77

Age, and performers' biases, 226–227, 228
Alcohol, in performing arts, 63
  in music business, 87, 88, 89
Altering of task, 154–155
American Psychological Association (APA)
  confidentiality standards of, 273
  Ethics Code of (APA Ethics Code), 252, 253,
    254, 255, 269, 271, 274–275, 252
  Division 13 of (Society of Consulting
    Psychology), 252–253
  Division 47 of (Exercise and Sport
    Psychology), 8
"Answer, the," consultants' claims to have, 239–
  240
Anthropologist, consultant as, 219, 230
Anxiety
  reframing of as attentiveness, 111
  vs. stress, 145
APA. *See* American Psychological Association
APA Ethics Code, 252, 253, 254, 255, 256, 269,
  271, 274–275
APA Insurance Trust, 253, 273
Appearance, of consultant, 218, 286–287. *See also*
  Presentation of consultant
Applied sport psychology, 4, 6–10
  and types of goals, 106
Aristotle, on excellence, 91
Arousal
  and imagery, 113
  optimal level of, 110
  pacing of, 159
Art of War, The (Sun Tzu), 53
Assessment
  as assistance from consultant, 202–204, 213
  of client's difficulties, 282

To protect the consultants' privacy, they were given pseudonyms.

Decreasing of demands, in coping with stress, 152–153, 154–156
Decreasing importance of outcome, in coping with stress, 166–168
Demands of performance, and stress, 133–140
"Desmond, Dr. Donna" (consultant, performing arts)
    on "anatomy as destiny," 60, 83
    on assessing competence, 268
    on ballet milieu, 61
    on consultants' recognition of performers' limitations, 234
    on eating disorders, 88
    on performance experience, 260
Developmental focus, in consultation, 212
Diaphragmatic breathing, 74–75, 77
    in coping with stress, 162
Direct observation, in assessing competence, 267
Disease or illness-based model, 13, 15
Distress, 132
Diversion, in pacing, 159, 160–161
Diversity, in broadcasting, 218, 230
Domain-specific knowledge, 281, 284–285
Domains of research, 20, 29–30
    commonalities among, 30
    See also Business; High-risk professions; Performing arts
Doubt, as suppressed in high-risk professions, 51–52
Drug use, in performing arts, 63–64
    in music business, 87
Dual relationships, 269–272

Eating disorders, among dancers, 76, 88, 89
Education, as assistance from consultant, 204–211
Egos, and actors, 65–66
Elite performance. *See* Peak performance
Emergency room physicians, 41, 44–46
    and assessment of situation 176–177
    and camaraderie, 43
    pressures on, 50
        and self-control, 52
    and relating to patients, 49
Emotion-focused strategies, for coping with stress, 152
Emotions
    in business, 36–37, 39
    coping with, 152 (*see also* Coping with stress)
    and high-risk professions, 45, 51–52, 56
    in Individual Zone of Optimal Functioning, 117
    and overlearning, 99, 104
    in performing arts, 51, 72–73, 76
    regulation of in performance, 178–180
Empathy, in effective consultation, 218
Energy management, 159–160
Erickson, Milton, 259

Errors, sensing of, 99
Ethical concerns, 251–254, 269
    advertising, 274
    and applicability of Ethics Code, 274–275
    and competence, 251, 252, 254–256
    confidentiality, 241, 273–274 (*see also* Confidentiality)
    and deficits in knowledge or experience, 258
    informed consent, 272–273
    multiple role relationships, 269–272
    recommendations to consultants on, 279–280
    unethical practice, 241–242
Ethical Principles of Psychologists and Code of Conduct (APA Ethics Code), 252, 253, 254, 255, 269, 271, 274–275, 252
Ethnicity, and performers' biases, 229, 230
Eustress, 132
"Evans, Dr. Edward" (consultant, business)
    on competence, 267
    on training as psychologist, 258
Excellence, psychology of (business community), 9
Excellent performance. *See* Peak performance
Executive coaching, 11, 12, 13, 36, 39
Expectations, as stressors, 138–140
Experience
    in assessing competence, 268
    consultant credibility from, 216–217
    consultants' discounting of, 238–239
    in performance by consultants, 260–262
Experience of performance, 193–197
Expert, 20
Exposure, as stressor, 136–138

Familiarity with consultants, 30
    in business, 37–38
    in high-risk professions, 53–55
    in performing arts, 74–75
Families
    and achievement as Navy SEAL, 48
    of actors, 69–70
Family businesses
    and confrontation, 11
    working with, 235, 258
Family/systems consultation, 11
Fear, consultant assistance with, 206
    vs. psychotherapy, 241
Feedback, from consultant, 203, 224–225
Fee structure, and consultation-therapy combination, 271
Females. *See* Gender; Women
Firefighters, unpredictable environment of, 50
"Fiske, Dr. Franklin" (consultant, business)
    on informal training, 262
    on performance experience, 261–262

About the Authors

Kate F. Hays, PhD, maintains a private practice, The Performing Edge, in Toronto, Ontario, Canada, with a specialized focus on performance enhancement for athletes, performing artists, and businesspeople. She earned her master's degree and doctorate in clinical psychology at Boston University in 1971. For the following 25 years, she directed a community mental health center and subsequently developed an individual and group private practice in New Hampshire. Her research, writing, teaching, and practice both in New Hampshire and, since 1997, in Toronto, have been directed toward the mental benefits of physical activity and the application of sport psychology techniques to other performance populations. Dr. Hays is the author of *Working It Out: Using Exercise In Psychotherapy* and *Move Your Body, Tone Your Mood,* and edited *Integrating Exercise, Sports, Movement and Mind: Therapeutic Unity.* She is the past president of the American Psychological Association's Division 47, Exercise and Sport Psychology.

Charles H. Brown, Jr., PhD, has been in private practice more than 20 years, totally independent of managed care. He earned his master's degree from Appalachian State University in 1974 and his doctorate in counseling psychology from the University of Southern Mississippi in 1979. From 1979 to 1997, he served as Director of Training at Family and Psychological Services (FPS) of Charlotte, North Carolina, where he provided postgraduate training in strategic systems interventions. He has been a leader in providing brief, solution-focused consultation that builds on the strengths and resources of the individual, relationship, and family. After a formal respecialization in sport psychology, Dr. Brown has broadened these skills to help athletes, performing artists, professionals, and executives perform to their full potential. He directs the *Make It Real* program at FPS, offering weekend retreats for high-performing couples striving for balance and excellence in their personal and professional lives.